Selected Essays

BOOKS BY

Robert Penn Warren

John Brown: The Making of a Martyr
Thirty-six Poems
Eleven Poems on the Same Theme
Night Rider
Selected Poems, 1923–1943
At Heaven's Gate
All the King's Men
The Circus in the Attic
World Enough and Time
Brother to Dragons
Band of Angels
Segregation: The Inner Conflict in the South
Promises: Poems 1954–1956
Selected Essays

Robert Penn Warren

Selected Essays

Random House   *New York*

First Printing

LIBRARY OF CONGRESS CATALOG CARD NUMBER: 58–7674

MANUFACTURED IN THE UNITED STATES OF AMERICA
By Kingsport Press, Inc., Kingsport, Tennessee

ACKNOWLEDGMENTS

The essay "Ernest Hemingway" is reprinted from MSA edition of *A Farewell to Arms*, by Ernest Hemingway. Copyright, 1949, by Charles Scribner's Sons. Used by permission of the publisher.

The quotation from David Daiches in the essay "Ernest Hemingway" is from *The Novel in the Modern World* (University of Chicago Press). Copyright, 1939, by University of Chicago.

"The Themes of Robert Frost" is from *The Writer and His Craft*, edited by Roy W. Cowden (Ann Arbor, 1954), The University of Michigan Press. Printed by permission.

The quotations from Thomas Wolfe in "The Hamlet of Thomas Wolfe" are from *Of Time and the River*. Copyright, 1935, by Charles Scribner's Sons. Used by permission of the publisher.

The lines from "A Still Moment" and "At The Landing" are from *The Wide Net and Other Stories*. Copyright, 1943, by Eudora Welty; the lines from "A Memory" are from *A Curtain of Green and Other Stories*. Copyright, 1937, by Eudora Welty. Used by permission of Harcourt, Brace and Company, Inc. The lines from "Flowering Judas" and "The Cracked Looking-Glass" are from *Flowering Judas and Other Stories*. Copyright, 1930, 1935, by Katherine Anne Porter; the lines from "Noon Wine" and "Old Mortality" are from *Pale Horse, Pale Rider*. Copyright, 1939, by Katherine Anne Porter. Used by permission of Harcourt, Brace and Company, Inc.

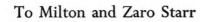

To Milton and Zaro Starr

Contents

Preface   xi

Pure and Impure Poetry (1942)   3

"The Great Mirage": Conrad and *Nostromo* (1951)   31

William Faulkner (1946–50)   59

Ernest Hemingway (1944–47)   80

The Themes of Robert Frost (1947)   118

Irony with a Center: Katherine Anne Porter (1941–52)   136

Love and Separateness in Eudora Welty (1944)   156

A Note on the Hamlet of Thomas Wolfe (1935)   170

Melville the Poet (1945)   184

A Poem of Pure Imagination: An Experiment in Reading (1945–46)   198

Preface

FOR SOME YEARS I was a teacher, or a part-time teacher, and most of my attempts at criticism, in the form of notes or textbooks, were directed straight at the classroom. At the same time, my deep and abiding desire was to write poetry and fiction, and even though I felt no competition between this desire and the profession I enjoyed, I turned most of my energy, when I left the classroom and the obligations of the classroom, toward writing poems and stories and novels. But now and then, over the years, I would try to write a critical essay aimed, hopefully, at an audience somewhat larger than that of the classroom. The pieces in this book are selected from among those attempts.

Though these essays are, in a sense, occasional pieces, drawn from over some years, they represent certain continuing interests and developing notions. It could scarcely be otherwise; they are all cut from the same bolt of goods. But they do not aspire to represent a complete theory of criticism. After all, no criticism—no matter how much more ambitious and systematic than these essays—would be complete. There is no complete criticism, and no complete critic. Even our own time, sometimes called, happily or unhappily, an age of criticism, is remarkable, not for a massive and systematic orthodoxy, but for the variety and internecine vindictiveness of voices; and even the "New Critics," who are so often referred to as a group, and at least are corralled together with the barbed wire of a label, are more remarkable for differences in fundamental principles than for anything they have in common. It sometimes seems hard to find much they do have in common except their enemies.

No, there is no complete criticism, and that, perhaps, is just as well. It is certainly just as well, if we conceive of a complete criticism as a sort of gigantic IBM machine—i.e., the "method"—into which deft fingers of filing clerks feed poems and plays and novels and stories, like punched cards. Who would punch the cards? Somebody has to punch them, if you have such a machine, and the hand that punches the cards rules the world. After all, even if you have such a machine, you have to trust the intelligence, tact, discipline, honesty, and sensitivity of that fallible human machine—the card-puncher.

Intelligence, tact, discipline, honesty, sensitivity —those are the things we have to depend on, after all, to give us what we prize in criticism, the insight. Insight into what? Into many different kinds of things, for those qualities may function in many different perspectives. Those qualities may give an insight into the nature and meaning of the thing being criticized, into the process by which it came to exist, into its relation to the world it came from and now exists in, into its value as a celebration of life.

There are, then, many different kinds of criticism. This fact, however, should not put a premium on whimsy, lack of system, amiable amateurism, and irresponsibility. It should, rather, make the critic more systematic, more responsible, more scrupulous in his craft, more anxious to understand exactly what kind of criticism he himself is trying to practice, and less ready to denigrate other kinds. It should make him remember that there is no end to wisdom, and that, with his own limited equipment of intelligence, tact, discipline, honesty, and sensitivity, his own chances of adding to its sum are slight indeed.

These pieces are not arranged chronologically, but the dates of composition are indicated in the table of contents. Except in three essays, I have done no rewriting, even though an idea or emphasis occasionally strikes me now as strange. I have, in general, merely struck out a few sentences here and there, for economy or to remove the tone of the platform. As for the exceptions, in the essay on William Faulkner and that on Katherine Anne Porter, I have added to the original versions certain sections drawn from other writing of mine on those subjects. And in the essay on *The Ancient Mariner* I have lifted some material from the notes into the text, have struck out some notes and added others, and in a few instances, in the hope of greater precision, have changed a formulation. Some of the pieces were, as I have implied above, composed as lectures. I have elsewhere gratefully acknowledged such sponsorships.

R. P. W.

Selected Essays

Pure and Impure Poetry

CRITICS are rarely faithful to their labels and their special strategies. Usually the critic will confess that no one strategy—the psychological, the moralistic, the formalistic, the historical—or combination of strategies, will quite work the defeat of the poem. For the poem is like the monstrous Orillo in Boiardo's *Orlando Innamorato*. When the sword lops off any member of the monster, that member is immediately rejoined to the body, and the monster is as formidable as ever. But the poem is even more formidable than the monster, for Orillo's adversary finally gained a victory by an astonishing feat of dexterity: he slashed off both the monster's arms and quick as a wink seized them and flung them into the river. The critic who vaingloriously trusts his method to account for the poem, to exhaust the poem, is trying to emulate this dexterity: he thinks that he, too, can win by throwing the lopped-off arms into the river. But he is doomed to failure. Neither fire nor water will suffice to prevent the rejoining of the mutilated members to the monstrous torso. There is only one way to conquer the monster: you must eat it, bones, blood, skin, pelt, and gristle. And even then the monster is not dead, for it lives in you, is assimilated into you, and you are different, and somewhat monstrous yourself, for having eaten it.

So the monster will always win, and the critic knows this. He does not want to win. He knows that he must always play stooge to the monster. All he wants to do is to give the monster—the poem— a chance to exhibit again its miraculous power, which is poetry.

With this fable, I shall begin by observing that poetry wants to be pure. And it always succeeds in this ambition. In so far as we have poetry at all, it is always pure poetry; that is, it is not non-poetry. The poetry of Shakespeare, the poetry of Pope, the poetry of Herrick, is pure, in so far as it is poetry at all. We call the poetry "higher" or "lower," we say "more powerful" or "less powerful" about it, and we are, no doubt, quite right in doing so. The souls that form the great rose of Paradise are seated in banks and tiers of ascending blessedness, but they are all saved, they are all perfectly happy; they are all "pure," for they have all been purged of mortal taint. This is not to say, however, that if we get poetry from only one source, say Shakespeare, such a single source ought to suffice us, in as much as we can always appeal to it; or that, since all poetry is equally pure, we engage in a superfluous labor in trying to explore or create new sources of poetry. No, for we can remember that every soul in the great rose is precious in the eyes of God. No soul is the substitute for another.

Poetry wants to be pure, but poems do not. At least, most of them do not want to be too pure. The poems want to give us poetry, which is pure, and the elements of a poem, in so far as it is a good poem, will work together toward that end, but many of the elements, taken in themselves, may actually seem to contradict that end, or be neutral toward the achieving of that end. Are we then to conclude that neutral or recalcitrant elements are simply an index to human frailty, and that in a perfect world there would be no dross in poems, which would, then, be perfectly pure? No, it does not seem to be merely the fault of our world, for the poems include, deliberately, more of the so-called dross than would appear necessary. They are not even as pure as they might be in this imperfect world. They mar themselves with cacophonies, jagged rhythms, ugly words and ugly thoughts, colloquialisms, clichés, sterile technical terms, headwork and argument, self-contradictions, clevernesses, irony, realism—all things which call us back to the world of prose and imperfection.

Sometimes a poet will reflect on this state of affairs, and grieve. He will decide that he, at least, will try to make one poem as pure as possible. So he writes:

> *Now sleeps the crimson petal, now the white;*
> *Nor waves the cypress in the palace walk;*
> *Nor winks the gold fin in the porphyry font.*
> *The fire-fly wakens; waken thou with me.*

We know the famous garden—the garden in Tennyson's "Princess." We know how all nature conspires here to express the purity of the moment: how the milk-white peacock glimmers like a ghost, and how like a ghost the unnamed "she" glimmers on to her tryst; how earth lies "all Danaë to the stars," as the beloved's heart lies open to the lover; and how, in the end, the lily folds up her sweetness, "and slips into the bosom of the lake," as the lovers are lost in the sweet dissolution of love.

And we know another poet and another garden. Or perhaps it is the same garden, after all, viewed by a different poet, Shelley.

> *I arise from dreams of thee*
> *In the first sweet sleep of night,*
> *When the winds are breathing low,*
> *And the stars are shining bright.*
> *I arise from dreams of thee,*
> *And a spirit in my feet*
> *Hath led me—who knows how?*
> *To thy chamber window, Sweet!*

We remember how, again, all nature conspires, how the wandering airs "faint," how the Champak's odors "pine," how the nightingale's complaint "dies upon her heart," as the lover will die upon the beloved's heart. Nature here strains out of nature, it wants to be called by another name, it wants to spiritualize itself by calling itself another name. How does the lover get to the chamber window?

He refuses to say how, in his semi-somnambulistic daze, he got there. He blames, he says, "a spirit in my feet," and hastens to disavow any knowledge of how that spirit operates. In any case, he arrives at the chamber window. Subsequent events and the lover's reaction toward them are somewhat hazy. We know only that the lover, who faints and fails at the opening of the last stanza and who asks to be lifted from the grass by a more enterprising beloved, is in a condition of delectable passivity, in which distinctions blur out in the "purity" of the moment.

Let us turn to another garden: the place, Verona; the time, a summer night, with full moon. The lover speaks:

> But, soft! what light through yonder
>   window breaks?
> It is the east . . .

But we know the rest, and know that this garden, in which nature for the moment conspires again with the lover, is the most famous of them all, for the scene is justly admired for its purity of effect, for giving us the very essence of young, untarnished love. Nature conspires beneficently here, but we may remember that beyond the garden wall strolls Mercutio, who can celebrate Queen Mab, but who is always aware that nature has other names as well as the names the pure poets and pure lovers put upon her. And we remember that Mercutio, outside the wall, has just said:

> . . . 'twould anger him
> To raise a spirit in his mistress' circle
> Of some strange nature, letting it there stand
> Till she had laid it and conjured it down.

Mercutio has made a joke, a bawdy joke. That is bad enough, but worse, he has made his joke witty and, worst of all, intellectually complicated in its form. Realism, wit, intellectual complication— these are the enemies of the garden purity.

But the poet has not only let us see Mercutio outside the garden wall. Within the garden itself, when the lover invokes nature, when he spiritualizes and innocently trusts her, and says,

Lady, by yonder blessed moon I swear,

the lady herself replies,

O! swear not by the moon, the inconstant moon,
That monthly changes in her circled orb.

The lady distrusts "pure" poems, nature spiritualized into forgetfulness. She has, as it were, a rigorous taste in metaphor, too; she brings a logical criticism to bear on the metaphor which is too easy; the metaphor must prove itself to her, must be willing to subject itself to scrutiny beyond the moment's enthusiasm. She injects the impurity of an intellectual style into the lover's pure poem.

And we must not forget the voice of the nurse, who calls from within, a voice which, we discover, is the voice of expediency, of half-measures, of the view that circumstances alter cases—the voice of prose and imperfection.

It is time to ask ourselves if the celebrated poetry of this scene, which as poetry is pure, exists despite the impurities of the total composition, if the effect would be more purely poetic were the nurse and Mercutio absent and the lady a more sympathetic critic of pure poems. I do not think so. The effect might even be more vulnerable poetically if the impurities were purged away. Mercutio, the lady, and the nurse are critics of the lover, who believes in pure poems, but perhaps they are necessary. Perhaps the lover can be accepted only in their context. The poet seems to say: "I know the worst that can be said on this subject, and I am giving fair warning. Read at your own risk." So the poetry arises from a recalcitrant and contradictory context; and finally involves that context.

Let us return to one of the other gardens, in which there is no Mercutio or nurse, and in which the lady is more sympathetic. Let us mar its purity

by installing Mercutio in the shrubbery, from
which the poet was so careful to banish him. You
can hear his comment when the lover says:

> *And a spirit in my feet*
> *Hath led me—who knows how?*
> *To thy chamber window, Sweet!*

And we can guess what the wicked tongue would
have to say in response to the last stanza.

It may be that the poet should have made early
peace with Mercutio, and appealed to his better nature. For Mercutio seems to be glad to co-operate
with a poet. But he must be invited; otherwise, he
is apt to show a streak of merry vindictiveness
about the finished product. Poems are vulnerable
enough at best. Bright reason mocks them like sun
from a wintry sky. They are easily left naked to
laughter when leaves fall in the garden and the cold
winds come. Therefore, they need all the friends
they can get, and Mercutio, who is an ally of reason and who himself is given to mocking laughter,
is a good friend for a poem to have.

On what terms does a poet make his peace with
Mercutio? There are about as many sets of terms
as there are good poets. I know that I have loaded
the answer with the word *good* here, that I have implied a scale of excellence based, in part at least, on
degree of complication. I shall return to this question. For the moment, however, let us examine an
anonymous sixteenth-century poem whose apparent innocence and simple lyric cry should earn it a
place in any anthology of "pure poetry."

> *Western wind, when will thou blow,*
> *The small rain down can rain?*
> *Christ, if my love were in my arms*
> *And I in my bed again!*

The lover, grieving for the absent beloved, cries
out for relief. Several kinds of relief are involved
in the appeal to the wind. First, there is the relief
that would be had from the sympathetic manifes-

tation of nature. The lover, in his perturbation of spirit, invokes the perturbations of nature. He invokes the beneficent perturbation,

> *Western wind, when will thou blow,*

as Lear invokes the destructive,

> *Blow, winds, and crack your cheeks! rage! blow!*

Second, there is the relief that would be had by the fulfillment of grief—the frost of grief, the drought of grief broken, the full anguish expressed, then the violence allayed in the peace of tears. Third, there is the relief that would be had in the excitement and fulfillment of love itself. There seems to be a contrast between the first two types of relief and the third type; speaking loosely, we may say that the first two types are romantic and general, the third type realistic and specific. So much for the first two lines.

In the last two lines, the lover cries out for the specific solace of his case: reunion with his beloved. But there is a difference between the two lines. The first is general, and romantic. The phrase "in my arms" does not seem to mean exactly what it says. True, it has a literal meaning, if we can look close at the words, but it is hard to look close because of the romantic aura—the spiritualized mist about them.[1] But with the last line the perfectly literal meaning suddenly comes into sharp focus. The mist is rifted and we can look straight at the words, which, we discover with a slight shock of surprise, do mean exactly what they say. The last line is realistic and specific. It is not even content to say,

> *And I in bed again!*

---

1. It may be objected here that I am reading the phrase "in my arms" as a twentieth-century reader. I confess the fact. Certainly, several centuries have passed since the composition of the little poem, and those centuries have thickened the romantic mist about the words, but it is scarcely to be believed that the sixteenth century was the clear, literal Eden dawn of poetry when words walked without the fig leaf.

It is, rather, more scrupulously specific, and says,

And I in my bed again!

All of this does not go to say that the realistic elements here are to be taken as canceling, or negating, the romantic elements. There is no ironical leer. The poem is not a celebration of carnality. It is a faithful lover who speaks. He is faithful to the absent beloved, and he is also faithful to the full experience of love. That is, he does not abstract one aspect of the experience and call it the whole experience. He does not strain nature out of nature; he does not overspiritualize nature. This nameless poet would never have said, in the happier days of his love, that he had been led to his Sweet's chamber window by "a spirit in my feet"; and he certainly would not have added the coy disavowal, "who knows how?" But because the nameless poet refused to overspiritualize nature, we can accept the spirituality of the poem.

Another poem gives us another problem.

Ah, what avails the sceptered race!
Ah, what the form divine!
What every virtue, every grace!
Rose Aylmer, all were thine.

Rose Aylmer, whom these wakeful eyes
May weep, but never see,
A night of memories and of sighs
I consecrate to thee.

This is another poem about lost love: a "soft" subject. Now, to one kind of poet the soft subject presents a sore temptation. Because it is soft in its natural state, he is inclined to feel that to get at its poetic essence he must make it softer still, that he must insist on its softness, that he must render it as "pure" as possible. At first glance, it may seem that Landor is trying to do just that. What he says seems to be emphatic, unqualified, and open. Not every power, grace, and virtue could avail to preserve his love. That statement insists on the pathetic contrast. And in the next stanza, wakeful-

ness and tearfulness are mentioned quite unasham-
edly, along with memories and sighs. It is all
blurted out, as pure as possible.

But only in the paraphrase is it "blurted." The
actual quality of the first stanza is hard, not soft.
It is a chiseled stanza, in which formality is insisted upon. We may observe the balance of the
first and second lines; the balance of the first half
with the second half of the third line, which re-
capitulates the structure of the first two lines; the
balance of the two parts of the last line, though
here the balance is merely a rhythmical and not a
sense balance as in the preceding instances; the
binders of discreet alliteration, repetition, and as-
sonance. The stanza is built up, as it were, of units
which are firmly defined and sharply separated,
phrase by phrase, line by line. We have the formal
control of the soft subject, ritual and not surrender.

But in the second stanza the rigor of this formality is somewhat abated, as the more general, specu-
lative emphasis (why cannot pomp, virtue, and
grace avail?) gives way to the personal emphasis,
as though the repetition of the beloved's name had,
momentarily, released the flood of feeling. The first
line of the second stanza spills over into the second;
the "wakeful eyes" as subject find their verb in the
next line, "weep," and the *wake-weep* alliteration,
along with the pause after *weep,* points up the disintegration of the line, just as it emphasizes the
situation. Then with the phrase "but never see" falling away from the long thrust of the rhetorical
structure to the pause after *weep,* the poem seems
to go completely soft, the frame is broken. But,
even as the poet insists on "memories and sighs,"
in the last two lines he restores the balance. Notice
the understatement of "A night." It says: "I know
that life is a fairly complicated affair, and that I
am committed to it and to its complications. I intend to stand by my commitment, as a man of integrity, that is, to live despite the grief. Since life
is complicated, I cannot, if I am to live, spare too
much time for indulging grief. I can give *a* night,

but not all nights." The lover, like the hero of Frost's poem "Stopping by Woods on a Snowy Evening," tears himself from the temptation of staring into the treacherous, delicious blackness, for he, too, has "promises to keep." Or he resembles the Homeric heroes who, after the perilous passage is made, after their energy has saved their lives, and after they have beached their craft and eaten their meal, can then set aside an hour before sleep to mourn the comrades lost by the way—the heroes who, as Aldous Huxley says, understand realistically a whole truth as contrasted with a half-truth.

Is this a denial of the depth and sincerity of the grief? The soft reader, who wants the poem pure, may be inclined to say so. But let us look at the last line to see what it gives us in answer to this question. The answer seems to lie in the word *consecrate*. The meter thrusts this word at us; we observe that two of the three metrical accents in the line fall on syllables of this word, forcing it beyond its prose emphasis. The word is important and the importance is justified, for the word tells us that the single night is not merely a lapse into weakness, a trivial event to be forgotten when the weakness is overcome. It is, rather, an event of the most extreme and focal importance, an event formally dedicated, "set apart for sacred uses," an event by which other events are to be measured. So the word *consecrate* formalizes, philosophizes, ritualizes the grief; it specifies what in the first stanza has been implied by style.

But here is another poem of grief, grief at the death of a child. It is "Bells for John Whiteside's Daughter," by John Crowe Ransom.[2]

> *There was such speed in her little body,*
> *And such lightness in her footfall,*
> *It is no wonder her brown study*
> *Astonishes us all.*

---

2. From *Selected Poems*, by John Crowe Ransom. Copyright, 1924, 1945, by Alfred A. Knopf, Inc. Used by permission.

Her wars were bruited in our high window.
We looked among orchard trees and beyond,
Where she took arms against her shadow,
Or harried unto the pond

The lazy geese, like a snow cloud
Dripping their snow on the green grass,
Tricking and stopping, sleepy and proud,
Who cried in goose, Alas,

For the tireless heart within the little
Lady with rod that made them rise
From their noon apple-dreams, and scuttle
Goose-fashion under the skies!

But now go the bells, and we are ready;
In one house we are sternly stopped
To say we are vexed at her brown study,
Lying so primly propped.

Another soft subject, softer, if anything, than the subject of "Rose Aylmer," and it presents the same problem. But the problem is solved in a different way.

The first stanza is based on two time-honored clichés: first, "Heavens, won't that child ever be still, she is driving me distracted"; and second, "She was such an active, healthy-looking child, who would've ever thought she would just up and die?" In fact, the whole poem develops these clichés, and exploits, in a backhand fashion, the ironies implicit in their interrelation. And in this connection, we may note that the fact of the clichés, rather than more original or profound observations at the root of the poem, is important; there is in the poem the contrast between the staleness of the clichés and the shock of the reality. Further, we may note that the second cliché is an answer, savagely ironical in itself, to the first: the child you wished would be still *is* still, despite all that activity which had interrupted your adult occupations.

But such a savage irony is not the game here. It is too desperate, too naked, in a word, too pure. And ultimately, it is, in a sense, a meaningless irony if left in its pure state, because it depends on a mechanical, accidental contrast in nature, void of moral content. The poem is concerned with modifications and modulations of this brute, basic irony, modulations and modifications contingent upon an attitude taken toward it by a responsible human being, the speaker of the poem. The savagery is masked, or ameliorated.

In this connection, we may observe, first, the phrase "brown study." It is not the "frosted flower," the "marmoreal immobility," or any one of a thousand such phrases which would aim for the pure effect. It is merely the brown study which astonishes—a phrase which denies, as it were, the finality of the situation, underplays the pathos, and merely reminds one of those moments of childish pensiveness into which the grownup cannot penetrate. And the phrase itself is a cliché—the common now echoed in the uncommon.

Next, we may observe that stanzas two, three, and four simply document, with a busy yet wavering rhythm (one sentence runs through the three stanzas), the tireless naughtiness which was once the cause of rebuke, the naughtiness which disturbed the mature goings-on in the room with the "high window." But the naughtiness is now transmuted into a kind of fanciful story-book dream world, in which geese are whiter than nature, and the grass greener, in which geese speak in goose language, saying "Alas," and have apple-dreams. It is a drowsy, delicious world, in which the geese are bigger than life, and more important. It is an unreal (now unreal because lost), stylized world. Notice how the phrase "the little lady with rod" works: the detached primness of "little lady"; the formal, stiff effect gained by the omission of the article before *rod;* the slightly unnatural use of the word *rod* itself, which sets some distance between us and the scene (perhaps with the hint of the fairy story, a magic wand, or a magic rod—not a common, everyday stick). But the stanzas tie back into the premises of the poem in other ways. The little girl, in her excess of energy, warred against her shadow. Is it crowding matters too hard to surmise that the shadow here achieves a sort of covert symbolic significance? The little girl lost her war against her "shadow," which was always with her. Certainly the phrase "tireless heart" has some rich connotations. And the geese which say "Alas!" conspire with the family to deplore the excessive activity of the child. (They do not conspire to express the present grief, only the past vexation—an inversion of the method of the pastoral elegy, or of the method of the first two garden poems.)

The business of the three stanzas, then, may be said to be twofold. First, they make us believe more fully in the child and therefore in the fact of the grief itself. They "prove" the grief, and they show the deliciousness of the lost world which will never look the same from the high window. Second, and contrariwise, they "transcend" the grief, or at least give a hint of a means for transcending immediate anguish: the lost world is, in one sense, redeemed out of time; it enters the pages of the picture book where geese speak, where the untrue is true, where the fleeting is fixed. What was had cannot, after all, be lost. (By way of comparison—a comparison which, because extreme, may be helpful— we may think of the transcendence in *La Recherche du Temps Perdu*.) The three stanzas, then, to state it in another way, have validated the first stanza and have prepared for the last.

The three stanzas have made it possible for us to say, when the bell tolls, "we are ready." Some kind of terms, perhaps not the best terms possible but some kind, has been made with the savage underlying irony. But the terms arrived at do not prevent the occasion from being a "stern" one. The transcendence is not absolute, and in the end is possible only because of an exercise of will and self-control. Because we control ourselves, we can say "vexed" and not some big word. And the word itself picks up the first of the domestic clichés on which the poem is based—the outburst of impatience at the naughty child who, by dying, has performed her most serious piece of naughtiness. But now the word comes to us charged with the burden of the poem, and further, as re-echoed here by the phrase "brown study," charged by the sentence in which it occurs: we are gathered formally, ritualistically, sternly together to say the word *vexed*.[3] *Vexed* becomes the ritualistic, the summarizing word.

I have used the words *pure* and *impure* often in the foregoing pages, and I confess that I have used them rather loosely. But perhaps it has been evident that I have meant something like this: the pure poem tries to be pure by excluding, more or less rigidly, certain elements which might qualify or contradict its original impulse. In other words, the pure poems want to be, and desperately, all of a piece. It has also been evident, no doubt, that the kinds of impurity which are admitted or excluded by the various little anthology pieces which have been presented, are different in the different poems. This is only to be expected, for there is not one doctrine of "pure poetry"—not one definition of what constitutes impurity in poems—but many.

And not all of the doctrines are recent. When, for example, one cites Poe as the father of *the* doctrine

---

3. It might be profitable, in contrast with this poem, to look at "After the Burial," by James Russell Lowell, a poem which is identical in situation. But in Lowell's poem the savagery of the irony is unqualified. In fact, the whole poem insists, quite literally, that qualification is impossible: the scheme of the poem is to set up the brute fact of death against possible consolations. It insists on "tears," the "thin-worn locket," the "anguish of deathless hair," "the smallness of the child's grave," the "little shoe in the corner." It is a poem which, we might say, does not progress, but ends where it begins, resting in savage irony from which it stems; or we might say that it is a poem without any "insides," for the hero of the poem is not attempting to do anything about the problem which confronts him—it is a poem without issue, without conflict, a poem of unconditional surrender. In other words. it tries to be a pure poem, pure grief, absolutely inconsolable. It is a strident poem, and strident in its rhythms. The fact that we know this poem to be an expression of a bereavement historically real makes it an embarrassing poem, as well. It is a naked poem.

of pure poetry, one is in error; Poe simply fathered *a* particular doctrine of pure poetry. One can find other doctrines of purity long antedating Poe. When Sir Philip Sidney, for example, legislated against tragicomedy, he was repeating a current doctrine of purity. When Ben Jonson told William Drummond that Donne, for not keeping of accent, deserved hanging, he was defending another kind of purity; and when Dryden spoke to save the ear of the fair sex from metaphysical perplexities in amorous poems, he was defending another kind of purity, just as he was defending another when he defined the nature of the heroic drama. The eighteenth century had a doctrine of pure poetry, which may be summed up under the word *sublimity*, but which involved two corollary doctrines, one concerning diction and the other concerning imagery. But at the same time that this century, by means of these corollary doctrines, was tidying up and purifying the doctrine derived from Longinus, it was admitting into the drama certain impurities which the theorists of the heroic drama would not have admitted.

But when we think of the modern doctrine of pure poetry, we usually think of Poe, as critic and poet, perhaps of Shelley, of the Symbolists, of the Abbé Bremond, perhaps of Pater, and certainly of George Moore and the Imagists. We know Poe's position: the long poem is "a flat contradiction in terms," because intense excitement, which is essential in poetry, cannot be long maintained; the moral sense and the intellect function more satisfactorily in prose than in poetry, and, in fact, "Truth" and the "Passions," which are for Poe associated with the intellect and the moral sense, may actually be inimical to poetry; vagueness, suggestiveness are central virtues, for poetry has for "its object an *indefinite* instead of a *definite* pleasure"; poetry is not supposed to undergo close inspection, only a cursory glance, for it, "above all things, is a beautiful painting whose tints, to minute inspection, are confusion worse confounded, but start out

boldly to the cursory glance of the connoisseur";
poetry aspires toward music, since it is concerned
with "indefinite sensations, to which music is an *essential*, since the comprehension of sweet sound is
our most indefinite conception"; melancholy is the
most poetical effect and enters into all the higher
manifestations of beauty. We know, too, the Abbé
Bremond's mystical interpretation, and the preface
to George Moore's anthology, and the Imagist manifesto.

But these views are not identical. Shelley, for
instance, delights in the imprecision praised and
practiced by Poe, but he has an enormous appetite
for "Truth" and the "Passions," which are, except
for purposes of contrast, excluded by Poe. The
Imagist manifesto, while excluding ideas, endorses
precision rather than vagueness in rendering the
image, and admits diction and objects which would
have seemed impure to Poe and to many poets of
the nineteenth century, and does not take much
stock in the importance of verbal music. George
Moore emphasizes the objective aspect of his pure
poetry, which he describes as "something which the
poet creates outside his own personality," and this
is opposed to the subjective emphasis in Poe and
Shelley; but he shares with both an emphasis on
verbal music, and with the former a distaste for
ideas.

But more recently, the notion of poetic purity has
emerged in other contexts, contexts which sometimes obscure the connection of the new theories
with the older theories. For instance, Max Eastman
has a theory. "Pure poetry," he says in *The Literary
Mind*, "is the pure effort to heighten consciousness." Mr. Eastman, we discover elsewhere in his
book, would ban idea from poetry, but his motive
is different from, say, the motive of Poe, and the
difference is important: Poe would kick out the
ideas because the ideas hurt the poetry, and Mr.
Eastman would kick out the ideas because the poetry hurts the ideas. Only the scientist, he tells us,
is entitled to have ideas on any subject, and the

rest of the citizenry must wait to be told what attitude to take toward the ideas which they are not
permitted to have except at second-hand. Literary
truth, he says, is truth which is "uncertain or com-
paratively unimportant." But he does assign the
poet a function—to heighten consciousness. In the
light of this context we would have to rewrite his
original definition: pure poetry is the pure effort to
heighten consciousness, but the consciousness
which is heightened must not have any connection
with ideas, must involve no attitude toward any
ideas.

Furthermore, to assist the poet in fulfilling the
assigned function, Mr. Eastman gives him a somewhat sketchy doctrine of "pure" poetic diction. For
instance, the word *bloated* is not admissible into a
poem because it is, as he testifies, "sacred to the
memory of dead fish," and the word *tangy* is,
though he knows not exactly how, "intrinsically poetic." The notion of a vocabulary which is intrinsically poetic seems, with Mr. Eastman, to mean a
vocabulary which indicates agreeable or beautiful
objects. So we might rewrite the original definition
to read: pure poetry is the pure effort to heighten
consciousness, but the consciousness which is
heightened must be a consciousness exclusively of
agreeable or beautiful objects—certainly not a consciousness of any ideas.

In a recent book, *The Idiom of Poetry*, Frederick
Pottle has discussed the question of pure poetry.
He distinguishes another type of pure poetry in addition to the types already mentioned. He calls it
the "Elliptical," and would include in it symbolist
and metaphysical poetry (old and new) and some
work by poets such as Collins, Blake, and Brown-
ing. He observes—without any pejorative implication, for he is a critical relativist and scarcely permits himself the luxury of evaluative judgments—
that the contemporary product differs from older
examples of the elliptical type in that "the modern
poet goes much farther in employing private experiences or ideas than would formerly have been

thought legitimate." To the common reader, he
says, "the prime characteristic of this kind of poetry
is not the nature of its imagery but its obscurity:
its urgent suggestion that you add something to the
poem without telling you what that something is."
This omitted "something" he interprets as the
prose "frame"—to use his word—the statement of
the occasion, the logical or narrative transitions, the
generalized application derived from the poem, etc.
In other words, this type of pure poetry contends
that "the effect would be more powerful if we could
somehow manage to feel the images fully and accurately without having the effect diluted by any
words put in to give us a 'meaning'—that is, if we
could expel all the talk *about* the imaginative realization and have the pure realization itself." [4]

For the moment I shall pass the question of the
accuracy of Mr. Pottle's description of the impulse
of Elliptical Poetry and present the question which
ultimately concerns him. How pure does poetry
need to be in practice? That is the question which
Mr. Pottle asks. He answers by saying that a great
degree of impurity *may* be admitted, and cites our
famous didactic poems, *The Faerie Queene, An Essay on Man, The Vanity of Human Wishes, The
Excursion.* That is the only answer which the relativist, and nominalist, can give. Then he turns to
what he calls the hardest question in the theory of

4. F. W. Bateson, in *English Poetry and the English Language,* discusses the modern elliptical practice in poetry.
Tennyson, he points out in connection with "The Sailor
Boy," dilutes his poetry by telling a story as well as writing a
poem, and "a shorter poem would have spoilt his story." The
claims of prose conquer the claims of poetry. Of the Victorians in general: "The dramatic and narrative framework of
their poems, by circumventing the disconcerting plunges
into *medias res* which are the essence of poetry, brings it
down to a level of prose. The reader knows where he is; it
serves the purpose of introduction and note." Such introduction and notes in the body of the poem itself are exactly
what Mr. Pottle says is missing in Elliptical Poetry. Mr.
Bateson agrees with Poe in accepting intensity as the criterion of the poetic effect, and in accepting the corollary that
a poem should be short. But he, contradicting Poe, seems to
admire precise and complicated incidental effects.

poetry: What kind of prosaism is acceptable and what is not? His answer, which he advances very modestly, is this:

. . . the element of prose is innocent and even salutary when it appears as—take your choice of three metaphors—a background on which the images are projected, or a frame in which they are shown, or a thread on which they are strung. In short, when it serves a *structural* purpose. Prose in a poem seems offensive to me when . . . the prosaisms are sharp, obvious, individual, and ranked co-ordinately with the images.

At first glance this looks plausible, and the critic has used the sanctified word *structural*. But at second glance we may begin to wonder what the sanctified word means to the critic. It means something rather mechanical—background, frame, thread. The structure is a showcase, say a jeweler's showcase, in which the little jewels of poetry are exhibited, the images. The showcase shouldn't be ornamental itself ("sharp, obvious, individual," Mr. Pottle says), for it would then distract us from the jewels; it should be chastely designed, and the jewels should repose on black velvet and not on flowered chintz. But Mr. Pottle doesn't ask what the relation among the bright jewels should be. Not only does the showcase bear no relation to the jewels, but the jewels, apparently, bear no relation to each other. Each one is a shining little focus of heightened interest, and all together they make only such a pattern, perhaps, as may make it easier for the eye to travel from one little jewel to the next, when the time comes to move on. Structure becomes here simply a device of salesmanship, a well-arranged showcase.

It is all mechanical. And this means that Mr. Pottle, after all, is himself an exponent of pure poetry. He locates the poetry simply in the images, the nodes of "pure realization." This means that what he calls the "element of prose" includes definition of situation, movement of narrative, logical transition, factual description, generalization, ideas. Such things, for him, do not participate in the poetic effect of the poem; in fact, they work against the poetic effect, and so, though necessary as a frame, should be kept from being "sharp, obvious, individual." [5]

I have referred to *The Idiom of Poetry*, first, because it is such an admirable and provocative book, sane, lucid, generous-spirited, and second, because, to my mind, it illustrates the insidiousness with which a doctrine of pure poetry can penetrate into the theory of a critic who is suspicious of such a doctrine. Furthermore, I have felt that Mr. Pottle's analysis might help me to define the common denominator of the various doctrines of pure poetry.

That common denominator seems to be the belief that poetry is an essence that is to be located at some particular place in a poem, or in some particular element. The exponent of pure poetry persuades himself that he has determined the particular something in which the poetry inheres, and then proceeds to decree that poems shall be composed, as nearly as possible, of that element and of nothing else. If we add up the things excluded by various critics and practitioners, we get a list about like this:

1. ideas, truths, generalizations, "meaning"
2. precise, complicated, "intellectual" images

---

5. Several other difficulties concerning Pottle's statement may suggest themselves. First, since he seems to infer that the poetic essence resides in the image, what view would he take of meter and rhythm? His statement, strictly construed, would mean that these factors do not participate in the poetic effect, but are simply part of the frame. Second, what view of dramatic poetry is implied? It seems again that a strict interpretation would mean that the story and the images bear no essential relation to each other, that the story is simply part of the frame. That is, the story, characters, rhythms, and ideas, are on one level, and the images, in which the poetry inheres, are on another. But Caroline Spurgeon, G. Wilson Knight, and other critics have given us some reason for holding that the images do bear some relation to the business of the other items. In fact, all of the items, as Jacques Maritain has said, "feelings, ideas, representations, are for the artist merely materials and means, still symbols." That is, they are all elements in a single expressive structure.

3. unbeautiful, disagreeable, or neutral materials
4. situation, narrative, logical transition
5. realistic details, exact descriptions, realism in general
6. shifts in tone or mood
7. irony
8. metrical variation, dramatic adaptations of rhythm, cacophony, etc.
9. meter itself
10. subjective and personal elements.

No one theory of pure poetry excludes all of these items, and, as a matter of fact, the items listed are not on the same level of importance. Nor do the items always bear the same interpretation. For example, if one item seems to be central to discussions of pure poetry, it is the first: "ideas," it is said, "are not involved in the poetic effect, and may even be inimical to it." But this view can be interpreted in a variety of ways. If it is interpreted as simply meaning that the paraphrase of a poem is not equivalent to the poem, that the poetic gist is not to be defined as the statement embodied in the poem with the sugar-coating as bait, then the view can be held by opponents as well as exponents of any theory of pure poetry. We might scale down from this interpretation to the other extreme interpretation that the poem should merely give the sharp image in isolation. But there are many complicated and confused variations possible between the two extremes. There is, for example, the interpretation that "ideas," though they are not involved in the poetic effect, must appear in poems to provide, as Mr. Pottle's prosaisms do, a kind of frame, or thread, for the poetry—a spine to support the poetic flesh, or a Christmas tree on which the baubles of poetry are hung.[6] T. S. Eliot has said something of this sort:

---

6. Such an interpretation seems to find a parallel in E. M. Forster's treatment of plot in fiction. Plot in his theory becomes a mere spine and does not really participate, except in a narrow, formal sense, in the fictional effect. By his

The chief use of the "meaning" of a poem, in the ordinary sense, may be (for here again I am speaking of some kinds of poetry and not all) to satisfy one habit of the reader, to keep his mind diverted and quiet, while the poem does its work upon him: much as the imaginary burglar is always provided with a bit of nice meat for the house-dog.

Here, it would seem, Mr. Eliot has simply inverted the old sugar-coated-pill theory: the idea becomes the sugar-coating and the "poetry" becomes the medicine. This seems to say that the idea in a poem does not participate in the poetic effect, and seems to commit Mr. Eliot to a theory of pure poetry. But to do justice to the quotation, we should first observe that the parenthesis indicates that the writer is referring to some sort of provisional and superficial distinction and not to a fundamental one, and second observe that the passage is out of its context. In the context, Mr. Eliot goes on to say that some poets "become impatient of this 'meaning' [explicit statement of ideas in logical order] which seems superfluous, and perceive possibilities of intensity through its elimination." This may mean either of two things. It may mean that ideas do not participate in the poetic effect, or it may mean that, though they do participate in the poetic effect, they need not appear in the poem in an explicit and argued form. And this second reading would scarcely be a doctrine of pure poetry at all, for it would involve poetic casuistry and not poetic principle.

We might, however, illustrate the second interpretation by glancing at Marvell's "Horatian Ode" on Cromwell. Marvell does not give us narrative; he does not give us an account of the issues behind the Civil War; he does not state the two competing ideas which are dramatized in the poem, the idea of "sanction" and the idea of "efficiency." But the effect of the poem does involve those two factors;

---

inversion of the Aristotelian principle the plot becomes merely a necessary evil.

and the reserved irony, scarcely resolved, which emerges from the historical situation, is an irony derived from unstated materials and ideas. It is, to use Mr. Pottle's term again, a pure poem in so far as it is elliptical in method, but it is anything but a pure poem if by purity we mean the exclusion of idea from participation in the poetic effect. And Mr. Eliot's own practice implies that he believes that ideas do participate in the poetic effect. Otherwise, why did he put the clues to his ideas in the notes at the end of *The Waste Land* after so carefully excluding any explicit statement of them from the body of the poem? If he is regarding those ideas as mere bait—the "bit of nice meat for the house-dog" —he has put the ideas in a peculiar place, in the back of the book—like giving the dog the meat on the way out of the house with the swag, or giving the mouse the cheese after he is in the trap.

All this leads to the speculation that Marvell and Mr. Eliot have purged away statement of ideas from their poems, not because they wanted the ideas to participate less in the poetry, but because they wanted them to participate more fully, intensely, and immediately. This impulse, then, would account for the characteristic types of image, types in which precision, complication, and complicated intellectual relation to the theme are exploited; in other words, they are trying—whatever may be their final success—to carry the movement of mind to the center of the process. On these grounds they are the exact opposite of poets who, presumably on grounds of purity, exclude the movement of mind from the center of the poetic process —from the internal structure of the poem—but pay their respect to it as a kind of footnote, or gloss, or application coming at the end. Marvell and Eliot, by their cutting away of frame, are trying to emphasize the participation of ideas in the poetic process. Then Elliptical Poetry is not, as Mr. Pottle says it is, a pure poetry at all; the elliptical poet is elliptical for purposes of inclusion, not exclusion.

But waiving the question of Elliptical Poetry, no

one of the other theories does—or could—exclude all the items on the list above. And that fact may instruct us. If all of these items were excluded, we might not have any poem at all. For instance, we know how some critics have pointed out that even in the strictest Imagist poetry idea creeps in— when the image leaves its natural habitat and enters a poem, it begins to "mean" something. The attempt to read ideas out of the poetic party violates the unity of our being and the unity of our experience. "For this reason," as Santayana puts it, "philosophy, when a poet is not mindless, enters inevitably into his poetry, since it has entered into his life; or rather, the detail of things and the detail of ideas pass equally into his verse, when both alike lie in the path that has led him to his ideal. To object to theory in poetry would be like objecting to words there; for words, too, are symbols without the sensuous character of the things they stand for; and yet it is only by the net of new connections which words throw over things, in recalling them, that poetry arises at all. Poetry is an attenuation, a rehandling, an echo of crude experience; it is itself a theoretic vision of things at arm's length."

Does this not, then, lead us to the conclusion that poetry does not inhere in any particular element but depends upon the set of relationships, the structure, which we call the poem?

Then the question arises: what elements cannot be used in such a structure? I should answer that nothing that is available in human experience is to be legislated out of poetry. This does not mean that anything can be used in *any* poem, or that some materials or elements may not prove more recalcitrant than others, or that it might not be easy to have too much of some things. But it does mean that, granted certain contexts, any sort of material, a chemical formula for instance, might appear functionally in a poem. It also may mean that, other things being equal, the greatness of a poet depends upon the extent of the area of experience which he can master poetically.

Can we make any generalizations about the nature of the poetic structure? First, it involves resistances, at various levels. There is the tension between the rhythm of the poem and the rhythm of speech (a tension which is very low at the extreme of free verse and at the extreme of verse such as that of "Ulalume," which verges toward a walloping doggerel); between the formality of the rhythm and the informality of the language; between the particular and the general, the concrete and the abstract; between the elements of even the simplest metaphor; between the beautiful and the ugly; between ideas (as in Marvell's poem); between the elements involved in irony (as in "Bells for John Whiteside's Daughter" or "Rose Aylmer"); between prosaisms and poeticisms (as in "Western Wind").

This list is not intended to be exhaustive; it is intended to be merely suggestive. But it may be taken to imply that the poet is like the jujitsu expert; he wins by utilizing the resistance of his opponent— the materials of the poem. In other words, a poem, to be good, must earn itself. It is a motion toward a point of rest, but if it is not a resisted motion, it is motion of no consequence. For example, a poem which depends upon stock materials and stock responses is simply a toboggan slide, or a fall through space. And the good poem must, in some way, involve the resistances; it must carry something of the context of its own creation; it must come to terms with Mercutio.

This is another way of saying that a good poem involves the participation of the reader; it must, as Coleridge puts it, make the reader into "an active creative being." Perhaps we can see this most readily in the case of tragedy: the determination of good or evil is not a "given" in tragedy, it is something to be earned in the process, and even the tragic villain must be "loved." We must kill him, as Brutus killed Caesar, not as butchers but as sacrificers. And all of this adds up to the fact that the structure is a dramatic structure, a movement through action toward rest, through complication toward simplicity of effect.

In the foregoing discussion, I have deliberately omitted reference to another type of pure poetry, a type which tends to become dominant in an age of political crisis and social disorientation. Perhaps the most sensible description of this type can be found in an essay by Herbert Muller:

If it is not the primary business of the poet to be eloquent about these matters [faith and ideals], it still does not follow that he has more dignity or wisdom than those who are, or that he should have more sophistication. At any rate the fact is that almost all poets of the past did freely make large, simple statements, and not in their prosy or lax moments.

Mr. Muller then goes on to illustrate by quoting three famous large, simple statements:

E'n la sua volontade è nostra pace

and

We are such stuff
As dreams are made on; and our little life
Is rounded with a sleep.

and

The mind is its own place, and in itself
Can make a heaven of hell, a hell of heaven.

Mr. Muller is here attacking the critical emphasis on ironic tension in poetry. His attack really involves two lines of argument. First, the poet is not wiser than the statesman, philosopher, or saint, people who are eloquent about faith and ideals and who say what they mean, without benefit of irony. This Platonic line of argument is, I think, off the point in the present context. Second, the poets of the past have made large, simple affirmations, have said what they meant. This line of argument is very much on the point.

Poets *have* tried very hard, for thousands of

years, to say what they mean. Not only have
they tried to say what they mean, they have tried
to prove what they mean. The saint proves his vision by stepping cheerfully into the fires. The poet,
somewhat less spectacularly, proves his vision by
submitting it to the fires of irony—to the drama of
his structure—in the hope that the fires will refine
it. In other words, the poet wishes to indicate that
his vision has been earned, that it can survive reference to the complexities and contradictions of experience. And irony is one such device of reference.

In this connection let us look at the first of Mr.
Muller's exhibits. The famous line occurs in Canto
III of the *Paradiso*. It is spoken by Piccarda Donati,
in answer to Dante's question as to why she does
not desire to rise higher than her present sphere,
the sphere of the moon. But it expresses, in un-
equivocal terms, a central theme of the *Commedia*,
as of Christian experience. On the one hand, it may
be a pious truism, fit for sampler work, and on the
other hand, it may be a burning conviction, tested
and earned. Dante, in his poem, sets out to show
how it has been earned and tested.

One set of ironic contrasts which centers on this
theme concerns, for instance, the opposition between the notion of human justice and the notion of
divine justice. The story of Paolo and Francesca is
so warm, appealing, and pathetic in its human
terms, and their punishment so savage and unre-
lenting, so incommensurable, it seems, with the
fault, that Dante, torn by the conflict, falls down as
a dead body falls. Or Farinata, the enemy of Dante's
house, is presented by the poet in terms of his
human grandeur, which now, in Hell, is transmuted
into a superhuman grandeur,

com' avesse l'inferno in gran dispitto.

Ulysses remains a hero, a hero who should draw
special applause from Dante, who defined the temporal end of man as the conquest of knowledge.
But Ulysses is damned, as the great Brutus is
damned, who hangs from the jaws of the fiend in

the lowest pit of traitors. So divine justice is set
over against human pathos, human dignity, human
grandeur, human intellect, human justice. And we
recall how Virgil, more than once, reminds Dante
that he must not apply human standards to the
sights he sees. It is this long conflict, which appears
in many forms, this ironic tension, which finally
gives body to the simple eloquence of the line in
question; the statement is meaningful, not for what
it says, but for what has gone before. It is earned.
It has been earned by the entire poem.

I do not want to misrepresent Mr. Muller. He
does follow his quotations by the sentence: "If they
are properly qualified in the work as a whole, they
may still be taken straight, they *are* [he italicizes
the word] taken so in recollection as in their immediate impact." But how can we take a line "straight,"
in either "recollection" or "immediate impact," unless we ignore what "properly qualified" the line in
"the work as a whole"? And if we do take it so, are
we not violating, very definitely, the poet's meaning,
for the poet means the *poem*, he doesn't mean the
line.

It would be interesting to try to develop the contexts of the other passages which Mr. Muller
quotes. But in any case, he is simply trying, in
his essay, to guard against what he considers to
be, rightly or wrongly, a too narrow description of
poetry; he is not trying to legislate all poetry
into the type of simple eloquence, the unqualified
statement of "faith and ideas." But we have also
witnessed certain, probably preliminary, attempts
to legislate literature into becoming a simple, unqualified, "pure" statement of faith and ideal. We
have seen the writers of the 1920's called the "irre-
sponsibles." We have seen writers such as Proust,
Eliot, Dreiser, and Faulkner called writers of the
"death drive." Why are these writers condemned?
Because they have tried, within the limits of their
gifts, to remain faithful to the complexities of the
problems with which they are dealing, because they
have refused to take the easy statement as solution,

because they have tried to define the context in which, and the terms by which, faith and ideals may be earned.

This method, however, will scarcely satisfy the mind which is hot for certainties; to that mind it will seem merely an index to lukewarmness, indecision, disunity, treason. The new theory of pure purity would purge out all complexities and all ironies and all self-criticism. And this theory will forget that the hand-me-down faith, the hand-me-down ideals, no matter what the professed content, is in the end not only meaningless but vicious. It is vicious because, as parody, it is the enemy of all faith.

"The Great Mirage":
CONRAD and *Nostromo*

EARLY in 1903, from Pent Farm, which he had rented from Ford Madox Ford, Joseph Conrad wrote to John Galsworthy: "Only with my head full of a story, I have not been able to write a single word— except the title, which shall be, I think: *Nostromo*." On July 8 of the same year, he wrote to R. B. Cunninghame Graham: "I am dying over that cursed *Nostromo* thing. All my memories of Central America seem to slip away. I just had a glimpse 25 years ago,—a short glance. That is not enough *pour bâtir un roman dessus.*" Then on September 1 of 1904, in a letter to Galsworthy, came the cry of triumph: "Finished! Finished! on the 30th in Hope's house in Stanford in Essex." Three days later, in a letter to William Rothenstein, the note of triumph has faded away:

> What the book is like, I don't know. I don't suppose it'll damage me: but I know that it is open to much intelligent criticism. For the other sort I don't care. Personally, I am not satisfied. It is something—but not *the* thing I tried for. There is no exultation, none of that temporary sense of achievement which is so soothing. Even the mere feeling of relief at having done with it is wanting. The strain has been too great, has lasted too long.

And the same day he wrote to Edward Garnett: "Nostromo is finished; a fact upon which my friends may congratulate me as upon a recovery from a dangerous illness."

It was not *the* book that Conrad had tried for. Let us grant that much, for who has ever written *the* book he tried for? But it remains Conrad's supreme effort. He had, as he was to say later in *A Personal Record,* "like the prophet of old 'wrestled with the Lord' for my creation, for the headlands of the coast, for the darkness of the Placid Gulf, the light on the snows, the clouds on the sky, and for the breath of life that had to be blown into the shapes of men and women, of Latin and Saxon, of Jew and Gentile." Here, in *A Personal Record,* the tone of fatigue and frustration has gone: the memory of the heroic struggle remains. And in 1920, in the Preface to *The Secret Agent,* which had been composed years before, just after *Nostromo,* Conrad refers to *Nostromo* as "an intense creative effort on what I suppose will remain my largest canvas."

In many ways *Nostromo* is more fully the fruit of a creative effort than is any other of his stories. It is not a story of those parts of the world that he had known best, the Malay Peninsula and the China seas—the parts where some critics, bemused by Conrad's exoticism and their own notion of his alienation from the modern world, would locate his best work. Rather it is a story of a part of the world that Conrad had never laid eyes on, the West Coast of South America. In general his fiction had depended, by his own account in the Preface to *Within the Tides*, on the conditions of his active life, even though more on "contacts, and very slight contacts at that, than on actual experiences." In the Author's Note to *Nostromo* we discover what "contact" had suggested Nostromo's story and how different the germ in real life is from the imaginative fulfillment. But the story of the stolen silver, suggested by the thievery of a cynical ruffian, and the figure of the Magnificent Capataz, suggested by old Dominic, padrone of the *Tremolino* in the days of Conrad's youth, and the severe charm of Antonia, suggested by Conrad's first love back in Poland, and even the skeptic Decoud, suggested perhaps by some deep, inner voice of Conrad himself, account for little of the finished novel. And they give us nothing of the land, remote and magisterial and vivid, that Conrad evoked in that supreme effort of his imagination.

For it was imagination and not recollection on which he had now to depend. Long before, in 1875 and 1876, when on the *Saint-Antoine* (running guns for a revolution), Conrad had been ashore for a few hours at ports on the Gulf of Mexico, but of the coast that might have given him a model for his Occidental Province and its people he knew nothing. There were books and hearsay to help, the odds and ends of information. But in the end, the land, its people, and its history had to be dreamed up, evoked out of the primal fecund darkness that always lies below our imagination.

The tempo of the book re-enacts for us the process of its creation: the stately vistas and massive involutions of the early chapters while the mists part, as it were, from the land; the nervous concentration of force and complication of event when the

individual passions sublimate themselves in historical process; the moment of pause and poise when
history has become anecdote and the creative conquest seems to have been complete; then, last, the
personal story of Nostromo, before Linda's final, un-
appeasable cry—"Never! Gian' Battista!"—rings
out over the dark Gulf, the part that is really a violent *coda* to the book, the product of the "volcanic
overflow" with which, Conrad tells us, he finished
his twenty months of agonized concentration. The
land and all in it was dreamed up, but it is one of
the most solid and significant dreams that we know,
more solid and significant than most of our actuali-
ties. It is, in my view, the masterwork of that *"puis-
sant rêveur,"* as Gustav Kahn once called Conrad.

Nostromo has not, however, been universally ac-
claimed. Some readers with whom it is dangerous
to disagree have not found it to their taste. For example, Joseph Warren Beach harbors objections to
the technique, as does Albert Guerard, Jr., who
finds the first part an "uncontrolled elaboration
of historical detail," and here and elsewhere misses
a detached narrator; Morton Zabel speaks of the
"dramatic impenetrability"; even F. R. Leavis, who
has done a perceptive and laudatory essay on the
novel and finds it Conrad's masterpiece, ends his
remarks by saying that the "reverberation of *Nostromo* has something hollow about it," and that
"with the color and life there is a suggestion of a
certain emptiness." My purpose is not to answer
these objections, though some answers will be implied if I do manage to carry out my purpose, the
purpose of saying what kind of book *Nostromo* is
and what it means.

We can begin with the proposition that *Nostromo* is central for Conrad's work. When *Nostromo*
appeared in 1904, Conrad had already published
eight books, and this work included *The Nigger of
the "Narcissus"* and *Lord Jim* and the famous novelettes "Heart of Darkness" and "Amy Foster."
Already the world of Conrad's imagination had
exhibited its characteristic persons and issues. Al-

ready we can find the themes of isolation and alienation, of fidelity and human solidarity, of moral
infection and redemption, of the paradox of action
and idea, of the "true lie," of the problem of history.
The characteristic themes and situations and persons had emerged, but had emerged piecemeal,
though in *Lord Jim* and "Heart of Darkness" Conrad had begun to move toward the massive synthesis and complex interfusion which was to engage
him in *Nostromo*. As the earlier fiction seems to
move toward *Nostromo*, so the later fiction seems
to represent, by and large, specializations and elab-
orations of elements that had been in suspension in
that work.

To take some examples, Dr. Monygham is an
older and more twisted Lord Jim, the man who had
failed the test, not like Jim by abandoning his post
and breaking the code of the sea, but by betraying
friends under the torture of a South American dic-
tator. His personal story, like the story of Jim, is
the attempt to restore himself to the human community and to himself, though he, unlike Jim, survives the attempt. Mitchell and Don Pépé belong to
the tribe of Captain MacWhirr of "Typhoon," those
men who by lack of imagination (and Conrad took
imagination to be a great gift and a great curse)
never see all that life may contain "of perfidy, of
violence, and of terror," and who, perhaps for that
very reason, may cling simply and nobly to duty
and fidelity.

Gould himself is a kind of cousin of Kurtz of
"Heart of Darkness," though Gould is doomed to
his isolation, not like Kurtz by avarice, vanity, and
violence, by refusing his mission as a light-bringer,
by repudiating the idea, but by accepting his mission as light-bringer and bearer of the idea. He accepts his mission, but ironically enough he falls a
victim to the impersonal logic of "material interests" and in the end is the slave of his silver, not by
avarice, not by vanity, certainly not vanity in any
simple sense, but because he has lost love to the
enormous abstraction of his historical role. As

Kurtz betrays his Intended to the Heart of Darkness, so Gould betrays his wife to what he takes to be the Heart of Light.

As for Emilia Gould, she is the victim of her husband's mission. Over against the abstractions, she sets up the human community, the sense of human solidarity in understanding and warmth and kindness outside the historical process. It is to her that the dying Nostromo makes his confession. It is she who compels the devotion of the bitter Dr. Monygham. Around her the other characters gather to warm their hands, as it were, at her flame. All but Charles Gould, bemused by his silver and his mission. Her role corresponds, in a way, to the role of Tekla in *Under Western Eyes,* who had been led into revolutionary activity by her sympathy for suffering, had been disillusioned by the character of the revolutionary prophet and tyrannical "feminist" whom she serves and by the abstractions he utters, and finds her fulfilment only when she can devote herself to the broken, dying, guilt-tortured Razumov. As Conrad puts it: "There was nothing in that task to become disillusioned about." But without that flicker of sardonic irony, he says of Mrs. Gould: "It had come into her mind that for life to be large and full, it must contain the care of the past and of the future in every passing moment of the present."

Somehow related to both Charles Gould and Emilia Gould stands the old Garibaldino, Giorgio Viola. He, like Emilia Gould, believes in the human bond, in a brotherhood of liberty, and has risked his life in the hope of bringing the day of liberty nearer to men; but like the idealism of Charles Gould, his idealism is tainted with abstraction. Tainted, but not destroyed, and some warmth remains in his nobility of purpose and his Roman rigor. Viola leans toward Nostromo, would take him as a son, and perhaps we find a symbolic force in this. For Nostromo is the natural man, the son of the people with the pride of the people, contemptuous of the *"hombres finos,"* with their soft hands inexpert on tiller or rifle, half magnificent unconscious animal and half the confused, conscious, tempted man,[1] who is virtuous merely by vanity, for until the combination of opportunity and rancor strikes him he wants nothing but "reputation," that full awareness of his identity ideally projected in the minds and on the tongues of men. As he says to Charles Gould, who wants to reward him for his heroism: "My name is known. . . . What more can you do for me?" This is the man whom old Viola would draw into his orbit by uniting him with Linda, the daughter who carried something of the Garibaldino's depth and fidelity. But Nostromo, who has lived by his vanity, though his vanity idealized, turns to the other daughter, Giselle, the "bad" daughter, and dies by consequence. Nostromo has natural grandeur; but natural grandeur unredeemed by principle, by idea, is not enough.

Without too much wrenching we may take Nostromo's significance as a parallel to that of Captain Brierly in *Lord Jim*. Brierly is the "natural" hero, his achievements all the product of luck and sound nerves and vanity; his suicide results when, seeing Jim on trial for cowardice, he realizes that the natural heroism is not enough and cannot find more in himself to sustain him. We may even say that Nostromo, too, commits a kind of suicide: he has destroyed the self by which he had lived. When, after the theft of the silver, he returns to the port but does not resume his work, he asks Captain Mitchell, "How can I look my cargadores in the face after

---

1. We may take as the key passage about Nostromo the moment at the end of Chapter VII of Part III, when Nostromo, having swum from the Isabels after the burying of the silver, goes to sleep in a "lair" of grass and then wakes: "He stood knee-deep among the whispering undulations of the green blades, with the lost air of a man just born into the world. Handsome, robust, and supple, he threw back his head, flung his arms open, and stretched himself with a slow twist of the waist and a leisurely growling yawn of white teeth, as natural and free from evil in the moment of waking as a magnificent and unconscious wild beast. Then, in the suddenly steadied glance fixed upon nothing from under a forced frown, appeared the man."

losing a lighter?" And Mitchell replies that it had merely been a fatality, that it could not have been helped. *"Si, si!"* Nostromo replies and turns away. It all now seems fated to Nostromo, fated because he had had nothing to depend on to prevent his succumbing and therefore cannot see how things could have been otherwise. But the whole passage bears a kind of double meaning: Nostromo's smile that wrenched Captain Mitchell's heart, and the *"Si, si!"* as he averts his head. He has lost what he had lived by.

Last, we turn to Decoud, the skeptic. He is one of the isolated men, not isolated by foreign blood and speech like the poor, gabbling hero of "Amy Foster," or by a crime like Kurtz or Lord Jim, or by his conception of his role or mission like Gould or Viola, or by personal history like Flora de Barral and Captain Anthony of *Chance* with their "mystic wound" that alienates them from each other.

Decoud's isolation is more like the isolation of Heyst of *Victory;* it is intellectual; that is, whatever its origin may be, even though in such a mystic wound as that of Flora, it presents itself to its victim, and to us, in terms of reason and argument, as a philosophy. But Decoud's philosophy is not the philosophy of Heyst. Heyst fancies himself as the absolute observer, who shrinks from all involvement in life except such involvement as his detached kindness permits. Decoud is a connoisseur of sensation, a *boulevardier,* a dilettante of experience, who "recognized no other virtue than intelligence, and had erected passions into duties." He has only tolerant amusement, tinged with scorn, for the Goulds, for "the sentimentalism of people that will never do anything for the sake of their passionate desire, unless it comes to them clothed in the fair robes of an idea."

But for Decoud, as the story develops, even his own skepticism becomes the subject of skepticism. With self-irony he observes how his passion for Antonia casts him in the role of the father of a revolution and the herald of Progress, and later in the role of heroic adventurer when he finds himself on the dark Gulf in the lighter with Nostromo and the load of silver. And referring to Charles Gould, whose sentimentalism he has just remarked on, he can say that such men "live on illusions which somehow or other help them to get a firm hold of the substance." Where Heyst comes to conversion with the last words, "Ah, Davidson, woe to the man whose heart has not learned while young to hope, to love—and to put its trust in life!" Decoud comes to his end with no vision beyond that which skepticism can achieve by preying upon skepticism, the objective recognition of the pragmatic efficacy of faith despite the fact that faith is an "illusion." What this signifies, however, in the total pattern of the novel we shall come to later.

So much for the main characters of *Nostromo* and their relation to the Conradian family of characters. But we cannot speak of the characters as such, for Conrad, in one sense, had little concern for character independently considered. He is no Dickens or Shakespeare, with relish for the mere variety and richness of personality. Rather, for him a character lives in terms of its typical involvement with situation and theme: the fable, the fable as symbol for exfoliating theme, is his central fact. Therefore, in placing the characters of *Nostromo* we have necessarily touched on the situations and themes. But let us linger a moment longer on this topic.

Conrad writes in *A Personal Record:* "Those who read me know my conviction that the world, the temporal world, rests on a few very simple ideas, so simple that they must be as old as the hills. It rests notably, among others, on the idea of Fidelity." Or again in his tribute to the Merchant Service in 1918, an essay called "Well Done": "For the great mass of mankind the only saving grace that is needed is steady fidelity to what is nearest to hand and heart in the short moment of each human effort." Fidelity and the sense of the job, the discipline of occupation which becomes a moral discipline with its own objective laws, this, for example, is what saves Marlow in "Heart of Darkness" as it had saved the Roman legionaries, those "handy men," when they had ventured into the dark heart of Britain.

Fidelity and the job sense make for the human community, the solidarity in which Conrad finds his final values, "the solidarity of all mankind in simple ideas and sincere emotions." It is through the realization of this community that man cures himself of that "feeling of life-emptiness" which had afflicted the young hero of *The Shadow-Line* before he came to his great test.

The characteristic story for Conrad becomes, then, the relation of man to the human communion. The story may be one of three types: the story of the MacWhirr or the Don Pépé or the Captain Mitchell, the man who lacks imagination and cannot see the "true horror behind the appalling face of things," and who can cling to fidelity and the job; the story of the Kurtz or Decoud, the sinner against human solidarity and the human mission; the story of the redemption, of Lord Jim, Heyst, Dr. Monygham, Flora de Barral, Captain Anthony, Razumov.

The first type of story scarcely engages Conrad. He admires the men of natural virtue, their simplicity, their dogged extroverted sense of obligation and self-respect. But his attitude toward them is ambivalent: they are men "thus fortunate—or thus disdained by destiny or by the sea." They live in a moral limbo of unawareness. They may not be damned like Kurtz or Decoud and achieve that strange, perverse exultation of horror or grim satisfaction by recognizing their own doom, or be saved like Dr. Monygham or Flora de Barral. We may almost say that their significance is in their being, not in their doing, that they have, properly speaking, no "story"; they are the static image of the condition which men who are real and who have real "stories" may achieve by accepting the logic of experience, but which, when earned, has a dynamic value the innocent never know. The man

who has been saved may reach the moment of fulfillment when he can spontaneously meet the demands of fidelity, but his spontaneity must have
been earned, and only by the fact of its having
been earned is it, at last, significant. Therefore, it
is the last type of story that engages Conrad most
fully, the effort of the alienated, whatever the cause
of his alienation, crime or weakness or accident
or the "mystic wound," to enter again the human
communion. And the crisis of this story comes
when the hero recognizes the terms on which he
may be saved, the moment, to take Morton Zabel's
phrase, of the "terror of the awakening."

In this general connection some critics have been
troubled by, or at least have commented on, the
fact that Conrad's prefaces and essays, and even his
autobiographical writings and letters, seem ambiguous, contradictory, false, or blandly misleading in
relation to the fiction. His comments on Fidelity,
such as that above from *A Personal Record,* and his
remarks on human solidarity seem so far away from
the dark inwardness of his work, this inwardness
taken either as the story of his heroes or as the nature of his creative process. When we read parts
of *A Personal Record,* for example, we see the image
of the false Conrad conjured up by reviewers long
ago, the image that William McFee complained
about: "a two-fisted shipmaster" telling us simply
how brave men behave. And we realize how far this
image is from the Conrad who suffered from gout,
malaria, rheumatism, neuralgia, dyspepsia, insomnia, and nerves; who, after the Congo experience
and its moral shock, says of himself, "I lay on my
back in dismal lodgings and expected to go out
like a burnt-out candle any moment. That was
nerves . . ."; who suffered "moments of cruel
blankness"; who on one occasion, years later, had
two doctors attending him, each unaware of the
other, and who at the same time emptied all medicine into the slop; who advised an aspiring writer
that "you must search the darkest corners of your
heart," and told the successful and simple-souled

Galsworthy, a sort of MacWhirr of literature, "the fact is you want more scepticism at the very fountain of your work. Scepticism, the tonic of minds, the tonic of life, the agent of truth—the way of art and salvation"; and who said of his own work, "For me, writing—the only possible writing—is just simply the conversion of nervous force into phrases."

But should we be troubled by this discrepancy between the two Conrads, the Conrad who praised the simple ideas and sincere emotions and the Conrad of the neurotic illnesses and the dark inwardness? No, we should not, but in saying that we should not I mean a little more than what has been offered elsewhere as a resolution of the discrepancy, the notion that the introverted and lonely Conrad, with a sizable baggage of guilts and fears, yearned, even as he mixed some contempt with his yearning, for the simplicity and certainty of the extroverted MacWhirrs of the world. I mean, in addition to this, a corollary of what has been said above about the story of awakening and redemption being the story that engaged Conrad most fully.

Perhaps the corollary can be stated in this fashion: If the central process that engaged Conrad is the process of the earned redemption, that process can only be rendered as "story," and any generalization about it would falsify the process. Instinctively or consciously, Conrad was willing to give the terms of the process, the poles of the situation, as it were, but not an abstract summary. The abstract summary would give no sense of the truth found within, in what, according to the Preface to *The Nigger of the "Narcissus,"* is "that lonely region of stress and strife."

There is another discrepancy, or apparent discrepancy, that we must confront in any serious consideration of Conrad—that between his professions of skepticism and his professions of faith. Already I have quoted his corrosive remark to Galsworthy, but that remark is not as radical as what he says in a letter to R. B. Cunninghame Graham:

The attitude of cold unconcern is the only reasonable one. Of course, reason is hateful—but why? Because it demonstrates (to those who have courage) that we, living, are out of life—utterly out of it. The mysteries of a universe made of drops of fire and clods of mud do not concern us in the least. The fate of humanity condemned ultimately to perish from cold is not worth troubling about . . .

Here, clearly enough, we see the trauma inflicted by nineteenth-century science, a "mystic wound" that Conrad suffered from in company with Hardy, Tennyson, Housman, Stevenson, and most men since their date.

Cold unconcern, an "attitude of perfect indifference" is, as he says in the letter to Galsworthy, "the part of creative power." But this is the same Conrad who speaks of Fidelity and the human communion, and who makes Kurtz cry out in the last horror and Heyst come to his vision of meaning in life. And this is the same Conrad who makes Marlow of "Heart of Darkness" say that what redeems is the "idea only," and makes the devoted Miss Haldin of *Under Western Eyes* say of her dead heroic brother, "Our dear one once told me to remember that men serve always something greater than themselves—the idea."

It is not some, but all, men who must serve the "idea." The lowest and the most vile creature must, in some way, idealize his existence in order to exist, and must find sanctions outside himself. This notion appears over and over in Conrad's fiction. For instance, there is the villainous Ricardo of *Victory*, one of the three almost allegorical manifestations of evil. "As is often the case with lawless natures, Ricardo's faith in any given individual was of a simple, unquestioning character. For a man must have some support in life." Or when Ricardo thinks of the tale of how Heyst had supposedly betrayed Morrison:

For Ricardo was sincere in his indignation before the elementary principle of loyalty to a chum violated in cold blood, slowly, in a patient duplicity of years. There are standards in villainy as in virtue, and the act as he pictured it to himself acquired an additional horror from the slow pace of that treachery so atrocious and so tame.

Then there is the villain Brown of *Lord Jim*. When, after Jim has allowed him to escape, he falls upon the unsuspecting men of Dain Waris, the act is not a "vulgar massacre":

Notice that even in this awful outbreak there is a superiority as of a man who carries right—the abstract thing—within the envelope of his common desires. It was not a vulgar and treacherous massacre; it was a lesson, a retribution. . . .

Even bloodthirstiness or villainy must appeal beyond itself to the "idea." The central passage of *Lord Jim*, Stein's speech about the "destructive element," is the basic text for this theme of Conrad:

A man that is born falls into a dream like a man who falls into the sea. If he tries to climb out into the air as inexperienced people endeavor to do, he drowns—*nicht wahr?* . . . No! I tell you! The way is to the destructive element submit yourself, and with the exertions of your hands and feet in the water make the deep, deep sea keep you up.

I take this, in the context of the action, to read as follows: It is man's fate to be born into the "dream" —the fate of all men. By the dream Conrad here means nothing more or less than man's necessity to justify himself by the "idea," to idealize himself and his actions into moral significance of some order, to find sanctions. But why is the dream like the sea, a "destructive element"? Because man, in one sense, is purely a creature of nature, an animal of black egotism and savage impulses. He should, to follow the metaphor, walk on the dry land of "nature," the real, naturalistic world, and not be dropped into the waters he is so ill equipped to survive in. Those men who take the purely "natural" view, who try to climb out of the sea, who deny the dream and man's necessity to submit to the idea, who refuse to create values that are, quite literally, "super-natural" and therefore human, are destroyed by the dream. They drown in it, and their agony is the agony of their frustrated humanity. Their failure is the failure to understand what is specifically human. They are the Kurtzes, the Browns, in so far as they are villains, but they are also all those isolated ones who are isolated because they have feared to take the full risk of humanity. To conclude the reading of the passage, man, as a natural creature, is not born to swim in the dream, with gills and fins, but if he submits in his own imperfect, "natural" way he can learn to swim and keep himself up, however painfully, in the destructive element. To surrender to the incorrigible and ironical necessity of the "idea," that is man's fate and his only triumph.

Conrad's skepticism is ultimately but a "reasonable" recognition of the fact that man is a natural creature who can rest on no revealed values and can look forward to neither individual immortality nor racial survival. But reason, in this sense, is the denial of life and energy, for against all reason man insists, as man, on creating and trying to live by certain values. These values are, to use Conrad's word, "illusions," but the last wisdom is for man to realize that though his values are illusions, the illusion is necessary, is infinitely precious, is the mark of his human achievement, and is, in the end, his only truth.

From this notion springs the motif of the "true lie," as we may term it, which appears several times in Conrad's fiction. For a first example, we may think of the end of "Heart of Darkness," when Marlow returns from the Congo to his interview with Kurtz's Intended, whose forehead, in the darkening room, "remained illumined by the unextinguishable light of belief and love." She demands to know her beloved's last words, and Marlow, confronted by her belief and love, manages to say: "The last word he pronounced was—your name." He is not able to tell her the literal truth, the words, "The horror!

The horror!" that Kurtz had uttered with his failing breath. If he had done so, "it would have been too dark—too dark altogether . . ." He has, literally, lied, but his lie is a true lie in that it affirms the "idea," the "illusion," belief and love.

Again, in *Under Western Eyes*, Miss Haldin speaks of bringing Razumov, supposedly the friend of her dead brother, to speak to the bereaved mother: "It would be a mercy if mamma could be soothed. You know what she imagines. Some explanation perhaps may be found, or—or even made up, perhaps. It would be no sin."

And even in *Nostromo* the lie that is true, that is no sin, reappears. The incorruptible capataz, dying, is on the verge of telling Mrs. Gould the secret of the stolen treasure, but she will not hear him. When she issues from the room, Dr. Monygham, with the "light of his temperamental enmity to Nostromo" shining in his eyes, demands to know if his long-nourished suspicion of the "incorruptible" Nostromo is correct. He longs to know, to soothe the old wound of his own corruptibility. "He told me nothing," Mrs. Gould says, steadily, and with her charitable lie affirms forever the ideal image of the dead capataz.

Skepticism is the reasonable view of the illusion, but skepticism, the attitude of the intelligence that would be self-sufficient, cannot survive, ironically enough, except by the presence of illusion. The fate of the skeptic Decoud, the "imaginative materialist," who had undertaken to be the natural man in that he had erected passions into duties, is the key parable, among many parables in Conrad, of the meaning of skepticism. Decoud had thought himself outside the human commitments, outside the influence of the "idea," the worshiper of reason, which told him that the only reality is sensation. In so far as his skepticism is "natural," he recognizes the skepticism of Nostromo, the natural man who, "like me, has come casually here to be drawn into the events for which his scepticism as well as mine seems to entertain a sort of passive contempt."

But Decoud's worship of nature and reason is not enough. As soon as he finds himself outside the human orbit, alone with sea and sky, he cannot live. Even skepticism demands belief to feed on; the opposite pole of the essential situation must be present for skepticism to survive.

Solitude from mere outward condition of existence becomes very swiftly a state of soul in which the affectation of irony and scepticism have no place. . . . After three days of waiting for the sight of some human face, Decoud caught himself entertaining a doubt of his own individuality. It had emerged into the world of cloud and water, of natural forces and forms of nature. In our activity alone do we find the sustaining illusion of an independent existence as against the whole scheme of things of which we form a helpless part.

Decoud has reached the ultimate stage of skepticism: his skepticism has dissolved his identity into nature. But even at this moment of his spiritual, and physical, death, he experiences the "first moral sentiment of his manhood," the vague awareness of "a misdirected life." Now both intelligence and passion are "swallowed up easily in this great unbroken solitude of waiting without faith." In this "sadness of a sceptical mind," he beholds "the universe as a succession of incomprehensible images." His act of shooting himself and letting his body fall into the sea is merely the literal repetition of an already accomplished fate: he is "swallowed up in the immense indifference of things."

How are we to reconcile the moral of the story of Decoud, or of Heyst, with Conrad's statements of a radical skepticism—or with even a radical pessimism, the notion of man as a savage animal driven by a black ego? Can we say, as F. R. Leavis says, that "Nostromo was written by a Decoud who wasn't a complacent dilettante, but was positively drawn towards those capable of 'investing their activities with spiritual value'—Monygham, Giorgio Viola, Señor Avellanos, Charles Gould"? Or can we say, as Albert Guerard, Jr., says, that against man's

heart of darkness we can "throw up only the bar-
rier of semi-military ethics; courage, order, tradition and unquestioned discipline; and as a last resort, the stoic's human awareness of his own plight,
a pessimism *'plus sombre que la nuit'* "? Both these
statements are, in one sense, true. They do describe
the bias of Conrad's temperament as I read it, but
they do not describe, to my satisfaction at least, the
work that Conrad produced out of that temperament. We must sometimes force ourselves to remember that the act of creation is not simply a
projection of temperament, but a criticism and
purging of temperament.

If Conrad repudiates the Decouds of the world,
even as they speak with, as Leavis says, his "personal *timbre*," he also has for the MacWhirrs of the
world, the creatures of "semi-military ethics," a
very ambivalent attitude, and some of the scorn of
a man who knows at least a little of the cost of
awareness and the difficulty of virtue. In other
words, his work itself is at center dramatic: it is
about the cost of awareness and the difficulty of
virtue, and his characteristic story is the story of
struggle and, sometimes, of redemption. Skepticism,
he wrote to Galsworthy, is "the tonic of minds,
the tonic of life, the agent of truth—the way of
art and salvation." This is, I suppose, a parallel to
Hardy's famous statement: ". . . if way to the Better there be, it exacts a full look at the Worst. . . ."
It is a way of saying that truth is not easy, but it is
also a way of saying that truth, and even salvation,
may be possible. Must we choose between the Decouds and the MacWhirrs? There is also Stein; and
Emilia Gould, who thought: "Our daily work must
be done to the glory of the dead, and for the good
of those who come after."

Let us turn, at long last, to *Nostromo*, the novel.
In this book Conrad endeavored to create a great,
massive, multiphase symbol that would render his
total vision of the world, his sense of individual
destiny, his sense of man's place in nature, his
sense of history and society.

First, *Nostromo* is a complex of personal stories, intimately interfused, a chromatic scale of attitudes, a study in the definition and necessity of "illusion" as Conrad freighted that word. Each character lives by his necessary idealization, up the scale from the "natural" man Nostromo, whose only idealization is that primitive one of his vanity, to Emilia Gould, who, more than any other, has purged the self and entered the human community.

The personal stories are related not only in the contact of person and person in plot and as carriers of variations of the theme of illusion, but also in reference to the social and historical theme. That is, each character is also a carrier of an attitude toward, a point of view about, society; and each is an actor in a crucial historical moment. This historical moment is presumably intended to embody the main issues of Conrad's time: capitalism, imperialism, revolution, social justice. Many of the personal illusions bear quite directly on these topics: Viola's libertarianism, with its dignity and leonine self-sufficiency and, even, contempt for the mob; Charles Gould's obsession in his mission; Avellanos' liberalism and Antonia's patriotic piety; Holroyd's concern with a "pure form of Christianity" which serves as a mask and justification for his imperialistic thirst for power; even the posturing and strutting "Caesarism" of Pedrito Montero, whose imagination had been inflamed by reading third-rate historical novels.

All readers of Conrad know the classic picture of imperialism at its brutal worst in "Heart of Darkness," the degradation and insanity of the process, and remember the passage spoken by Marlow:

"The conquest of the earth, which mostly means the taking it away from those who have a different complexion or slightly flatter noses than ourselves, is not a pretty thing when you look into it too much. What redeems it is the idea only."

In "Heart of Darkness" we see the process absolutely devoid of "idea," with lust, sadism, and greed

rampant. In *Nostromo* we see the imperialistic process in another perspective, as the bringer of order
and law to a lawless land, of prosperity to a land
of grinding poverty. At least, that is the perspective
in which Charles Gould sees himself and his
mine:

"What is wanted here is law, good faith, order, security.
Anyone can declaim about these things, but I pin my
faith to material interests. Only let the material interests
once get a firm footing, and they are bound to impose
the conditions on which alone they can continue to exist. That's how your money-making is justified here in
the face of lawlessness and disorder. It is justified because the security which it demands must be shared
with an oppressed people."

This passage and Gould's conception of his own
role may be taken as the central fact of the social
and historical theme of *Nostromo*. But how does
Conrad intend us to regard this passage? Albert
Guerard, Jr., in his careful and brilliant study of
Conrad, says that the mine "corrupts Sulaco, bringing civil war rather than progress." That strikes me
as far too simple. There has been a civil war but
the forces of "progress"—i.e., the San Tomé mine
and the capitalistic order—have won. And we must
admit that the society at the end of the book is
preferable to that at the beginning.

Charles Gould's statement, and his victory, are,
however, hedged about with all sorts of ironies.
For one thing—and how cunning is this stroke!—
there is Decoud's narrative, the letter written to his
sister in the midst of the violence, that appears at
the very center of the book; and the voice of the
skeptic tells us how history is fulfilled. For another thing—and this stroke is even more cunning
—old Captain Mitchell, faithful-hearted and stupid,
the courageous dolt, is the narrator of what he
pleases to call the "historical events." His is the
first human voice we have heard, in Chapter II
of Part I, after the mists part to exhibit the great
panorama of the mountains, campo, city, and gulf;

and in Chapter X of Part III, just after Nostromo
has made his decision to ride to Cayta and save
the Concession and the new state, the voice of Captain Mitchell resumes. He is speaking long after-
ward, to some nameless distinguished visitor, and
now all the violence and passion and the great
anonymous forces of history come under the unconscious irony of his droning anecdotes. We can say
of Captain Mitchell what Conrad says of Pedrito
Montero, inflamed by his bad novels read in a Pari-
sian garret: his mind is "wrapped . . . in the fu-
tilities of historical anecdote." Captain Mitchell's
view is, we may say, the "official view": "Progress"
has triumphed, the world has achieved itself, there
is nothing left but to enjoy the fruits of the famous
victory. Thus the very personalities of the narrators
function as commentary (in a triumph of technical
virtuosity) as their voices are interpolated into Conrad's high and impersonal discourse.

But we do not have to depend merely on this subtle commentary. Toward the end of the book, at a
moment of pause when all seems to be achieved on
a sort of Fiddler's Green at the end of history, a
party has gathered in the garden of the Casa Gould.
They discuss in a desultory way the possibility of
a new revolution, and the existence of secret socie-
ties in which Nostromo, despite his secret treasure
and growing wealth, is a great force. Emilia Gould
demands: "Will there never be any peace?" And
Dr. Monygham replies:

"There is no peace and no rest in the development of
material interests. They have their law and their justice.
But it is founded on expediency, and is inhuman; it is
without rectitude, and without the continuity and force
that can be found only in a moral principle. Mrs. Gould,
the time approaches when all that the Gould Concession
stands for shall weigh as heavily upon the people as the
barbarism, cruelty, and misrule of a few years back."

The material interests have fulfilled their historical mission, or are in the process of fulfilling it.
Even Charles Gould, long before, in defining his

mission to bring order through the capitalistic development, had not seen that order as the end, only
as a phase. He had said: "A better justice will come
afterwards. That's our ray of hope." And in this
connection we may recall in *Under Western Eyes*
how, after hearing the old teacher of languages give
his disillusioned view of revolution, Miss Haldin
can still say: "I would take liberty from any hand
as a hungry man would snatch at a piece of bread.
The true progress must begin after." In other words,
the empire-builder and hard-bitten realist Gould
and the idealistic girl join to see beyond the era of
material interests and the era of revolution the
time of "true progress" and the "better justice."
Somewhere, beyond, there will be, according to Miss
Haldin's version, the period of concord:

I believe that the future will be merciful to us all. Revolutionist and reactionary, victim and executioner, be-
trayer and betrayed, they shall all be pitied together
when the light breaks on our black sky at last. Pitied and
forgotten; for without that there can be no union and
no love.

Emilia Gould, trapped in her "merciless nightmare"
in the "Treasure House of the World," leans over
the dying capataz and hears him say, "But there is
something accursed in wealth." Then he begins to
tell her where the treasure is hidden. But she bursts
out: "Let it be lost for ever."

If in this moment of vision, Emilia Gould and
(in a sense that we shall come to) Conrad himself
repudiate the material interests as merely a step
toward justice, what are we to make of revolution?
We may remember that Conrad most anxiously
meditated the epigraphs of his various books, and
that the epigraph of *Nostromo* is the line from
Shakespeare: "So foul a sky clears not without a
storm." It is innocent to think that this refers
merely to the "storm" which is the action of the
novel, the revolution that has established the order
of material interests in Sulaco. If the sky has
cleared at the end of that episode, even now in the

new peace we see, as Dr. Monygham sees, the blacker and more terrible thunderheads piling up on the far horizon.

"Heart of Darkness" and *Nostromo* are, in one sense, an analysis and unmasking of capitalism as it manifested itself in the imperialistic adventure. Necessarily this involves the topic of revolution. The end of *Nostromo* leaves the sky again foul, and in the years immediately after finishing that novel Conrad turns to two studies of revolution, *The Secret Agent*, begun in 1905 and published in 1907, and *Under Western Eyes*, begun in 1908 and published in 1911. These books are in their way an analysis and unmasking of revolution to correspond to the already accomplished analysis and unmasking of capitalism and imperialism. In the world of revolution we find the same complex of egotism, vanity, violence, and even noble illusion. As the old teacher of languages in *Under Western Eyes* puts it:

A violent revolution falls into the hands of the narrow-minded fanatics and of tyrannical hypocrites at first. Afterwards comes the turn of all the pretentious intellectual failures of the time. Such are the chiefs and the leaders. You will notice that I have left out the mere rogues. The scrupulous and the just, the noble, humane, and devoted natures; the unselfish and the intelligent may begin a movement—but it passes away from them. They are not the leaders of a revolution. They are its victims: the victims of disgust, of disenchantment— often of remorse. Hopes grotesquely betrayed, ideal caricatured—that is the definition of revolutionary success. There have been in every revolution hearts broken by such successes.

We could take this, in appropriate paraphrase, as a summary of the situation at the end of *Nostromo*. There is the same irony of success. There has been the same contamination of the vision in the very effort to realize the vision. As Emilia Gould reflects: "There was something inherent in the necessities of successful action which carried with it the moral degradation of the idea."

Man, however, is committed to action. The

Heysts, who repudiate action, find their own kind of damnation. Wisdom, then, is the recognition of man's condition, the condition of the creature made without gills or fins but dropped into the sea, the necessity of living with the ever renewing dilemma of idea as opposed to nature, morality to action, "utopianism" to "secular logic" (to take Razumov's terms from *Under Western Eyes*), justice to material interests. Man must make his life somehow in the dialectical process of these terms, and in so far as he is to achieve redemption he must do so through an awareness of his condition that identifies him with the general human communion, not in abstraction, not in mere doctrine, but immediately. The victory is never won, the redemption must be continually re-earned. And as for history, there is no Fiddler's Green, at least not near and soon. History is a process fraught with risks, and the moral regeneration of society depends not upon shifts in mechanism but upon the moral regeneration of men. But nothing is to be hoped for, even in the most modest way, if men lose the vision of the time of concord, when "the light breaks on our black sky at last." That Platonic vision is what makes life possible in its ruck and confusion, if we are to take Conrad's word from the essay called "Books":

I would require from him [the artist] many acts of faith of which the first would be the cherishing of an undying hope; and hope, it will not be contested, implies all the piety of effort and renunciation. It is the God-sent form of trust in the magic force and inspiration belonging to the life of this earth. We are inclined to forget that the way of excellence is in the intellectual, as distinguished from emotional, humility. What one feels so hopelessly barren in declared pessimism is just its arrogance. It seems as if the discovery made by many men at various times that there is much evil in the world were a source of proud and unholy joy unto some of the modern writers. That frame of mind is not the proper one in which to approach seriously the art of fiction. It gives an author—goodness only knows why—an elated sense of

his own superiority. And there is nothing more dangerous than such an elation to that absolute loyalty towards
his own feelings and sensations an author should keep
hold of in his most exalted moments of creation.

To be hopeful in an artistic sense it is not necessary
to think that the world is good. It is enough to believe
that there is no impossibility of its being made so.

Nothing, however, is easy or certain. Man is pre-
cariously balanced in his humanity between the
black inward abyss of himself and the black outward abyss of nature. What Conrad meant by and
felt about man's perilous balance must already be
clear, if I can make it clear at all. But now I shall
speak of *Nostromo* as an image of this.

The setting of the story, the isolation of Sulaco,
is in itself significant. The serrated wall of the
Cordillera, hieratic and snow-capped, behind the
Campo, the Azuera and the Golfo Placido define
a little world that comes to us as complete—as a
microcosm, we may say, of the greater world and
its history. Man is lost in this overwhelming scene.
The story of the two gringos, spectral and alive, on
the peninsula of Azuera is, of course, a fable of
greed and of the terrifying logic of material interests unredeemed. But it is also a fable, here at the
threshold of *Nostromo,* of man lost in the blankness of nature. At the center of the book, to resume
the same theme, we find the story of Decoud, who
loses his identity into the "world of cloud and water, of natural forces and forms of nature." When
he commits suicide, he falls into the "immense indifference of things." Then at the very end of the
novel, in the last paragraph, Dr. Monygham, in the
police-galley, hears the wild, faithful cry uttered by
Linda, the name of Nostromo: "Never! Gian' Battista!"

It was another of Nostromo's successes, the greatest, the
most enviable, the most sinister of all. In that true cry
of love and grief that seemed to ring aloud from Punta
Mala to Azuera and away to the bright line of the horizon, overhung by a big white cloud shining like a mass
of solid silver, the genius of the magnificent capataz de

cargadores dominated the dark gulf containing his con-
quests of treasure and love.

This, too, is a fable: the passionate cry in the
night that is a kind of triumph in the face of the
immense indifference of things. It is a fable with
a moral not unlike that of the second of Yeats's
"Two Songs from a Play":

> *Whatever flames upon the night*
> *Man's own resinous heart has fed.*

Or to take another fable, one from Conrad's essay on Henry James:

When the last aqueduct shall have crumbled to pieces,
the last airship fallen to the ground, the last blade of
grass have died upon a dying earth, man, indomitable
by his training in resistance to misery and pain, shall
set this undiminished light of his eyes against the feeble
glow of the sun. . . .
For my own part, from a short and cursory acquaintance with my kind, I am inclined to think that the last
utterance will formulate, strange as it may appear, some
hope now to us utterly inconceivable.

I have tried to define my reading of Conrad's
work in general and of *Nostromo* in particular. In
these matters there is not, and should not be, an
ultimate "reading," a final word and orthodoxy of
interpretation. In so far as a work is vital, there
will continually be a development, an extrapolation
of significance. But at any one moment each of us
must take the risk of his sensibility and his logic
in making a reading. I have taken this risk, and
part of the risk is the repudiation, or at least criticism, of competing interpretations.

There is one view, not uncommonly encountered,
that Conrad did not intend his fiction to have
"meaning." We encounter, for example, the comment of Edward Crankshaw: "Bothering about
what Conrad meant in 'Heart of Darkness' is as irrelevant as bothering about what Mozart meant in
the Haffner Symphony." Conrad himself gives
some support to this view in his skeptical bias, in

his emphasis on the merely spectacular value of life, and in not a few of his remarks on his literary intentions, particularly in the famous one: "My task which I am trying to achieve is, by the power of the written word, to make you hear, to make you feel—it is, before all, to make you *see*."

All of this seems to me, however, to mean nothing more than that Conrad was an artist, that he wanted, in other words, to arrive at his meanings immediately, through the sensuous renderings of passionate experience, and not merely to define meanings in abstraction, as didacticism or moralizing. Conrad made no split between literature and life. If anything, he insisted on the deepest inward relationship. As he put it about the writer in the essay "Books": "It is in the impartial practice of life, if anywhere, that the promise of perfection for his art can be found, rather than in the absurd formulas trying to prescribe this or that particular method of technique or conception."

Over and over again, Conrad implies what he says in the Author's Note to *Chance*: "But every subject in the region of intellect and emotion must have a morality of its own if it is treated at all sincerely; and even the most artful writer will give himself (and his morality) away in about every third sentence." And even to the famous sentence about his intention being, before all, to make us *"see,"* we find an addition: "That—and no more, and it is everything." To seeing in its fullest sense, to "our sympathetic imagination," as Conrad says in "Autocracy and War," we must look "for the ultimate triumph of concord and justice."

If in *A Personal Record* Conrad declares himself an "imperfect Esthete," in the same sentence he admits that he is "no better philosopher." Leavis goes so far as to affirm that Conrad cannot be said to have a philosophy: "He is not one of those writers who clear up their fundamental attitudes for themselves in such a way that we may reasonably, in talking of them, use that portentous term." In discussing this remark, as I am about to do, I run

the risk of making Conrad's work seem too schematic and of implying that he somehow sat down
and worked out a philosophy which he then projected, with allegorical precision, into fiction. I
mean nothing of the sort, but I do mean to say that
in my judgment Leavis takes Conrad's work as too
much a casual matter of temperament. For I think
that even if Conrad is as "imperfect" philosopher as
esthete, he is still, in the fullest sense of the term,
a philosophical novelist.

The philosophical novelist, or poet, is one for
whom the documentation of the world is constantly
striving to rise to the level of generalization about
values, for whom the image strives to rise to symbol, for whom images always fall into a dialectical
configuration, for whom the urgency of experience,
no matter how vividly and strongly experience may
enchant, is the urgency to know the meaning of experience. This is not to say that the philosophical
novelist is schematic and deductive. It is to say
quite the contrary, that he is willing to go naked
into the pit, again and again, to make the same
old struggle for his truth. But we cannot better Conrad's own statement for the philosophical novelist,
the kind of novelist he undertook, quite consciously,
to be: "Even before the most seductive reveries I
have remained mindful of that sobriety of interior
life, that asceticism of sentiment, in which alone
the naked form of truth, such as one conceives it,
can be rendered without shame."

For him the very act of composition was a way of
knowing, a way of exploration. In one sense this is
bound to be true of all composition, but the matter
of degree and self-consciousness is important in
our present distinction, even crucial. We know a
little of how *Nostromo* came to be, how it rose out
of a feeling of blankness, how its composition was,
in sober fact, an exploration and a growth, how the
"great mirage," as Edward Garnett called it, took
shape until it could float before us, vivid and severe, one of the few mastering visions of our historical moment and our human lot.

WILLIAM FAULKNER

AT THE age of fifty-three, William Faulkner has written nineteen books which for range of effect, philosophical weight, originality of style, variety of characterization, humor, and tragic intensity are without equal in our time and country. Let us grant, even so, that there are grave defects in Faulkner's work. Sometimes the tragic intensity becomes mere sensationalism, the technical virtuosity mere complication, the philosophical weight mere confusion of mind. Let us grant that much, for Faulkner is a very uneven writer. The unevenness is, in a way, an index to his vitality, his willingness to take risks, to try for new effects, to make new explorations of material and method. And it is, sometimes at least, an index to a very important fact about Faulkner's work. The fact is that he writes of two Souths: he reports one South and he creates another. On one hand he is a perfectly straight realistic writer, and on the other he is a symbolist.

Let us speak first of that realistic South, the South which we can recognize by its physical appearance and its people. In this realistic way we can recognize that county which Faulkner calls Yoknapatawpha County, the county in which most of his stories occur and most of his people live. Jefferson, the county seat of Yoknapatawpha County, is already the most famous county seat in the nation, and is as solidly recognizable as anybody's home town. There is Miss Emily's house, the big squarish frame house, once white, decorated with cupolas and spires and scrolled balconies, in the heavily lightsome style of the seventies, once on the most select street but now surrounded by garages and cotton gins, lifting its stubborn and coquettish decay above the cotton wagons and gasoline pumps. There is Uncle Gavin's law office. There is the cedar-bemused cemetery. There is the jail where a hundred years ago, or near, the jailer's daughter, a young girl, scratched her name with a diamond on a windowpane. There are the neat small new one-story houses designed in Florida and California, set with matching garages in their neat plots of clipped grass and tedious flower beds. Then beyond that town where we recognize every item, the country stretches away, the plantation houses, the cotton fields the back country of Frenchman's Bend, where Snopeses and Varners live, the Beat Four section, where the Gowrie clan holds the land and brawls and makes whiskey in the brush.

We know everything about Yoknapatawpha County. Its 2,400 square miles lie between the hills of north Mississippi and the rich black bottom lands. No land in all fiction lives more vividly in its physical presence than this county of Faulkner's imagination—the pine-winey afternoons, the nights with a thin sickle of moon like the heel print of a boot in wet sand, the tremendous reach of the big river in flood, yellow and sleepy in the afternoon, and the little piddling creeks, that run backward one day and forward the next and come busting down on a man full of dead mules and hen houses, the ruined plantation which was Popeye's hangout, the swamps and fields and dusty roads, the last remnants of the great original forests, "green with gloom" in summer, "if anything actually dimmer than they had been in November's gray dissolution, where even at noon the sun fell only in windless dappling upon earth which never completely dried." A little later I shall speak of what the physical world means to Faulkner, but for the moment I wish only to insist on its vividness, its recognizability.

This county has a population of 15,611 persons, who spill in and out of Faulkner's books with the startling casualness of life, not explaining them-

selves or asking to be explained, offering their being with no apology, as though we, the readers,
were the intruders on their domain. They compose
a society with characters as various as the Bundrens of *As I Lay Dying;* the Snopeses of *The Hamlet* and several stories; the Gowries of *Intruder in
the Dust;* Ike McCaslin of "The Bear" and "Delta
Autumn"; Percy Grimm, the gun-mad Nazi proto-
type of *Light in August;* Temple Drake, the dubious little heroine of *Sanctuary;* the Compsons, the
ruined great family; Christmas, the tortured and
self-torturing mulatto of *Light in August;* Dilsey,
the old Negro woman, heroic and enduring, who
stands at the center of *The Sound and the Fury;*
Wash, the no-good poor-white; and Sutpen, the
violent bearer of the great design which the Civil
War had brought to nothing, in *Absalom, Absalom;*
and the tall convict of *The Wild Palms.* No land
in all fiction is more painstakingly analyzed from
the sociological point of view. The descendants of
the old families, the descendants of bushwhackers
and carpetbaggers, the swamp rats, the Negro cooks
and farm hands, the bootleggers and gangsters,
tenant farmers, college boys, county-seat lawyers,
country storekeepers, peddlers—all are here in
their fullness of life and their complicated in-
terrelations. The marks of class, occupation, and
history are fully rendered, and we know completely
their speech, food, dress, houses, manners, and
attitudes.

Faulkner not only gives us the land and the people as we can see them today; he gives us glimpses
of their history. His stories go back to the time
when the Indians occupied Yoknapatawpha County
and held slaves, and the first Compson came
with a small, light-waisted, strong-hocked mare
that could do two furlongs in under a half-minute,
and won all the races from Ikkemotubbe's young
braves until Ikkemotubbe swapped him a square
mile of that land for the little mare. We know how
Sartorises, the aristocrats, and Sutpens, nameless,
driven, rancorous, ambitious men, seized the land,

created a society, fought a war to defend that society, lost the war, and watched their world change
and the Snopeses arise. The past is dramatized in
situation after situation, in its full complication.
It is a recognizable past, not a romanticized past,
though we find many characters in Faulkner who
are themselves romantics about that past, Quentin
of *The Sound and the Fury* or Hightower of *Light
in August.*

The land, the people, and their history—they
come to us at a realistic level, at the level of recognition. This realistic, recognizable world is one of
the two Souths about which Faulkner writes. As
a realist he knows this world; it is the world he
lives in and carries on his daily business in. To
represent this world with full fidelity is in itself a
great achievement, and I would not underrate it.
But this achievement is not Faulkner's claim to
our particular attention. That claim is the world
he creates out of the materials of the world he
presents. Yoknapatawpha County, its people and
its history, is also a parable—as Malcolm Cowley
has called it, a legend.

We can approach the significance of this legend
by thinking of the land and its history as a fate or
doom—words that are often on Faulkner's page.
From the land itself, from its rich soil yearning
to produce, and from history, from an error or sin
committed long ago and compounded a thousand
times over, the doom comes. That is, the present
is to be understood, and fully felt, only in terms of
the past.

The men who seized the land from the Indians
were determined to found an enduring and stable
order. They brought to this project imagination and
rectitude and strength and integrity and cunning
and endurance, but their project—or their great
"design," to use Sutpen's word from *Absalom, Absalom*—was doomed from the first. It was "accurst"
—to use one of Faulkner's favorite words—by
chattel slavery. There is a paradox here. The fact
of slavery itself was not a single, willed act. It was

a natural historical growth. But it was an evil, and
all its human and humane mitigations and all its
historical necessity could not quiet the bad conscience it engendered. The Civil War began the fulfillment of the doom. The war was fought with
courage and fortitude and strength but with divided
conscience. Not that the enemy was the bearer of
light—the enemy was little better than a blind instrument of doom or fate. After the Civil War the
attempt to rebuild according to the old plan and
for the old values was defeated by a combination
of forces: the carpetbaggers, the carriers of Yankee
exploitation—or better, a symbol of it, for the real
exploiters never left their offices fifteen hundred
miles away—and the Snopeses, a new exploiting
indigenous class descended from the bushwhackers
and landless whites.

Meanwhile, most of the descendants of the old
order are in various ways incompetent. For one
thing, in so far as they carry over into the new
world the code of behavior prescribed by the old
world, some sense of honor and honesty, they
are at a disadvantage in dealing with the Snopeses,
who have no code, who are pure pragmatists. But
often the descendant of the old order clings to the
letter of his tradition and forgets the spirit. George
Marion O'Donnell, in one of the first perceptive
essays ever published on Faulkner, pointed out
the story "There Was a Queen" as an example of
this. The heroine, in order to get possession of
certain obscene and insulting letters written her
by a Snopes, gives herself to a detective who has
blackmailed her. That is, to protect her reputation,
she is willing to perform the act which will render
the reputation a mere sham.

We find something of the same situation with the
whining Mrs. Compson, the mother in *The Sound
and the Fury*, who with her self-pity and insistence
on her "tradition" surrenders all the decency which
the tradition would have prescribed, the honor and
courage. Or the exponents of the tradition may
lose all contact with reality and escape into a dream

world of alcohol or rhetoric or madness or sexual dissipation. Or they fall in love with defeat and death, like Quentin Compson, who commits suicide at Harvard. Or they lose nerve and become cowardly drifters. Or, worst of all, they try to come to terms with reality by adopting Snopesism, like the last Jason of *The Sound and the Fury*, whose portrait is one of the most terrifying in all literature—the paranoidal self-deceiver, who plays the cotton market and when he loses, screams about those "kikes" in New York who rob him, who himself robs the daughter of his sister Caddy over the years and in the end makes her into the desperate and doomed creature she becomes, who under the guise of responsibility for his family—the ailing mother, the idiot brother, the wild niece—tortures them all with an unflagging sadistic pleasure.

The point to insist on here is that you do not characteristically have noble examples of antique virtue beset by little and corrupt men. There are a few such examples of the antique virtue—old Ike McCaslin, for example, whom we shall come to later—but the ordinary situation is to find the descendant of the old order contributing, actively or passively, to his own ruin and degradation. He is not merely a victim, and he frequently misunderstands his own tradition.

Over against these people there stand, as we have said, the forces of "modernism," embodied in various forms. There are, of course, the Snopeses, the pure exploiters, descendants of barn-burners and bushwhackers, of people outside of society, belonging to no side, living in a kind of limbo, not even having the privilege of damnation, reaching their apotheosis in Flem Snopes, who becomes a bank president in Jefferson. But there is also Popeye, the gangster of *Sanctuary*, with eyes like "rubber knobs," a creature with "that vicious depthless quality of stamped tin," the man who "made money and had nothing he could do with it, spend it for, since he knew that alcohol would kill him

like poison, who had no friends and had never
known a woman." Popeye is a kind of dehumanized
robot, a mere mechanism, an abstraction, and as
such he is a symbol for what Faulkner thinks of
as modernism, for the society of finance capitalism.

It is sometimes said that Faulkner's theme is
the disintegration of the Southern traditional life.
For instance, Malcolm Cowley, in his fine introduction to the *Portable Faulkner*, says that the
violence of Faulkner's work is "an example of the
Freudian method turned backward, being full of
sexual nightmares that are in reality social symbols. It is somehow connected in the author's mind
with what he regards as the rape and corruption
of the South." And Maxwell Geismar, whose lack
of comprehension of Faulkner strikes me as monu-
mental, interprets Faulkner's work as merely Southern apologetics, as "the extreme hallucinations" of
a "cultural psychosis."

It is true that Faulkner deals almost exclusively
with the Southern scene, it is true that the conflict
between past and present is a constant concern
for him, it is true that the Civil War is always
behind his work as a kind of backdrop, and it is
true, or at least I think it is true, that in Faulkner's
work there is the implication that Northern arms
were the cutting edge of modernism. But granting
all this, I should put the emphasis not in terms of
South and North, but in terms of issues common
to our modern world.

The Faulkner legend is not merely a legend of
the South but of a general plight and problem. The
modern world is in moral confusion. It does suffer
from a lack of discipline, of sanction, of community of values, of a sense of mission. We don't have
to go to Faulkner to find that out—or to find that
it is a world in which self-interest, workableness,
success provide the standards of conduct. It was a
Yankee who first referred to the bitch goddess Success. It is a world in which the individual has lost
his relation to society, the world of the power

state in which man is a cipher. It is a world in which man is the victim of abstraction and mechanism, or at least, at moments, feels himself to be. It can look back nostalgically upon various worlds of the past, Dante's world of the Catholic synthesis, Shakespeare's world of Renaissance energy, or the world of our grandfathers who lived before Shiloh and Gettysburg, and feel loss of traditional values and despair in its own aimlessness and fragmentation. Any of those older worlds, so it seems now, was a world in which, as one of Faulkner's characters puts it, men "had the gift of living once or dying once instead of being diffused and scattered creatures drawn blindly from a grab bag and assembled"—a world in which men were, "integer for integer," more simple and complete.

At this point we must pause to consider an objection. Someone will say, and quite properly, that there never was a golden age in which man was simple and complete. Let us grant that. But we must grant that even with that realistic reservation man's conception of his own role and position has changed from time to time. It is unhistorical to reduce history to some dead level, and the mere fact that man in the modern world is worried about his role and position is in itself significant.

Again, it may be objected, and quite properly, that any old order that had satisfied human needs would have survived; that it is sentimental to hold that an old order is killed from the outside by certain wicked people or forces. But when this objection is applied to Faulkner it is based on a misreading of his work. The old order, he clearly indicates, did *not* satisfy human needs, did *not* afford justice, and therefore was "accurst" and held the seeds of its own ruin. But the point is this: the old order, even with its bad conscience and confusion of mind, even as it failed to live up to its ideal, cherished the concept of justice. Even in terms of the curse, the old order as opposed to the new order (in so far as the new order is equated with Snopesism) allowed the traditional man to define himself as human by setting up codes, ideas of virtue, however mistaken; by affirming obligations, however arbitrary; by accepting the risks of humanity. But Snopesism has abolished the concept, the very possibility of entertaining the idea of virtue. It is not a question of one idea and interpretation. It is simply that no idea of virtue is conceivable in the world in which practical success is the criterion.

Within the traditional world there had been a notion of truth, even if man in the flow of things could not readily define or realize his truth. Take, for instance, a passage from "The Bear."

'All right,' he said. 'Listen,' and read again, but only one stanza this time and closed the book and laid it on the table. 'She cannot fade, though thou has not thy bliss,' McCaslin said: 'Forever wilt thou love, and she be fair.'

'He's talking about a girl,' he said.

'He had to talk about something,' McCaslin said. Then he said, 'He was talking about truth. Truth is one. It doesn't change. It covers all things which touch the heart—honor and pride and pity and justice and courage and love. Do you see now?'

The important thing, then, is the presence of the concept of truth—that covers all things which touch the heart and define the effort of man to rise above the mechanical process of life.

When it is said, as it is sometimes said, that Faulkner is "backward-looking," the answer lies, I think, in the notion expressed above. The "truth" is neither of the past nor of the future. Or rather, it is of both. The constant ethical center of Faulkner's work is to be found in the glorification of human effort and human endurance, which are not confined to any one time. It is true that Faulkner's work contains a savage attack on modernity, but the values he admires *are* found in our time. The point is that they are found most often in people who are outside the stream of the dominant world, the "loud world," as it is called in *The Sound and the Fury*. Faulkner's world is full of "good" people—Byron Bunch, Lucas Beauchamp, Dilsey, Ike McCaslin, Uncle Gavin, Benbow, the justice of the peace in *The Hamlet*, Ratliff of the same book, Hightower of *Light in August*—we could make an impressive list, probably a longer list from Faulkner than from any other modern writer. "There are good men everywhere, at all times," Ike McCaslin says in "Delta Autumn."

It is not ultimately important whether the traditional order (Southern or other) as depicted by Faulkner fits exactly the picture which critical historical method provides. Let it be granted that Faulkner does simplify the matter. What remains important is that his picture of the traditional order has a symbolic function in contrast to the modern world which he gives us. It is a way of embodying his values—his "truth."

In speaking of the relation of the past to the present, I have mentioned the curse laid upon the present, the Southern present at least, by slavery. But also, as I have said, Faulkner is not concerned ultimately with the South, but with a general philosophical view. Slavery merely happens to be the particular Southern curse. To arrive at his broader philosophical view, we can best start with his notions of Nature.

For one thing, one of the most impressive features of Faulkner's work is the vivid realization of the natural background. It is accurately observed, as accurately as in Thoreau, but observation provides only the stuff from which Faulkner's characteristic effects are gained. It is the atmosphere that counts, the infusion of feeling, the symbolic weight. Nature provides a backdrop—of lyric beauty, as in the cow episode of *The Hamlet;* of homely charm, as in the trial scene after the spotted horses episode of the same book; of sinister, brooding force, as in the river episodes from *The Wild Palms*—a backdrop for the human action and passion.

Nature is, however, more than a backdrop. There is an interrelation between man and nature, some-

thing not too unlike the Wordsworthian communion. At least, at moments, there is the communion,
the interrelation. The indestructible beauty is there,
beyond man's frailty. "God created man," Ike
McCaslin says in "Delta Autumn," "and He created
the world for him to live in and I reckon He created
the kind of world He would have wanted to live in
if He had been a man."

Ideally, if man were like God, as Ike McCaslin
puts it, man's attitude toward nature would be one
of pure contemplation, pure participation in nature's great forms and appearances, pure communion. The appropriate attitude for this communion
is love, for with Ike McCaslin, who is as much
Faulkner's spokesman as any other character, the
moment of love is equated with godhood. But since
man "wasn't quite God himself," since he lives in
the world of flesh, he must be a hunter, user, and
violator. To return to McCaslin's words: God "put
them both here: man and the game he would follow and kill, foreknowing it. I believe He said, 'So
be it.' I reckon He even foreknew the end. But He
said, 'I will give him his chance. I will give him
warning and foreknowledge too, along with the
desire to follow and the power to slay. The woods
and the fields he ravages and the game he devas-
tates will be the consequence and signature of his
crime and guilt, and his punishment.' "

There is, then, a contamination implicit in the
human condition—a kind of Original Sin, as it
were—the sin of use, exploitation, violation. So
slavery is but one of the many and constant forms
of that Original Sin. But it is possible—and necessary if man is to strive to be human—to achieve
some measure of redemption through love. For
instance, in "The Bear," the great legendary beast
which is pursued from year to year to the death is
also an object of love and veneration, and the symbol of virtue; and the deer hunt of "Delta Autumn"
is for old Ike McCaslin a ritual of renewal. Those
who have learned the right relationship to nature
—"the pride and humility" which Ike as a boy

learns from the half-Negro, half-Indian Sam Fathers (he learns it appropriately from an outcast)
—are set over against those who do not have it.
In "The Bear," General Compson speaks up to Cass
McCaslin to defend the wish of the boy Ike McCaslin to stay an extra week in the woods:

"You've got one foot straddled into a farm and the other
foot straddled into a bank; you aint even got a good
hand-hold where this boy was already an old man long
before you damned Sartorises and Edmondses invented
farms and banks to keep yourselves from having to find
out what this boy was born knowing and fearing too
maybe but without being afraid, that could go ten miles
on a compass because he wanted to look at a bear none
of us had ever got near enough to put a bullet in and
looked at the bear and came the ten miles back on the
compass in the dark; maybe by God that's the why and
the wherefore of farms and banks."

The Sartorises and Edmondses, according to
General Compson, have in their farms and banks
something of the contamination, they have cut
themselves off from the fundamental truth which
young Ike already senses. But the real contamination is that of the pure exploiters, the apostles of
abstractionism, those who have the wrong attitude toward nature and therefore toward other
men.

We have a nice fable of this in the opening of
Sanctuary, in the contrast between Benbow, the
traditional man, and Popeye, the symbol of
modernism. While the threat of Popeye keeps Benbow crouching by the spring, he hears a Carolina
wren sing, and even under these circumstances
tries to recall the local name for it. And he says
to Popeye: "And of course you dont know the name
of it. I dont suppose you'd know a bird at all,
without it was singing in a cage in a hotel lounge,
or cost four dollars on a plate." Popeye, as we
may remember, spits in the spring (he hates nature and must foul it), is afraid to go through the
woods ("Through all them trees?" he demands

when Benbow points out the short cut), and when an owl whisks past them in the twilight, he claws at Benbow's coat with almost hysterical fear. "It's just an owl," Benbow explains. "It's nothing but an owl."

The pure exploiters are, however, caught in a paradox. Though they may gain ownership and use of a thing, they never really have it. Like Popeye, they are impotent. For instance, Flem Snopes, the central character and villain of *The Hamlet*, who brings the exploiter's mentality to the quiet country of Frenchman's Bend, finally marries Eula Varner, a kind of fertility goddess or earth goddess; but his ownership is meaningless, for she never refers to him as anything but "that man"—she does not even have a name for him—and he had got her only after she had given herself willingly to one of the hot-blooded boys of the neighborhood. In fact, nothing can, in one sense, be "owned." Ike McCaslin, in "The Bear," says of the land which had come down to him:

'It was never Father's and Uncle Buddy's to bequeath to me to repudiate because it was never Grandfather's to bequeath them to bequeath me to repudiate because it was never old Ikkemotubbe's to sell to Grandfather for bequeathment and repudiation. Because it was never Ikkemotubbe's fathers' fathers' to bequeath Ikkemotubbe to sell to Grandfather or any man because on the instant when Ikkemotubbe discovered, realized, that he could sell it for money, on that instant it ceased ever to have been his forever, father to father to father, and the man who bought it bought nothing.'

In other words, reality cannot be bought. It can only be had by love.

The right attitude toward nature and man is love. And love is the opposite of the lust for power over nature or over other men, for God gave the earth to man, we read in "The Bear," not "to hold for himself and his descendants inviolable title forever, generation after generation, to the oblongs and squares of the earth, but to hold the earth mutual and intact in the communal anonymity of brotherhood, and all the fee He [God] asked was pity and humility and sufferance and endurance and the sweat of his face for bread." It is the failure of this pity that curses the earth and brings on the doom. For the rape of nature and the rape of man are always avenged. Mere exploitation without love is always avenged because the attitude which commits the crime in itself leads to its own punishment, so that man finally punishes himself. It is along this line of reasoning that we can read the last page of "Delta Autumn":

This land which man has deswamped and denuded and derivered in two generations so that white men can own plantations and commute every night to Memphis and black men own plantations and ride in jim crow cars to Chicago to live in millionaires' mansions on Lakeshore Drive, where white men rent farms and live like niggers and niggers crop on shares and live like animals, where cotton is planted and grows man-tall in the very cracks of the sidewalks, and usury and mortgage and bankruptcy and measureless wealth, Chinese and African and Aryan and Jew, all breed and spawn together until no man has time to say which one is which nor cares. . . . No wonder the ruined woods I used to know dont cry for retribution! he thought: *The people who have destroyed it will accomplish its revenge.*

Despite the emphasis on the right relation to nature, and the communion with nature, the attitude toward nature in Faulkner's work does not involve a sinking into nature. In Faulkner's mythology man has "suzerainty over the earth," he is not of the earth, and it is the human virtues that count —"pity and humility and endurance." If we take even the extreme case of the idiot Snopes and his fixation on the cow in *The Hamlet* (a scene whose function in the total order of the book is to show that even the idiot pervert is superior to Flem), a scene in which the human being appears as close as possible to the "natural" level, we find that the scene is the most lyrical in Faulkner's work: even

the idiot is human and not animal, for only human
desires, not animal desires, must clothe themselves
in poetry. I think that George Marion O'Donnell is
right in pointing to the humanism-naturalism opposition in Faulkner's work, and over and over
again we find that the point of some story or novel
has to do with the human effort to break out of
the mechanical round of experience at the merely
"natural" level—"not just to eat and evacuate and
sleep warm," as Charlotte Rittenmeyer says in
The Wild Palms, "so we can get up and eat and
evacuate in order to sleep warm again," or not
just to raise cotton to buy niggers to raise cotton
to buy niggers, as it is put in another place. Even
when a character seems to be caught in the iron
ring of some compulsion, of some mechanical process, the effort may be discernible. And in Quentin's
attempt in *The Sound and the Fury* to persuade his
sister Caddy, who is pregnant by one of the town
boys of Jefferson, to confess that she has committed
incest with him, we find among other things the
idea that "the horror" of the crime and the "clean
flame" of guilt would be preferable to the meaninglessness of the "loud world." More is at stake in
Quentin's attitude than the snobbery of a Compson,
which would prefer incest to the notion that his
sister has had to do with one of the underbred
town boys.

And that leads us to the question of class and
race. There is a current misconception on this
point, the notion that Faulkner's Snopesism is a
piece of snobbery. It is true that the Snopeses are
poor whites, descendants of bushwhackers (those
who had no side in the Civil War but tried to make
a good thing out of it), but any careful reader
should realize that a Snopes is not to be equated
with a poor white. For instance, the book most
fully about the poor white, *As I Lay Dying,* is
charged with sympathy and poetry. There are a
hundred touches like that in Cash's soliloquy about
the phonograph:

I reckon it's a good thing we ain't got ere a one of them. I reckon I wouldn't never get no work done a-tall for listening to it. I don't know if a little music ain't about the nicest thing a fellow can have. Seems like when he comes in tired of a night, it ain't nothing could rest him like having a little music played and him resting.

Or like the long section devoted to Addie Bundren, a section full of eloquence like that of this paragraph:

And then he died. He did not know he was dead. I would lie by him in the dark, hearing the dark land talking of God's love and His beauty and His sin; hearing the dark voicelessness in which the words are the deeds, and the other words that are not deeds, that are just the gaps in peoples' lacks, coming down like the cries of geese out of the wild darkness in the old terrible nights, fumbling at the deeds like orphans to whom are pointed out in a crowd two faces and told, That is your father, your mother.

The whole of *As I Lay Dying* is based on the heroic effort of the Bundren family to fulfill the promise to the dead mother to take her body to Jefferson; and the fact that Anse Bundren, after the effort is completed, immediately gets him a new wife, "the duck-shaped woman," does not negate the heroism of the effort or the poetry in which it is clothed. We are told by one critic that "what should have been the drama of the Bundrens thus becomes in the end a sort of brutal farce," and that we are "unable to feel the tragedy because the author has refused to accept the Bundrens, as he did accept the Compsons, as tragic." Rather, I should say, the Bundrens come off a little better than the latter-day Compsons, the whining, self-deluding mother, the promiscuous Caddy, the ineffectual Quentin, and the rest, including the vile Jason. The Bundrens at least are capable of the heroic effort. What the conclusion indicates is that even such a fellow as Anse Bundren, in the grip of an idea, in terms of promise or code, can rise above his ordinary level; Anse falls back at the end, but only after the prop of the obligation has been removed. And we can recall that Wash Jones has been capable of some kind of obscure dream, as his attachment to Sutpen indicates, and that in the end, in his murder of Sutpen, he achieves dignity and manhood.

The final evidence that the Snopeses are not to be equated with "poor white" comes in *The Hamlet.* The point of the book is the assault made by the Snopes family on a community of plain, hard-working small farmers. And if the corruption of Snopesism does penetrate into the community, there is no one here, not even Flem Snopes, who can be compared to Jason of *The Sound and the Fury,* the Compson who has embraced Snopesism.

As for the poor white, there has been a grave misconception in some quarters concerning the Negro in Faulkner's work. In one of Faulkner's books it is said that every white child is born crucified on a black cross, and remarks like this have led to the notion that Faulkner "hates" Negroes—or at least all Negroes except the favored black servitors. For instance, we find Maxwell Geismar exclaiming what a "strange inversion" it is to take the Negro, who is the "tragic consequence," and to exhibit him as the "evil cause" of the failure of the old order in the South. But all this is to misread the text. It is slavery, not the Negro, which is defined quite flatly as the curse, and the Negro is the black cross in so far as he is the embodiment of the curse, the reminder of the guilt, the incarnation of the problem. The black cross is, then, the weight of the white man's guilt, the white man who now sells salves and potions to "bleach the pigment and straighten the hair of Negroes that they might resemble the very race which for two hundred years had held them in bondage and from which for another hundred years not even a bloody civil war would have set them completely free." The curse is still operative, as the crime is still compounded.

The actual role of the Negro in Faulkner's fiction is consistently one of pathos or heroism. There is

Dilsey, under whose name in the Compson gene-
alogy Faulkner writes, "They endured," and whose
role in *The Sound and the Fury* is to be the very
ethical center of the book, the vessel of virtue and
compassion. Then there is the Negro in "Red
Leaves," the slave held by Indians who is hunted
down to be killed at the funeral of the chief. When
he is overtaken, one of the Indians says to him,
"You ran well. Do not be ashamed," and when he
walks among the Indians, he is "the tallest there,
his high, close, mud-caked head looming above
them all." And old Sam Fathers is the fountain of
the wisdom which Ike McCaslin, Faulkner's philosopher, finally gains, and the repository of the virtues central for Faulkner—"an old man, son of a
Negro slave and an Indian king, inheritor on the
one hand of the long chronicle of a people who
had learned humility through suffering and learned
pride through the endurance which survived the
suffering, and on the other side the chronicle of a
people even longer in the land than the first, yet
who now existed there only in the solitary brotherhood of an old and childless Negro's alien blood and
the wild and invincible spirit of an old bear." Even
Christmas in *Light in August* is a mixture of pathos
and heroism. With his mixed blood, he is the lost,
suffering, enduring creature, and even the murder
he commits at the end is a fumbling attempt to
define his manhood, an attempt to break out of the
iron ring of mechanism, for the woman whom he
kills has become a figure of the horror of the human which has surrendered human attributes.

Or for a general statement let us take a passage
from "The Bear":

'Because they will endure. They are better than we are.
Stronger than we are. Their vices are vices aped from
white men or that white men and bondage have taught
them: improvidence and intemperance and evasion—
not laziness: evasion: of what white men had set them
to, not for their aggrandisement or even comfort but his
own—' and McCaslin

'All right. Go on: Promiscuity. Violence. Instability

and lack of control. Inability to distinguish between mine and thine—' and he

'How distinguish, when for two hundred years mine did not even exist for them?' and McCaslin

'All right. Go on. And their virtues—' and he

'Yes. Their own. Endurance—' and McCaslin

'So have mules:' and he

'—and pity and tolerance and forbearance and fidelity and love of children—' and McCaslin

'So have dogs:' and he

'—whether their own or not or black or not. And more: what they got not only from white people but not even despite white people because they had it already from the old free fathers a longer time free than us because we have never been free—'

It is in *Intruder in the Dust,* however, that his views of the Negro are most explicit and best dramatized. Lucas Beauchamp, the stiff-necked and high-nosed old Negro man, is accused on good evidence of having shot a white man in the back, and is lodged in the Jefferson jail with a threat of lynching. The lynching is averted and Lucas's innocence established by a boy and an old lady. But what is important about the book is two-fold: First, there is the role of Lucas as hero, the focus of dignity and integrity. Second, there is the quite explicit and full body of statement, which comes to us through the lips of Gavin, the lawyer-uncle of the boy who saves Lucas. To quote Gavin:

'. . . the postulate that Sambo is a human being living in a free country and hence must be free. That's what we are really defending [against the North]: the privilege of setting him free ourselves: which we will have to do for the reason that nobody else can since going on a century ago now the North tried it and have been admitting for seventy-five years now that they failed. So it will have to be us. Soon now this sort of thing [the lynching] wont even threaten anymore. It shouldn't now. It should never have. Yet it did last Saturday and it probably will again, perhaps once more, perhaps twice more. But then no more, it will be finished; the shame will still be there of course but then the whole chronicle of man's immortality is in the suffering he has endured, his struggle toward the stars in the stepping-stones of his expiations. Someday Lucas Beauchamp can shoot a white man in the back with the same impunity to lynch-rope or gasoline as a white man; in time he will vote anywhen and anywhere a white man can and send his children to the same school anywhere the white man's children go and travel anywhere the white man travels as the white man does it. But it won't be next Tuesday. . . .'

This is not the whole passage, or even the burden of the whole passage, but it merits our lingering. The motive behind the notion of "defending" against the North is not merely resentment at easy Phariseeism. It is something else, two other things in fact. First, the realization that legislation in itself never solves a really fundamental question. Legislation can only reflect a solution already arrived at. Second, the problem is finally one of understanding and, in a sense, conversion: conversion and, as the passage puts it, expiation. That is, the real problem is a spiritual and moral one. The story of *Intruder in the Dust* is, in a sense, the education of the boy, and the thing he learns is a lesson in humanity. This can be brought to focus on two parallel episodes. He sees Lucas on the street one day, and Lucas walks past him without recognition. Later he realizes that Lucas had been grieving for his dead wife. Again, in the cemetery where the body of a Gowrie had been exhumed, he sees old Stub Gowrie, the father of the man Lucas had presumably killed, and realizes that this head of the brawling, mean, lawless Gowrie clan is grieving, too. The recognition of grief, the common human bond, that is his education.

That is the central fact in Faulkner's work, the recognition of the common human bond, a profound respect for the human. There are, in one way, no villains in his work, except those who deny the human bond. Even some of the Snopes family are, after all, human: the son of the barn-burner in the story "Barn-Burning," or Mink in *The Hamlet*. The

point about the Gowries in *Intruder in the Dust* is
the same: the Gowries seem to be the enemy, the
pure villains, but in the end there is the pure grief
on old Stub's face, and he is human, after all.

If respect for the human is the central fact of
Faulkner's work, what makes that fact significant
is that he realizes and dramatizes the difficulty of
respecting the human. Everything is against it, the
savage egotism, the blank appetite, stupidity and
arrogance, even virtues sometimes, the misreading
of our history and tradition, our education, our
twisted loyalties. That is the great drama, however,
the constant story. His hatred of "modernism"—
and we must quote the word to give it his special
meaning—arises because he sees it as the enemy
of the human, as abstraction, as mechanism, as irresponsible power, as the cipher on the ledger or
the curve on a graph.

And the reference to modernism brings us back
to the question of the past and the present. But what
of the future? Does Faulkner come to a dead end,
setting up traditional virtues against the blank
present, and let the matter stand there? No, he
does not. But he holds out no easy solutions for
man's "struggle toward the stars in the stepping-
stones of his expiations." He does, however, give
a sense of the future, though as a future of struggle
in working out that truth referred to in "The Bear."
We can remember that old Ike McCaslin, at the
end of "Delta Autumn" gives General Compson's
hunting horn to the mulatto girl who has been deserted by her young kinsman, saying, "We will have
to wait." And *The Sound and the Fury,* which is
Faulkner's *Waste Land,* ends with Easter and the
promise of resurrection.

ERNEST HEMINGWAY

IN MAY, 1929, in *Scribner's Magazine,* the first installment of *A Farewell to Arms* appeared. The novel was completed in the issue of October, and was published in book form the same year. Ernest Hemingway was already regarded, by a limited literary public, as a writer of extraordinary freshness and power, as one of the makers, indeed, of a new American fiction. *A Farewell to Arms* more than justified the early enthusiasm of the connoisseurs for Hemingway, and extended his reputation from them to the public at large. Its great importance was at once acknowledged, and its reputation has survived through the changing fashions and interests of many years.

What was the immediate cause of its appeal? It told a truth about the first world war, and a truth about the generation who had fought it and whose lives, because of the war, had been wrenched from the expected pattern and the old values. Other writers had told or were to tell similar truths about this war. John Dos Passos in *Three Soldiers*, E. E. Cummings in *The Enormous Room*, William Faulkner in *Soldier's Pay*, Maxwell Anderson and Laurence Stallings in *What Price Glory*? All these writers had presented the pathos and endurance and gallantry of the individual caught and mangled in the great anonymous mechanism of a modern war fought for reasons that the individual could not understand, found insufficient to justify the event, or believed to be no reasons at all. And *A Farewell to Arms* was not the first book to record the plight of the men and women who, because of the war, had been unable to come to terms with life in the old way. Hemingway himself in *The Sun Also Rises*, 1926, had given the picture of the dislocated life of young English and American expatriates in the bars of Paris, the "lost generation," as Gertrude Stein defined them. But before that, F. Scott Fitzgerald, who had been no nearer to the war than an officers' training camp, had written of the lost generation. For the young people about whom Fitzgerald wrote, even when they were not veterans and even when their love stories were enacted in parked cars, fraternity houses, and country clubs and not in the cafés and hotels of Paris, were like Hemingway's expatriates under the shadow of the war and were groping to find some satisfaction in a world from which the old values had been withdrawn. Hemingway's expatriates had turned their backs on the glitter of the Great Boom of the 1920's, and Fitzgerald's young men were usually drawn to the romance of wealth and indulgence, but this difference is superficial. If Hemingway's young men begin by repudiating the Great Boom, Fitzgerald's young men end with disappointment in what even success has to offer. "All the sad young men" of Fitzgerald—to take the title of one of his collections of stories—and the "lost generation" of Hemingway are seekers for landmarks and bearings in a terrain for which the maps have been mislaid.

A Farewell to Arms, which appeared ten years after the first world war and on the eve of the collapse of the Great Boom, seemed to sum up and bring to focus an inner meaning of the decade being finished. It worked thus, not because it disclosed the end results that the life of the decade was producing—the discontents and disasters that were beginning to be noticed even by unreflective people—but because it cut back to the beginning of the process, to the moment that had held within itself the explanation of the subsequent process.

Those who had grown up in the war, or in its shadow could look back nostalgically, as it were, to the lost moment of innocence of motive and purity of emotion. If those things had been tar-

nished or manhandled by the later business of living, they had, at least, existed, and on a grand scale.
If they had been tarnished or manhandled, it was
not through the fault of the individual who looked
back to see the image of the old simple and heroic
self in Frederick or Catherine, but through the impersonal grindings of the great machine of the universe. *A Farewell to Arms* served, in a way, as the
great romantic alibi for a generation, and for those
who aped and emulated that generation. It showed
how cynicism or disillusionment, failure of spirit
or the worship of material success, debauchery or
despair, might have been grounded in heroism,
simplicity, and fidelity that had met unmerited defeat. The early tragedy could cast a kind of flatter-
ing and extenuating afterglow over what had come
later. The battlefields of *A Farewell to Arms* explained the bars of *The Sun Also Rises*—and explained the young Krebs, of the story "Soldier's
Home," who came back home to a Middle-Western
town to accept his own slow disintegration.

This is not said in disparagement of *A Farewell
to Arms*. It is, after all, a compliment to the
hypnotic force of the book. For the hypnotic force
of the book was felt from the first, and it is not unusual for such a book to be relished by its first readers for superficial reasons and not for the essential
virtues that may engage those who come to it later.

In accounting for the immediate appeal of *A
Farewell to Arms*, the history of the author himself
is of some importance. In so far as the reader knew
about Ernest Hemingway in 1929, he knew about a
young man who seemed to typify in his own experience the central experience of his generation.
Behind the story of *A Farewell to Arms* and his
other books there was the shadow of his own story
that could stamp his fiction with the authenticity of
a document and, for the more impressionable, with
the value of a revelation. He could give an ethic
and a technique for living, even in the face of defeat or frustration, and yet his own story was the

story that we have always loved: the American success story.

He was born in Oak Park, Illinois, in the Middle West—that region which it was fashionable to condemn (after Mencken and Sinclair Lewis) as romanceless, but which became endowed, paradoxically enough, with the romance of the American average. His father was a physician. There were two boys and four girls in the family. In the summers the family lived in northern Michigan, where there were Indians, and where lake, streams, and forests gave boyhood pursuits their appropriate setting. In the winters he went to school in Oak Park. He played football in high school, ran away from home, returned and, in 1917, graduated. After graduation he was for a short time a reporter on the *Kansas City Star*, but the war was on and he went to Italy as a volunteer ambulance driver. He was wounded and decorated, and after his recovery served in the Italian army as a soldier. For a time after the war he was a foreign correspondent for the *Toronto Star*, in the Near East.

In the years after the war Hemingway set about learning, quite consciously and with rigorous self-discipline, the craft and art of writing. During most of his apprenticeship he lived in Paris, one of the great number of expatriates who were drawn to the artistic capital of the world to learn to be writers, painters, sculptors, or dancers, or simply to enjoy on a low monetary exchange the freedom of life away from American or British conventions. "Young America," writes Ford Madox Ford, "from the limitless prairies leapt, released, on Paris. They stampeded with the madness of colts when you let down the slip-rails between dried pasture and green. The noise of their advancing drowned all sounds. Their innumerable forms hid the very trees on the boulevards. Their perpetual motion made you dizzy." And of Hemingway himself: "He was presented to me by Ezra [Pound] and Bill Bird and had rather the aspect of an Eton-Oxford, huskyish young captain of a midland regiment of His Britannic Majesty. . . . Into that animated din would drift Hemingway, balancing on the point of his toes, feinting at my head with hands as large as hams and relating sinister stories of Paris landlords. He told them with singularly choice words in a slow voice." [1]

The originality and force of Hemingway's early stories, published in little magazines and in limited editions in France, were recognized from the first by many who made their acquaintance. The seeds of his later work were in those stories of *In Our Time*, concerned chiefly with scenes of inland American life and a boy's growing awareness of that life in contrast to vivid flashes of the disorder and brutality of the war years and the immediate postwar years in Europe. There are both contrast and continuity between the two elements of *In Our Time*. There is the contrast between the lyric rendering of one aspect of the boyhood world and the realistic rendering of the world of war, but there is also a continuity, because in the boyhood world there are recurring intimations of the blackness into which experience can lead even in the peaceful setting of Michigan.

With the publication of *The Sun Also Rises*, in 1926, Hemingway's work reached a wider audience, and at the same time defined more clearly the line his genius was to follow and his role as one of the spokesmen for a generation. But *A Farewell to Arms* gave him his first substantial popular success and established his reputation. It was a brilliant and compelling novel; it provided the great alibi; it crowned the success story of the American boy from the Middle West, who had hunted and fished, played football in high school, been a newspaper reporter, gone to war and been wounded and decorated, wandered exotic lands as a foreign correspondent, lived the free life of the Latin Quarter of Paris, and, at the age of thirty, written a best

1. Introduction to the Modern Library edition of *A Farewell to Arms*.

seller—athlete, sportsman, correspondent, soldier, adventurer, and author.

It would be possible and even profitable to discuss *A Farewell to Arms* in isolation from Hemingway's other work. But Hemingway is a peculiarly personal writer, and for all the apparent objectivity and self-suppression in his method as a writer, his work, to an uncommon degree, forms a continuous whole. One part explains and interprets another part. It is true that there have been changes between early and late work, that there has been an increasing self-consciousness, that attitudes and methods that in the beginning were instinctive and simple have become calculated and elaborated. But the best way to understand one of his books is, nevertheless, to compare it with both earlier and later pieces and seek to discern motives and methods that underlie all of his work.

Perhaps the simplest way into the whole question is to consider what kind of world Hemingway writes about. A writer may write about his special world merely because he happens to know that world, but he may also write about that special world because it best dramatizes for him the issues and questions that are his fundamental concerns—because, in other words, that special world has a kind of symbolic significance for him. There is often—if we discount mere literary fashion and imitation— an inner and necessary reason for the writer's choice of his characters and situations. What situations and characters does Hemingway write about?

They are usually violent. There is the hard-drinking and sexually promiscuous world of *The Sun Also Rises;* the chaotic and brutal world of war, as in *A Farewell to Arms, For Whom the Bell Tolls,* many of the inserted sketches of *In Our Time,* the play *The Fifth Column,* and some of the stories; the world of sport, as in "Fifty Grand," "My Old Man," "The Undefeated," "The Snows of Kilimanjaro"; the world of crime, as in "The Killers," "The

Gambler, the Nun, and the Radio," and *To Have and Have Not*. Even when the situation of a story does not fall into one of these categories, it usually involves a desperate risk, and behind it is the shadow of ruin, physical or spiritual. As for the typical characters, they are usually tough men, experienced in the hard worlds they inhabit, and not obviously given to emotional display or sensitive shrinking—men like Rinaldi or Frederick Henry of *A Farewell to Arms*, Robert Jordan of *For Whom the Bell Tolls*, Harry Morgan of *To Have and Have Not*, the big-game hunter of "The Snows of Kilimanjaro," the old bullfighter of "The Undefeated," or the pugilist of "Fifty Grand." Or if the typical character is not of this seasoned order, he is a very young man, or boy, first entering the violent world and learning his first adjustment to it.

We have said that the shadow of ruin is behind the typical Hemingway situation. The typical character faces defeat or death. But out of defeat or death the character usually manages to salvage something. And here we discover Hemingway's special interest in such situations and characters. His heroes are not squealers, welchers, compromisers, or cowards, and when they confront defeat they realize that the stance they take, the stoic endurance, the stiff upper lip mean a kind of victory. If they are to be defeated they are defeated upon their own terms; some of them have even courted their defeat; and certainly they have maintained, even in the practical defeat, an ideal of themselves—some definition of how a man should behave, formulated or unformulated—by which they have lived. They represent some notion of a code, some notion of honor, that makes a man a man, and that distinguishes him from people who merely follow their random impulses and who are, by consequence, "messy."

In case after case, we can illustrate this "principle of sportsmanship," as Edmund Wilson has called it, at the center of a story or novel. Robert Jordan, in *For Whom the Bell Tolls*, is somehow happy as he lies, wounded, behind the machine gun that is to cover the escape of his friends and his sweetheart from Franco's Fascists. The old bull-fighter, in "The Undefeated," continues his incompetent fight even under the jeers and hoots of the crowd, until the bull is dead and he himself is mortally hurt. Francis Macomber, the rich young sportsman who goes lion-hunting in "The Short, Happy Life of Francis Macomber," and who has funked it and bolted before a wounded lion, at last learns the lesson that the code of the hunter demands that he go into the bush after an animal he has wounded. Brett, the heroine of *The Sun Also Rises*, gives up Romero, the young bullfighter with whom she is in love, because she knows she will ruin him, and her tight-lipped remark to Jake, the newspaper man who is the narrator of the novel, might almost serve as the motto of Hemingway's work: "You know it makes one feel rather good deciding not to be a bitch."

It is the discipline of the code that makes man human, a sense of style or good form. This applies not only in isolated, dramatic cases such as those listed above, but is a more pervasive thing that can give meaning, partially at least, to the confusions of living. The discipline of the soldier, the form of the athlete, the gameness of the sportsman, the technique of an artist can give some sense of the human order, and can achieve a moral significance. And here we see how Hemingway's concern with war and sport crosses his concern with literary style. If a writer can get the kind of style at which Hemingway, in *Green Hills of Africa*, professes to aim, then "nothing else matters. It is more important than anything else he can do." It is more important because, ultimately, it is a moral achievement. And no doubt for this reason, as well as for the reason of Henry James's concern with cruxes of a moral code, he is, as he says in *Green Hills of Africa*, an admirer of the work of Henry James, the devoted stylist.

But to return to the subject of Hemingway's

world: the code and the discipline are important because they can give meaning to life that otherwise seems to have no meaning or justification. In other words, in a world without supernatural sanctions, in the God-abandoned world of modernity, man can realize an ideal meaning only in so far as he can define and maintain the code. The effort to do so, however limited and imperfect it may be, is the characteristically human effort and provides the tragic or pitiful human story. Hemingway's attitude on this point is much like that of Robert Louis Stevenson in "Pulvis et Umbra":

Poor soul, here for so little, cast among so many hardships, filled with desires so incommensurate and so inconsistent, savagely surrounded, savagely descended, irremediably condemned to prey upon his fellow lives: who should have blamed him had he been of a piece with his destiny and a being merely barbarous? And we look and behold him instead, filled with imperfect virtues . . . an ideal of decency, to which he would rise if it were possible; a limit of shame, below which, if it be possible, he will not stoop. . . . Man is indeed marked for failure in his effort to do right. But where the best consistently miscarry how tenfold more remarkable that all should continue to strive; and surely we should find it both touching and inspiriting, that in a field from which success is banished, our race should not cease to labor. . . . It matters not where we look, under what climate we observe him, in what stage of society, in what depth of ignorance, burthened with what erroneous morality; by campfires in Assiniboia, the snow powdering his shoulders, the wind plucking his blanket, as he sits, passing the ceremonial calumet and uttering his grave opinions like a Roman senator; on ships at sea, a man inured to hardship and vile pleasures, his brightest hope a fiddle in a tavern and a bedizened trull who sells herself to rob him, and he for all that, simple, innocent, cheerful, kindly like a child, constant to toil, brave to drown, for others; . . . in the brothel, the discard of society, living mainly on strong drink, fed with affronts, a fool, a thief, the comrade of thieves, and even here keeping the point of honor and the touch of pity, often repaying the world's scorn with service, often standing firm upon a scruple, and at a certain cost, rejecting riches:—everywhere some virtue cherished or affected, everywhere some decency of thought or carriage, everywhere the ensign of man's ineffectual goodness! . . . under every circumstance of failure, without hope, without help, without thanks, still obscurely fighting the lost fight of virtue, still clinging, in the brothel or on the scaffold, to some rag of honor, the poor jewel of their souls! They may seek to escape, and yet they cannot; it is not alone their privilege and glory, but their doom; they are condemned to some nobility. . . .

Hemingway's code is more rigorous than Stevenson's and perhaps he finds fewer devoted to it, but, like Stevenson, he can find his characteristic hero and characteristic story among the discards of society, and, like Stevenson, is aware of the touching irony of that fact. But for the moment the important thing in the parallel is that, for Stevenson, the world in which this drama of pitiful aspiration and stoic endurance is played out, is apparently a violent and meaningless world—"our rotary island loaded with predatory life and more drenched with blood . . . than ever mutinied ship, scuds through space."

Neither Hemingway nor Stevenson invented this world. It had already appeared in literature before their time, and that is a way of saying that this cheerless vision had already begun to trouble men. It is the world we find pictured (and denied) in Tennyson's "In Memoriam"—the world in which human conduct is a product of "dying Nature's earth and lime." It is the world pictured (and not denied) in Hardy and Housman, a world that seems to be presided over by blind Doomsters (if by anybody), as Hardy put it in his poem "Hap," or made by some brute and blackguard (if by anybody), as Housman put it in his poem "The Chestnut Casts Its Flambeaux." It is the world of Zola or Dreiser or Conrad or Faulkner. It is the world of, to use Bertrand Russell's phrase, "secular hurryings through space." It is the God-abandoned world, the world of Nature-as-all. We know where the literary men got this picture. They got it from the scientists of the nineteenth century. This is Hemingway's world, too, the world with nothing at center.

Over against this particular version of the naturalistic view of the world, there was, of course, an argument for Divine Intelligence and a Divine purpose, an argument that based itself on the beautiful system of nature, on natural law. The closely knit order of the natural world, so the argument ran, implies a Divine Intelligence. But if one calls Hemingway's attention to the fact that the natural world is a world of order, his reply is on record in a story called "A Natural History of the Dead." There he quotes from the traveler Mungo Park, who, naked and starving in an African desert, observed a beautiful little moss-flower and meditated thus:

Can the Being who planted, watered, and brought to perfection, in this obscure part of the world, a thing which appears of so small importance, look with unconcern upon the situation and suffering of creatures formed after his own image? Surely not. Reflections like these would not allow me to despair: I started up and, disregarding both hunger and fatigue, travelled forward, assured that relief was at hand; and I was not disappointed.

And Hemingway continues:

With a disposition to wonder and adore in like manner, as Bishop Stanley says [the author of *A Familiar History of Birds*], can any branch of Natural History be studied without increasing that faith, love and hope which we also, everyone of us, need in our journey through the wilderness of life? Let us therefore see what inspiration we may derive from the dead.

Then Hemingway presents the picture of a modern battlefield, where the bloated and decaying bodies give a perfect example of the natural order of chemistry—but scarcely an argument for faith, hope, and love. That picture is his answer to the argument that the order of nature implies meaning in the world.

In one of the stories, "A Clean, Well-Lighted

Place," we find the best description of what under-lies Hemingway's world of violent action. In the early stages of the story we see an old man sitting late in a Spanish café. Two waiters are speaking of him.

"Last week he tried to commit suicide," one waiter said.

"Why?"

"He was in despair."

"What about?"

"Nothing."

"How do you know it was nothing?"

"He has plenty of money."

The despair beyond plenty of money—or beyond all the other gifts of the world: its nature becomes a little clearer at the end of the story when the older of the two waiters is left alone, reluctant too to leave the clean, well-lighted place:

Turning off the electric light he continued the con-versation with himself. It is the light of course but it is necessary that the place be clean and pleasant. You do not want music. Certainly you do not want music. Nor can you stand before a bar with dignity although that is all that is provided for these hours. What did he fear? It was not fear or dread. It was a nothing that he knew too well. It was all a nothing and a man was nothing too. It was only that and light was all it needed and a certain cleanness and order. Some lived in it and never felt it but he knew it all was nada y pues nada y nada y pues nada. Our nada who art in nada, nada be thy name thy kingdom nada thy will be nada in nada as it is in nada. Give us this nada our daily nada and nada us our nada as we nada our nadas and nada us not into nada but deliver us from nada; pues nada. Hail nothing full of nothing, nothing is with thee. He smiled and stood before a bar with a shining steam pressure coffee machine.

"What's yours?" asked the barman.

"Nada."

At the end the old waiter is ready to go home:

Now, without thinking further, he would go home to his room. He would lie in bed and finally, with daylight, he would go to sleep. After all, he said to himself, it is probably only insomnia. Many must have it.

And the sleepless man—the man obsessed by death, by the meaninglessness of the world, by nothingness, by nada—is one of the recurring symbols in the work of Hemingway. In this phase Hemingway is a religious writer. The despair beyond plenty of money, the despair that makes a sleeplessness beyond insomnia, is the despair felt by a man who hungers for the sense of order and assurance that men seem to find in religious faith, but who cannot find grounds for his faith.

Another recurring symbol is the violent man. But the sleepless man and the violent man are not contradictory; they are complementary symbols. They represent phases of the same question, the same hungering for meaning in the world. The sleepless man is the man brooding upon nada, upon chaos, upon Nature-as-all. (For Nature-as-all equals moral chaos; even its bulls and lions and kudu are not admired by Hemingway as creatures of conscious self-discipline; their courage has a meaning only in so far as it symbolizes human courage.) The violent man is the man taking an action appropriate to the realization of the fact of nada. He is, in other words, engaged in the effort to discover human values in a naturalistic world.

Before we proceed with this line of discussion, it might be asked, "Why does Hemingway feel that the quest necessarily involves violence?" Now, at one level, the answer to this question would involve the whole matter of the bias toward violence in modern literature. But let us take it in its more immediate reference. The typical Hemingway hero is the man aware, or in the process of becoming aware, of nada. Death is the great nada. Therefore whatever code or creed the hero gets must, to be good, stick even in the face of death. It has to be good in the bull ring or on the battlefield and not merely in the study or lecture room. In fact, Hemingway is anti-intellectual, and has a great contempt for any type of solution arrived at without the testings of immediate experience.

So aside from the question of a dramatic sense that would favor violence, and aside from the mere matter of personal temperament (for Hemingway describes himself on more than one occasion as obsessed by death), the presentation of violence is appropriate in his work because death is the great nada. In taking violent risks man confronts in dramatic terms the issue of nada that is implicit in all of Hemingway's world.

But to return to our general line of discussion. There are two aspects to this violence that is involved in the quest of the Hemingway hero, two aspects that seem to represent an ambivalent attitude toward nature.

First, there is the conscious sinking into nature, as we may call it. On this line of reasoning we would find something like this: if there is at center only nada, then the only sure compensation in life, the only reality, is gratification of appetite, the relish of sensation.

Continually in the stories and novels one finds such sentences as this from *Green Hills of Africa:* ". . . drinking this, the first one of the day, the finest one there is, and looking at the thick bush we passed in the dark, feeling the cool wind of the night and smelling the good smell of Africa, I was altogether happy." What is constantly interesting in such sentences is the fact that happiness, a notion that we traditionally connect with a complicated state of being, with notions of virtue, of achievement, etc., is here equated with a set of merely agreeable sensations. For instance, in "Cross-Country Snow," one of the boys, George, says to the other, Nick, who in story after story is a sort of shadow of Hemingway himself, "Maybe we'll never go skiing again, Nick." And Nick replies, "We've got to. It isn't worth while if you can't." The sensations of skiing are the end of life. Or in another story, "Big

Two-Hearted River: Part II," a story that is full of
the sensation-as-happiness theme, we find this remark about Nick, who has been wading in a trout
stream: "Nick climbed out onto the meadow and
stood, water running down his trousers and out of
his shoes, his shoes squelchy. He went over and sat
on the logs. He did not want to rush his sensations
any." The careful relish of sensation—that is what
counts, always.

This intense awareness of the world of the senses
is, of course, one of the things that made the early
work of Hemingway seem, upon its first impact, so
fresh and pure. Physical nature is nowhere rendered with greater vividness than in his work, and
probably his only competitors in this department of
literature are William Faulkner, among the modern,
and Henry David Thoreau, among the older American writers. The meadows, forests, lakes, and trout
streams of America, and the arid, sculpturesque
mountains of Spain, appear with astonishing immediacy, an immediacy not dependent upon descriptive flourishes. But not only the appearance
of landscape is important; a great deal of the freshness comes from the discrimination of sensation,
the coldness of water in the "squelchy" shoes after
wading, the tangy smell of dry sagebrush, the
"cleanly" smell of grease and oil on a field piece.[2]
Hemingway's appreciation of the aesthetic qualities
of the physical world is important, but a peculiar
poignancy is implicit in the rendering of those
qualities; the beauty of the physical world is a background for the human predicament, and the very
relishing of the beauty is merely a kind of desperate
and momentary compensation possible in the midst
of the predicament.

This careful relishing of the world of the senses
comes to a climax in drinking and sex. Drink is
the "giant-killer," the weapon against man's thought
of nada. And so is sex, for that matter, though

---

2. Commented on by Ford Madox Ford in his introduction to
the Modern Library edition of *A Farewell to Arms*.

when sexual attraction achieves the status of love, the process is one that attempts to achieve a meaning rather than to forget meaninglessness in the world. In terms of drinking and sex, the typical Hemingway hero is a man of monel-metal stomach and Homeric prowess in the arts of love. And the typical situation is love, with some drinking, against the background of nada—of civilization gone to pot, of war, or of death—as we get it in all of the novels in one form or another, and in many of the stories.

It is important to remember, however, that the sinking into nature, even at the level of drinking and mere sexuality, is a self-conscious act. It is not the random gratification of appetite. We see this quite clearly in *The Sun Also Rises* in the contrast between Cohn, who is merely a random dabbler in the world of sensation, who is merely trying to amuse himself, and the initiates like Jake and Brett, who are aware of the nada at the center of things and whose dissipations, therefore, have a philosophical significance. The initiate in Hemingway's world raises the gratification of appetite to the level of a cult and a discipline.

The cult of sensation, as we have already indicated, passes over very readily into the cult of true love, for the typical love story is presented primarily in terms of the cult of sensation. (*A Farewell to Arms,* as we shall see when we come to a detailed study of that novel, is closely concerned with this transition.) Even in the cult of true love it is the moment that counts, and the individual. There is never any past or future to the love stories, and the lovers are always isolated, not moving within the framework of obligations of an ordinary human society. The notion of the cult—a secret cult composed of those who have been initiated into the secret of nada—is constantly played up.

In *A Farewell to Arms,* for instance, Catherine and Frederick are two against the world, a world that is, literally as well as figuratively, an alien world. The peculiar relationship between Frederick and the priest takes on a new significance if viewed in terms of the secret cult. We shall come to this topic later, but for the moment we can say that the priest is a priest of Divine Love, the subject about which he and Frederick converse in the hospital, and that Frederick himself is a kind of priest, one of the initiate in the end, of the cult of profane love. This same pattern of two against the world with an understanding confidant or interpreter, reappears in *For Whom the Bell Tolls*—with Pilar, the gipsy woman who understands "love," substituting for the priest of *A Farewell to Arms*.

The initiates of the cult of love are those who are aware of nada, but their effort, as members of the cult, is to find a meaning to put in place of the nada. That is, there is an attempt to make the relationship of love take on a religious significance in so far as it can give meaning to life. This general topic is not new with the work of Hemingway. It is one of the literary themes of the nineteenth century—and has, as a matter of fact, a longer history than that.

If the cult of love arises from and states itself in the language of the cult of sensation, it is an extension of the sinking-into-nature aspect of the typical Hemingway violence; but in so far as it involves a discipline and a search for a "faith," it leads us to the second aspect of the typical violence.

The violence, although in its first aspect it represents a sinking into nature, at the same time, in its second aspect, represents a conquest of nature, and of nada in man. It represents such a conquest, not because of the fact of violence, but because the violence appears in terms of a discipline, a style, and a code. It is, as we have already seen, in terms of a self-imposed discipline that the heroes make one gallant, though limited, effort to redeem the incoherence of the world: they attempt to impose some form upon the disorder of their lives, the technique of the bullfighter or sportsman, the discipline of the soldier, the fidelity of the lover, or even the code of the gangster, which, though brutal and apparently dehumanizing, has its own ethic. (Ole Anderson, in "The Killers," is willing to take his medicine without whining, and even recognizes some necessity and justice in his plight. Or the dying Mexican, in "The Gambler, the Nun, and the Radio," refuses to squeal despite the detective's argument: "One can, with honor, denounce one's assailant.")

If it is said that Frederick in *A Farewell to Arms* does not, when he deserts, exhibit the discipline of the soldier, the answer is simple: his obligation has been constantly presented as an obligation to the men in his immediate command, and he and the men in his command have never recognized an obligation to the total war—they recognize no meaning in the war and are bound together only by a squad sense and by their immediate respect for each other; when Frederick is separated from his men his obligation is gone. His true obligation then becomes the fidelity to Catherine.

The discipline, the form, is never quite capable of subduing the world, but fidelity to it is part of the gallantry of defeat. By fidelity to it the hero manages to keep one small place "clean" and "well-lighted," and manages to retain, or achieve for one last moment, his dignity. There should be, as the old Spanish waiter reflects, a "clean, well-lighted place" where one could keep one's dignity at the late hour.

We have said earlier that the typical Hemingway character is tough and, apparently, insensitive. But only apparently, for the fidelity to a code, to the discipline, may be the index to a sensitivity that allows the characters to see, at moments, their true plight. At times, and usually at times of stress, it is the tough man in the Hemingway world, the disciplined man, who is actually aware of pathos or tragedy. The individual toughness (which may be taken to be the private discipline demanded by the world) may find itself in conflict with the natural human reactions; but the Hemingway hero, though he may be aware of the claims of the natural reac-

tion, the spontaneous human emotion, cannot surrender to it because he knows that the only way to
hold on to the definition of himself, to "honor" or
"dignity," is to maintain the discipline, the code.
For example, when pity appears in the Hemingway
world—as in "The Pursuit Race"—it does not appear in its maximum but in its minimum manifestation.

What this means in terms of style and method
is the use of understatement. This understatement,
stemming from the contrast between the sensitivity
and the superimposed discipline, is a constant aspect of the work, an aspect that was caught in a
cartoon in the *New Yorker*. The cartoon showed a
brawny, muscle-knotted forearm and a hairy hand
that clutched a rose. It was entitled "The Soul of
Ernest Hemingway." Just as there is a margin of
victory in the defeat of the Hemingway characters,
so there is a little margin of sensitivity in their brutal
and apparently insensitive world. Hence we have
the ironical circumstance—a central circumstance
in creating the pervasive irony of Hemingway's
work—that the revelation of the values characteristic of his work arises from the most unpromising
people and the most unpromising situations—the
little streak of poetry or pathos in "The Pursuit
Race," "The Killers," "My Old Man," "A Clean,
Well-Lighted Place," or "The Undefeated." We
have a perfect example of it in the last-named
story. After the defeat of the old bullfighter, who
is lying wounded on an operating table, Zurito, the
picador, is about to cut off the old fellow's pigtail,
the mark of his profession. But when the wounded
man starts up, despite his pain, and says, "You
couldn't do a thing like that," Zurito says, "I was
joking." Zurito becomes aware that, after all, the
old bullfighter is, in a way, undefeated, and deserves
to die with his coleta on.

This locating of the poetic, the pathetic, or the
tragic in the unpromising person or situation is not
unique with Hemingway. It is something with which
we are acquainted in a great deal of our literature

since the Romantic Movement. In such literature, the sensibility is played down, and an antiromantic surface sheathes the work; the point is in the contrast. The impulse that led Hemingway to the simple character is akin to the one that drew Wordsworth to the same choice. Wordsworth felt that his unsophisticated peasants were more honest in their responses than the cultivated man, and were therefore more poetic. Instead of Wordsworth's peasant we have in Hemingway's work the bullfighter, the soldier, the revolutionist, the sportsman, and the gangster; instead of Wordsworth's children we have the young men like Nick, the person just on the verge of being initiated into the world. There are, of course, differences between the approach of Wordsworth and that of Hemingway, but there is little difference on the point of marginal sensibility. In one sense, both are anti-intellectual, and in such poems as "Resolution and Independence" or "Michael" one finds even closer ties.

I have just indicated a similarity between Wordsworth and Hemingway on the grounds of a romantic anti-intellectualism. But with Hemingway it is far more profound and radical than with Wordsworth. All we have to do to see the difference is to put Wordsworth's Preface to the *Lyrical Ballads* over against any number of passages from Hemingway. The intellectualism of the eighteenth century had merely put a veil of stereotyped language over the world and a veil of snobbism over a large area of human experience. That is Wordsworth's indictment. But Hemingway's indictment of the intellectualism of the past is that it wound up in the mire and blood of 1914 to 1918; that it was a pack of lies leading to death. We can put over against the Preface of Wordsworth, a passage from *A Farewell to Arms:*

I was always embarrassed by the words sacred, glorious, and sacrifice and the expression in vain. We had heard them, sometimes standing in the rain almost out of earshot, so that only the shouted words came through, and had read them, on proclamations that were slapped up by billposters over other proclamations, now for a long time, and I had seen nothing sacred, and the things that were glorious had no glory and the sacrifices were like the stockyards at Chicago if nothing was done with the meat except to bury it. There were many words that you could not stand to hear and finally only the names of places had dignity. . . . Abstract words such as glory, honor, courage, or hallow were obscene beside the concrete names of villages, the numbers of roads, the names of rivers, the numbers of regiments and the dates.

I do not mean to say that the general revolution in style, and the revolt against the particular intellectualism of the nineteenth century, was a result of the first world war. As a matter of fact, that revolt was going on long before the war, but for Hemingway, and for many others, the war gave the situation a peculiar depth and urgency.

Perhaps we might scale the matter thus: Wordsworth was a revolutionist—he truly had a new view of the world—but his revolutionary view left great tracts of the world untouched; the Church of England, for instance. Arnold and Tennyson, a generation or so later, though not revolutionists themselves, are much more profoundly stirred by the revolutionary situation than ever Wordsworth was; that is, the area of the world involved in the debate was for them greater. Institutions are called into question in a more fundamental way. But they managed to hang on to their English God and their English institutions. With Hardy, the area of disturbance has grown greater, and what can be salvaged is much less. He, like the earlier Victorians, had a strong sense of community to sustain him in the face of the universe that was for him, as not finally for Arnold and Tennyson, unfriendly, or at least neutral and Godless. But his was a secret community, different from that of social institutions. It was a human communion that, as a matter of fact, was constantly being violated by institutions. Their violation of it is, in fact, a constant source of subject matter and a constant spring of irony. Nevertheless, Hardy could refer to himself as a meliorist. He could not keep company with Wordsworth or Tennyson or Arnold; and when Hardy, having been elected an Honorary Fellow of Magdalene College, Cambridge, was to be formally admitted, the Master, Doctor Donaldson (as we know from A. C. Benson's *Diary*) was much afraid that Hardy might dislike the religious service. The occasion, however, went off very well, even though Hardy, after impressing the Master with his knowledge of ecclesiastical music, did remark, "Of course it's only a sentiment to me now." Hardy listened to a sermon by the Archdeacon of Zanzibar, who declared that God was "a God of *desire*—who both hated and loved—not a mild or impersonal force." But even though Hardy could not accept the God of the Bishop of Zanzibar, he still had faith in the constructive power of the secret community.

Now, in Hemingway we see something very like Hardy's secret community, but one much smaller, one whose definition has become much more specialized. Its members are those who know the code. They recognize each other, they know the password and the secret grip, but they are few in number, and each is set off against the world like a wounded lion ringed round by waiting hyenas (*Green Hills of Africa* gives us the hyena symbol—the animal whose death is comic because it is all hideously "appetite": wounded, it eats its own intestines). Furthermore, this secret community is not constructive; Hemingway is no meliorist. In fact, there are hints that somewhere in the back of his mind, and in behind his work, there is a kind of Spenglerian view of history: our civilization is running down. We get this most explicitly in *Green Hills of Africa:*

A continent ages quickly once we come. The natives live in harmony with it. But the foreigner destroys, cuts down the trees, drains the water, so that the water supply is altered and in a short time the soil, once the sod is turned under, is cropped out and, next, it starts to blow away as it has blown away in every old country and as I had seen it start to blow in Canada. The earth gets tired of being exploited. A country wears out quickly unless man puts back in it all his residue and that of all his beasts. When he quits using beasts and uses machines, the earth defeats him quickly. The machine can't reproduce, nor does it fertilize the soil, and it eats what he cannot raise. A country was made to be as we found it. We are the intruders and after we are dead we may have ruined it but it will still be there and we don't know what the next changes are. I suppose they all end up like Mongolia.

I would come back to Africa but not to make a living from it. . . . But I would come back to where it pleased me to live; to really live. Not just let my life pass. Our people went to America because that was the place for them to go then. It had been a good country and we had made a bloody mess of it and I would go, now, somewhere else as we had always had the right to go somewhere else and as we had always gone. You could always come back. Let the others come to America who did not know that they had come too late. Our people had seen it at its best and fought for it when it was well worth fighting for. Now I would go somewhere else.

This is the most explicit statement, but the view is implicit in case after case. The general human community, the general human project, has gone to pot. There is only the little secret community of, paradoxically enough, individualists who have resigned from the general community, and who are strong enough to live without any of the illusions, lies, and big words of the herd. At least, this is the case up to the novel *To Have and Have Not,* which appeared in 1937. In that novel and in *For Whom the Bell Tolls,* Hemingway attempts to bring his individualistic hero back to society, to give him a common stake with the fate of other men.

But to return to the matter of Wordsworth and Hemingway. What in Wordsworth is merely simple or innocent is in Hemingway violent: the gangster or bullfighter replaces the leech-gatherer or the child. Hemingway's world is a more disordered world, and sensibility of his characters is more ironically in contrast with their world. The most immediate consideration here is the playing down of the sensibility as such, the sheathing of it in the code of toughness. Gertrude Stein's tribute is here relevant: "Hemingway is the shyest and proudest and sweetest-smelling storyteller of my reading." But this shyness manifests itself in the irony. In this, of course, Hemingway's irony corresponds to the Byronic irony. But the relation to Byron is even more fundamental. The pity is valid only when it is wrung from the man who has been seasoned by experience. Therefore a premium is placed on the fact of violent experience. The "dumb ox" character, commented on by Wyndham Lewis, represents the Wordsworthian peasant; the character with the code of the tough guy, the initiate, the man cultivating honor, gallantry, and recklessness, represents the Byronic aristocrat.

The failures of Hemingway, like his successes, are rooted in this situation. The successes occur in those instances where Hemingway accepts the essential limitations of his premises—that is, when there is an equilibrium between the dramatization and the characteristic Hemingway "point," when the system of ironies and understatements is coherent. On the other hand, the failures occur when we feel that Hemingway has not respected the limitations of his premises—that is, when the dramatization seems to be "rigged" and the violence, therefore, merely theatrical. The characteristic irony, or understatement, in such cases, seems to be too self-conscious. For example, let us glance at Hemingway's most spectacular failure, *To Have and Have Not*. The point of the novel is based on the contrast between the smuggler and the rich owners of the yachts along the quay. But the irony is essentially an irony without any center of reference. It is superficial, for, as Philip Rahv indicates, the only difference between the smuggler and the rich is that the rich were successful in their buccaneering. The revelation that comes to the smuggler dying in his launch—"a man alone ain't got no . . . chance"—is a meaningless revelation, for it has no reference

to the actual dramatization. It is, finally, a failure
in intellectual analysis of the situation.

There is, I believe, a good chance that *For Whom
the Bell Tolls* will not turn out to be Hemingway's
best novel (an honor I should reserve for *A Farewell
to Arms*) primarily because in this most ambitious
of the novels Hemingway does not accept the
limitations of his premises. I do not mean to imply
that it is on a level with *To Have and Have Not*.
There is a subtler irony in the later novel. I have
pointed out that the irony in *To Have and Have Not*
is that of the contrast between the smuggler and
the rich in the yachts along the pier; that is, it is a
simple irony, in direct line with the ostensible surface direction of the story. But the irony in *For
Whom the Bell Tolls* runs counter to the ostensible
surface direction of the story. As surface, we have a
conflict between the forces of light and the forces of
darkness, freedom versus fascism, etc. Hero and
heroine are clearly and completely and romantically
aligned on the side of light. We are prepared to see
the Fascist atrocities and the general human kindness of the Loyalists. It happens to work out the
other way. The scene of horror is the massacre by
the Loyalists, not by the Fascists. Again, in the attack on El Sordo's hill by the Fascists, we are introduced to a young Fascist lieutenant, whose bosom
friend is killed in the attack. We are suddenly given
this little human glimpse—against the grain of the
surface. But this incident, we discover later, is
preparation for the very end of the novel. We leave
the hero lying wounded, preparing to cover the re-
treat of his friends. The man who is over the sights
of the machine gun as the book ends is the Fascist
lieutenant, whom we have been made to know as
a man, not as a monster. This general ironical conditioning of the overt story line is reflected also in
the attitude of Anselmo, who kills but cannot believe in killing. In other words, the irony here is
much more functional, and more complicated, than
that of *To Have and Have Not;* the irony affirms

that the human values may transcend the party lines.

Much has been said to the effect that *To Have and Have Not* and *For Whom the Bell Tolls* represent a basic change of point of view, an enlargement of what I have called the secret community. Now no doubt that is the intention behind both books, but the temper of both books, the good one and the bad one, is the old temper, the cast of characters is the old cast, and the assumptions lying far below the explicit intention are the old assumptions.

The monotony and self-imitation, into which Hemingway's work sometimes falls, are again an effect of a failure in dramatization. Hemingway, apparently, can dramatize his "point" in only one basic situation and with only one set of characters. He has, as we have seen, only two key characters, with certain variations from them by way of contrast or counterpoint. His best women characters, by the way, are those who most nearly approximate the men; that is, they embody the masculine virtues and point of view characteristic of Hemingway's work.

But the monotony is not merely a monotony deriving from the characters as types; it derives, rather, from the limitations of the author's sensibility, which seems to come alive in only one issue. A more flexible sensibility, one capable of making nicer discriminations, might discover great variety in such key characters and situations. But Hemingway's successes are due, in part at least, to the close co-ordination that he sometimes achieves between the character and the situation, and the sensibility as it reflects itself in the style.

The style characteristically is simple, even to the point of monotony. The characteristic sentence is simple, or compound; and if compound, there is no implied subtlety in the co-ordination of the clauses. The paragraph structure is, characteristically, based on simple sequence. There is an obvious relation between this style and the characters and situations with which the author is concerned—a relation of dramatic decorum. (There are, on the other hand, examples, especially in the novels, of other, more fluent, lyrical effects, but even here this fluency is founded on the conjunction *and;* it is a rhythmical and not a logical fluency. And the lyrical quality is simply a manifestation of that marginal sensibility, as can be demonstrated by an analysis of the occasions on which it appears.)

But there is a more fundamental aspect of the question, an aspect that involves not the sensibility of the characters but the sensibility of the author. The short, simple rhythms, the succession of coordinate clauses, the general lack of subordination —all suggest a dislocated and ununified world. The figures who live in this world live a sort of hand-to-mouth existence perceptually, and conceptually they hardly live at all. Subordination implies some exercise of discrimination—the sifting of reality through the intellect. But in Hemingway we see a romantic anti-intellectualism.

In Wordsworth, too, we see this strain of anti-intellectualism. He, too, wishes to clear away the distorting sophistications of the intellect, and to keep his eye on the object. The formulations of the intellect create the "veil of familiarity" that he would clear away. His mode, too, was to take unpromising material and reveal in it the lyric potentiality. He, too, was interested in the margin of sensibility. He, too, wished to respect the facts, and could have understood Hemingway's rejection of the big abstract words in favor of "the concrete names of villages, the numbers of roads, the names of rivers, the numbers of regiments and the dates."

The passage from *A Farewell to Arms* from which the above quotation comes is, of course, the passage most commonly used to explain the attitude behind Hemingway's style. But we can put with it other passages of a similar import, and best of all a sentence from the story "Soldier's Home." Krebs, the boy who has been through the war and who comes back home to find himself cut off from life, had "acquired the nausea in regard to experience that is the result of untruth or exaggeration." He is a casualty, not of bullet or bayonet, but of the big, abstract words. Hemingway's style is, in a way, an attempt to provide an antidote for that "nausea."

A *Farewell to Arms* is a love story. It is a compelling story at the merely personal level, but it is much more compelling and significant when we see the figures of the lovers silhouetted against the flame-streaked blackness of war, of a collapsing world, of nada. For there is a story behind the love story. That story is the quest for meaning and certitude in a world that seems to offer nothing of the sort. It is, in a sense, a religious book; if it does not offer a religious solution it is nevertheless conditioned by the religious problem.

The very first scene of the book, though seemingly casual, is important if we are to understand the deeper motivations of the story. It is the scene at the officers' mess where the captain baits the priest. "Priest every night five against one," the captain explains to Frederick. But Frederick, we see in this and later scenes, takes no part in the baiting. There is a bond between him and the priest, a bond that they both recognize. This becomes clear when, after the officers have advised Frederick where he should go on his leave to find the best girls, the priest turns to him and says that he would like to have him to go to Abruzzi, his own province:

"There is good hunting. You would like the people and though it is cold it is clear and dry. You could stay with my family. My father is a famous hunter."

"Come on," said the captain. "We go whorehouse before it shuts."

"Goodnight," I said to the priest.

"Goodnight," he said.

In this preliminary contrast between the officers, who invite the hero to go the brothel, and the priest, who invites him to go to the cold, clear, dry country, we have in its simplest form the issue of the novel.

Frederick does go with the officers that night, and on his leave he does go to the cities, "to the smoke of cafés and nights when the room whirled and you needed to look at the wall to make it stop, nights in bed, drunk, when you knew that that was all there was, and the strange excitement of waking and not knowing who it was with you, and the world all unreal in the dark and so exciting that you must resume again unknowing and not caring in the night, sure that this was all and all and all and not caring." Frederick, at the opening of the novel, lives in the world of random and meaningless appetite, knowing that it is all and all and all, or thinking that he knows that. But behind that there is a dissatisfaction and disgust. Upon his return from his leave, sitting in the officers' mess, he tries to tell the priest how he is sorry that he had not gone to the clear, cold, dry country—the priest's home, which takes on the shadowy symbolic significance of another kind of life, another view of the world. The priest had always known that other country.

He had always known what I did not know and what, when I learned it, I was always able to forget. But I did not know that then, although I learned it later.

What Frederick learns later is the story behind the love story of the book.

But this theme is not merely stated at the opening of the novel and then absorbed into the action. It appears later, at crucial points, to define the line of meaning in the action. When, for example, Frederick is wounded, the priest visits him in the hospital. Their conversation makes even plainer the religious background of the novel. The priest has said that he would like to go back after the war to the Abruzzi. He continues:

"It does not matter. But there in my country it is understood that a man may love God. It is not a dirty joke."

"I understand."

He looked at me and smiled.

"You understand but you do not love God."

"No."

"You do not love Him at all?" he asked.

"I am afraid of him in the night sometimes."

"You should love Him."

"I don't love much."

"Yes," he said. "You do. What you tell me about in the nights. That is not love. That is only passion and lust. When you love you wish to do things for. You wish to sacrifice for. You wish to serve."

"I don't love."

"You will. I know you will. Then you will be happy."

We have here two important items. First, there is the definition of Frederick as the sleepless man, the man haunted by nada. Second, at this stage in the novel, the end of Book I, the true meaning of the love story with Catherine has not yet been defined. It is still at the level of appetite. The priest's role is to indicate the next stage of the story, the discovery of the true nature of love, the "wish to do things for." And he accomplishes this by indicating a parallel between secular love and Divine Love, a parallel which implies Frederick's quest for meaning and certitude. And to emphasize further this idea, Frederick, after the priest leaves, muses on the high, clean country of the Abruzzi, the priest's home that has already been endowed with the symbolic significance of the religious view of the world.

In the middle of Book II (chapter xviii), in which the love story begins to take on the significance that the priest had predicted, the point is indicated by a bit of dialogue between the lovers.

"Couldn't we be married privately some way? Then if anything happened to me or if you had a child."

"There's no way to be married except by church or state. We are married privately. You see, darling, it would mean everything to me if I had any religion. But I haven't any religion."

"You gave me the Saint Anthony."

"That was for luck. Some one gave it to me."

"Then nothing worries you?"

"Only being sent away from you. You're my religion. You're all I've got."

Again, toward the end of Book IV (chapter xxxv), just before Frederick and Catherine make their escape into Switzerland, Frederick is talking with a friend, the old Count Greffi, who has just said that he thought H. G. Wells's novel *Mr. Britling Sees It Through* a very good study of the English middle-class soul. But Frederick twists the word *soul* into another meaning.

"I don't know about the soul."

"Poor boy. We none of us know about the soul. Are you *Croyant*?"

"At night."

Later in the same conversation the Count returns to the topic:

"And if you ever become devout pray for me if I am dead. I am asking several of my friends to do that. I had expected to become devout myself but it has not come." I thought he smiled sadly but I could not tell. He was so old and his face was very wrinkled, so that a smile used so many lines that all gradations were lost.

"I might become very devout," I said. "Anyway, I will pray for you."

"I had always expected to become devout. All my family died very devout. But somehow it does not come."

"It's too early."

"Maybe it is too late. Perhaps I have outlived my religious feeling."

"My own comes only at night."

"Then too you are in love. Do not forget that is a religious feeling."

So here we find, again, Frederick defined as the sleepless man, and the relation established between secular love and Divine Love.

In the end, with the death of Catherine, Frederick discovers that the attempt to find a substitute for universal meaning in the limited meaning of the personal relationship is doomed to failure. It is doomed because it is liable to all the accidents of a world in which human beings are like the ants running back and forth on a log burning in a camp-fire and in which death is, as Catherine says just before her own death, "just a dirty trick." But this is not to deny the value of the effort, or to deny the value of the discipline, the code, the stoic endur-ance, the things that make it true—or half true—that "nothing ever happens to the brave."

This question of the characteristic discipline takes us back to the beginning of the book, and to the context from which Frederick's effort arises. We have already mentioned the contrast between the officers of the mess and the priest. It is a con-trast between the man who is aware of the issue of meaning in life and those who are unaware of it, who give themselves over to the mere flow of accident, the contrast between the disciplined and the undisciplined. But the contrast is not merely between the priest and the officers. Frederick's friend, the surgeon Rinaldi, is another who is on the same "side" of the contrast as the priest. He may go to the brothel with his brother officers, he may even bait the priest a little, but his personal relationship with Frederick indicates his affilia-tions; he is one of the initiate. Furthermore, he has the discipline of his profession, and, as we have seen, in the Hemingway world, the discipline that seems to be merely technical, the style of the artist or the form of the athlete or bullfighter, may be an index to a moral value. "Already," Rinaldi says, "I am only happy when I am working." (Already the seeking of pleasure in sensation is inadequate for Rinaldi.) This point appears more sharply in the re-marks about the doctor who first attends to Freder-ick's wounded leg. He is incompetent and does not wish to take the responsibility for a decision.

Before he came back three doctors came into the room. I have noticed that doctors who fail in the prac-tice of medicine have a tendency to seek one another's company and aid in consultation. A doctor who cannot take out your appendix properly will recommend to you a doctor who will be unable to remove your tonsils with success. These were three such doctors.

In contrast with them there is Doctor Valentini, who is competent, who is willing to take responsibility, and who, as a kind of mark of his role, speaks the same lingo, with the same bantering, ironical tone, as Rinaldi—the tone that is the mark of the initiate.

So we have the world of the novel divided into two groups, the initiate and the uninitiate, the aware and the unaware, the disciplined and the undisciplined. In the first group are Frederick, Catherine, Rinaldi, Valentini, Count Greffi, the old man who cut the paper silhouettes "for pleasure," and Passini, Manera, and the other ambulance men in Frederick's command. In the second group are the officers of the mess, the incompetent doctors, the "legitimate hero" Ettore, and the "patriots"—all the people who do not know what is really at stake, who are deluded by the big words, who do not have the discipline. They are the messy people, the people who surrender to the flow and illusion of things. It is this second group who provide the context of the novel, and more especially the context from which Frederick moves toward his final complete awareness.

The final awareness means, as we have said, that the individual is thrown back upon his private discipline and his private capacity to endure. The hero cuts himself off from the herd, the confused world, which symbolically appears as the routed army at Caporetto. And, as Malcolm Cowley has pointed out,[3] the plunge into the flooded Tagliamento,

---

3. Introduction to the *Portable Hemingway*, The Viking Press. In this general connection one may consider the strategic advantage that Hemingway has in that it is the Italian army from which his hero deserts. If his hero had, for instance, deserted from the American army, the American reader's resistance to accepting the act would have been much greater—the reader's own immediate loyalties, etc., would

when Frederick escapes from the battle police, has the significance of a rite. By this "baptism" Frederick is reborn into another world; he comes out into the world of the man alone, no longer supported by and involved in society.

Anger was washed away in the river along with my obligation. Although that ceased when the carabiniere put his hands on my collar. I would like to have had the uniform off although I did not care much about the outward forms. I had taken off the stars, but that was for convenience. It was no point of honor. I was not against them. I was through. I wished them all the luck. There were the good ones, and the brave ones, and the calm ones and the sensible ones, and they deserved it. But it was not my show any more and I wished this bloody train would get to Maestre and I would eat and stop thinking.

So Frederick, by a decision, does what the boy [4] Nick does as the result of the accident of a wound. He makes a "separate peace." And from the waters of the flooded Tagliamento arises the Hemingway hero in his purest form, with human history and obligation washed away, ready to enact the last phase of his appropriate drama, and learn from his inevitable defeat the lesson of lonely fortitude.

---

have been betrayed by Frederick's act. And by the same token the resistance to the symbolic meaning of the act—the resigning from society—would have been much greater. The reader is led to accept the act because the desertion is from a "foreign" army. The point is indicated in a passage of dialogue between Frederick and Catherine. Frederick complains that he doesn't want them to have to live in secret and on the run like criminals.

"I feel like a criminal. I've deserted from the army."

"Darling, *please* be sensible. It's not deserting from the army. It's only the Italian army."

It may be objected that since Hemingway himself saw service on the Italian front it is only natural that his story should be laid there and that by consequence the fact has no symbolic significance and no significance as fictional strategy. But the fact that circumstances of personal history dictated the setting of the story does not prevent the author from seizing on and using the advantages inherent in the situation.

4. *In Our Time*, chapter vi.

This is not the time to attempt to give a final appraisal of Hemingway's work as a whole or even of this particular novel—if there is ever a time for a "final" appraisal. But we may touch on some of the objections which have been brought against his work.

First, there is the objection that his work is immoral or dirty or disgusting. This objection appeared in various quarters against *A Farewell to Arms* at the time of its first publication. For instance, Robert Herrick wrote that if suppression were to be justified at all it would be justified in this case. He said that the book had no significance, was merely a "lustful indulgence," and smelled of the "boudoir," and summarized his view by calling it "garbage." [5] That objection has, for the most part, died out, but its echoes can still be occasionally heard, and now and then at rare intervals some bigot or high-minded but uninstructed moralist will object to the inclusion of *A Farewell to Arms* in a college course.

The answer to this moralistic objection is fundamentally an answer to the charge that the book has no meaning. The answer would seek to establish the fact that the book does deal seriously with a moral and philosophical issue, which, for better or worse, does exist in the modern world in substantially the terms presented by Hemingway. This means that the book, even if it does not end with a solution that is generally acceptable, still embodies a moral effort and is another document of the human effort to achieve ideal values. As for the bad effect it may have on some readers, the best answer is perhaps to be found in a quotation from Thomas Hardy, who is now sanctified but whose most famous novels, *Tess of the D'Urbervilles* and *Jude the Obscure*, once suffered the attacks of the dogmatic moralists, and one of whose books was burned by a bishop:

---

5. "What Is Dirt?" *Bookman*, November, 1929.

Of the effects of such sincere presentation on weak minds, when the courses of the characters are not exemplary and the rewards and punishments ill adjusted to deserts, it is not our duty to consider too closely. A novel which does moral injury to a dozen imbeciles, and has bracing results upon intellects of normal vigor, can justify its existence; and probably a novel was never written by the purest-minded author for which there could not be found some moral invalid or other whom it was capable of harming.[6]

Second, there is the objection that Hemingway's work, especially of the period before *To Have and Have Not*, has no social relevance, that it is off the main stream of modern life, and that it has no concern with the economic structure of society. Critics who hold this general view regard Hemingway, like Joseph Conrad and perhaps like Henry James, as an exotic. There are several possible lines of retort to this objection. One line is well stated in the following passage by David Daiches if we substitute the name of Hemingway for Conrad:

Thus it is no reproach to Conrad that he does not concern himself at all with the economic and social background underlying human relationships in modern civilization, for he never sets out to study those relationships. The Marxists cannot accuse him of cowardice or falsification, because in this case the charge is not relevant [though it might be relevant to *To Have and Have Not* or to *For Whom the Bell Tolls*]. That, from the point of view of the man with a theory, there are accidents in history, no one can deny. And if a writer chooses to discuss those accidents rather than the events which follow the main stream of historical causation, the economic, or other, determinist can only shrug his shoulder and maintain that these events are less instructive to the students than are the major events which he chooses to study; but he cannot accuse the writer of falsehood or distortion.[7]

---

6. "The Profitable Reading of Fiction," in *Life and Art, Essays, Notes and Letters*.
7. For a contrary view of the work of Conrad, see my essay on p. 31.

That much is granted by one of the ablest critics of the group who would find Hemingway an exotic. But a second line of retort would fix on the word *instructive* in the foregoing passage, and would ask what kind of instruction, if any, is to be expected of fiction, as fiction. Is the kind of instruction expected of fiction in direct competition, at the same level, with the kind of instruction offered in Political Science I or Economics II? If that is the case, then out with Shakespeare and Keats and in with Upton Sinclair.

Perhaps *instruction* is not a relevant word, after all, for this case. This is a very thorny and debatable question, but it can be ventured that what good fiction gives us is the stimulation of a powerful image of human nature trying to fulfill itself, and not instruction in an abstract sense. The economic man and political man are important aspects of human nature and may well constitute part of the *materials* of fiction. Neither the economic nor the political man is the complete man; other concerns may still be important enough to engage the attention of a writer—such concerns as love, death, courage, the point of honor, and the moral scruple. A man has to live with other men in terms not only of economic and political arrangements but also of moral arrangements; and he has to live with himself, he has to define himself. It can truly be said that these concerns are all interrelated in fact, but it might be dangerously dogmatic to insist that a writer should not bring one aspect into sharp, dramatic focus.

And it might be dangerously dogmatic to insist that Hemingway's ideas are not relevant to modern life. The mere fact that they exist and have stirred a great many people is a testimony to their relevance. Or to introduce a variation on that theme, it might be dogmatic to object to his work on the ground that he has few basic ideas. The history of literature seems to show that good artists may have very few *basic* ideas. They may have many ideas, but the ideas do not lead a life of democratic give-

and-take, of genial camaraderie. No, there are usually one or two basic, obsessive ones. Like Savonarola, the artist may well say: *"Le mie cose erano poche e grandi."* And the ideas of the artist are grand simply because they are intensely felt, intensely realized—not because they are, by objective standards, by public, statistical standards, "important." No, that kind of public, statistical importance may be a condition of their being grand but is not of the special essence of their grandeur. (Perhaps not even the condition—perhaps the grandeur inheres in the fact that the artistic work shows us a parable of meaning—how idea is felt and how passion becomes idea through order.)

An artist may need few basic ideas, but in assessing his work we must introduce another criterion in addition to that of intensity. We must introduce the criterion of area. An artist's basic ideas do not operate in splendid isolation; to a greater or lesser degree, they prove themselves by their conquest of other ideas. Or again differently, the focus is a focus of experience, and the area of experience involved gives us another criterion of condition, the criterion of area. Perhaps an example would be helpful here. We have said that Hemingway is concerned with the scruple of honor, that this is a basic idea in his work. But we find that he applies this idea to a relatively small area of experience. In fact, we never see a story in which the issue involves the problem of definition of the scruple, nor do we ever see a story in which honor calls for a slow, grinding, day-to-day conquest of nagging difficulties. In other words, the idea is submitted to the test of a relatively small area of experience, to experience of a hand-picked sort, and to characters of a limited range.

But within that range, within the area in which he finds congenial material and in which competing ideas do not intrude themselves too strongly, Hemingway's expressive capacity is very powerful and the degree of intensity is very great. He is concerned not to report variety of human nature or

human situation, or to analyze the forces operating
in society, but to communicate a certain feeling
about, a certain attitude toward, a special issue.
That is, he is essentially a lyric rather than a dramatic writer, and for the lyric writer virtue depends upon the intensity with which the personal
vision is rendered rather than upon the creation of
a variety of characters whose visions are in conflict
among themselves. And though Hemingway has not
given—and never intended to give—a documented
diagnosis of our age, he has given us one of the
most compelling symbols of a personal response to
our age.

The Themes

of ROBERT FROST

A LARGE body of criticism has been written on
the poetry of Robert Frost, and we know the labels
which have been used: nature poet, New England
Yankee, symbolist, humanist, skeptic, synecdochist,
anti-Platonist, and many others. These labels have
their utility, true or half true as they may be. They
point to something in our author. But the important
thing about a poet is the kind of poetry he writes.
We are not interested primarily in his "truth" as
such—as label, as samplerwork—but in the de-

gree to which it is an organizing and vitalizing principle in his poem. For only in so far as it operates as such a principle—in so far as the poem becomes truly expressive—does the truth have meaning at all.

In any case, I do not want to begin by quarreling with the particular labels. Instead, I want to begin with some poems and try to see how their particular truths are operative within the poems themselves. I know perfectly well that there are some readers of poetry who object to this process. They say that it is a profanation, that they simply want to enjoy the poem. We all want to enjoy the poem. And we can be comforted by the fact that the poem, if it is true poem, will, like the baby's poor kitty-cat, survive all the pinching and prodding and squeezing which love will lavish upon it. It will have nine lives too. Further, and more importantly, the perfect intuitive and immediate grasp of a poem in the totality of its meaning and structure—the thing we desire—may come late rather than early—on the fiftieth reading rather than on the first. Perhaps we must be able to look forward as well as back as we move through the poem—be able to sense the complex of relationships and implications—before we can truly have that immediate grasp.

But we know that some poets flinch when faced with any critical discussion of their poems. The critic may so readily turn into the dogmatist who wants to extract the message from the poem and throw the poem away—just as the sentimentalist wants to enjoy his own feelings provoked by the poem and throw the poem away. Frost himself has been especially shy of the dogmatists and has not shown too much sympathy with a reader who, to quote him, "stands at the end of a poem ready in waiting to catch you by both hands with enthusiasm and drag you off your balance over the last punctuation mark into more than you meant to say."

Or we have the case of Yeats. An admirer sent Yeats an interpretation of one of his poems and asked if it was right. Yeats replied, grudgingly, that it was, but added that he did not think poets ought to interpret their own poems, or give the green light to the interpretations of other people, for this would serve to limit the poems.

A good poem is a massive, deep, and vital thing, but this does not imply that a poem is a stimulus to which any response, so long as it is intense, is appropriate. It does not mean that the poem is merely a body of material which the reader may fancifully reorder according to his whim. But it does imply that, though the poem is a controlled focus of experience, within the terms of that control many transliterations are possible as variants of the root attitude expressed. (There are many ways to state the theme of a poem.)

To turn to the poems: The poets may make their protests and reservations, but discussions will continue. As a starting point I am taking one of Frost's best-known and most widely anthologized pieces, "Stopping by Woods on a Snowy Evening." [1] But we shall not be content to dwell exclusively on this poem, attractive as it is, for it will quite naturally lead us into some other poems. It will lead us to the other poems because it represents but one manifestation of an impulse very common in Frost's poetry. Here is the poem:

> *Whose woods these are I think I know.*
> *His house is in the village though;*
> *He will not see me stopping here*
> *To watch his woods fill up with snow.*
>
> *My little horse must think it queer*
> *To stop without a farmhouse near*
> *Between the woods and frozen lake*
> *The darkest evening of the year.*

He gives his harness bells a shake
To ask if there is some mistake.
The only other sound's the sweep
Of easy wind and downy flake.

The woods are lovely, dark and deep.
But I have promises to keep,
And miles to go before I sleep,
And miles to go before I sleep.

Now, the poem we are dealing with may be said to be simple—that is, the event presented is, in it-self, simple and the poet says, quite simply, what the event presumably means. But this does not mean that the implications of the event are not complex; the area of experience touched upon by the poem is "suggestive" or "haunting." And all good poems, even the simplest, work, it seems to me, in exactly that way. They drop a stone into the pool of our being, and the ripples spread.

The poem does, in fact, look simple. A man driving by a dark woods stops to admire the scene, to watch the snow falling into the special dark-ness. He remembers the name of the man who owns the woods and knows that the man, snug in his house in the village, cannot begrudge him a look. He is not trespassing. The little horse is restive and shakes the harness bells. The man decides to drive on, because, as he says, he has promises to keep—he has to get home to deliver the groceries for sup-per—and he has miles to go before he can afford to stop, before he can sleep.

At the literal level that is all the poem has to say. But if we read it at that level, we shall say, and quite rightly, that it is the silliest stuff we ever saw. That is what the Amazon queen in Shake-speare's *Midsummer Night's Dream* said to her husband as she watched the play Bottom and his fellows were giving in honor of her marriage. But Theseus, her husband, replied: "The best in this kind are but shadow and the worst are no worse if imagination amend them." We shall try to be a little less literal-minded than the Amazon queen and shall try to see what reality our little poem is a shadow of.

> *Whose woods these are I think I know.*
> *His house is in the village though;*
> *He will not see me stopping here*
> *To watch his woods fill up with snow.*

With that first stanza we have a simple contrast, the contrast between the man in the village, snug at his hearthside, and the man who stops by the woods. The sane, practical man has shut himself up against the weather; certainly he would not stop in the middle of the weather for no reason at all. But, being a practical man, he does not mind if some fool stops by his woods so long as the fool merely looks and does not do any practical damage, does not steal firewood or break down fences. With this stanza we seem to have a contrast between the sensitive and the insensitive man, the man who uses the world and the man who contemplates the world. And the contrast seems to be in favor of the gazer and not the owner—for the purposes of the poem at least. In fact, we may even have the question: Who is the owner, the man who is miles away or the man who can really see the woods?

With the second stanza another contrast emerges:

> *My little horse must think it queer*
> *To stop without a farmhouse near*
> *Between the woods and frozen lake*
> *The darkest evening of the year.*

Here we have the horse-man contrast. The horse is practical too. He can see no good reason for stopping, not a farmhouse near, no oats available. The horse becomes an extension, as it were, of the man in the village—both at the practical level, the level of the beast which cannot understand why a man would stop, on the darkest evening of the year, to stare into the darker darkness of the snowy woods. In other words, the act of stopping is the specially

human act, the thing that differentiates the man
from the beast. The same contrast is continued into
the third stanza—the contrast between the impatient shake of the harness bells and the soothing
whish of easy wind and downy flake.

To this point we would have a poem all right,
but not much of a poem. It would set up the essential contrast between, shall we say, action and contemplation, but it would not be very satisfying because it would fail to indicate much concerning
the implications of the contrast. It would be a rather
too complacent poem, too much at ease in the Zion
of contemplation.

But in the poem the poet actually wrote, the
fourth and last stanza brings a very definite turn,
a refusal to accept either term of the contrast developed to this point.

> *The woods are lovely, dark and deep.*
> *But I have promises to keep,*
> *And miles to go before I sleep,*
> *And miles to go before I sleep.*

The first line proclaims the beauty, the attraction of the scene—a line lingering and retarded in
its rhythm. But with this statement concerning
the attraction—the statement merely gives us what
we have already dramatically arrived at by the fact
of the stopping—we find the repudiation of the attraction. The beauty, the peace, is a sinister beauty,
a sinister peace. It is the beauty and peace of surrender—the repudiation of action and obligation.
The darkness of the woods is delicious—but treacherous. The beauty which cuts itself off from action
is sterile; the peace which is a peace of escape
is a meaningless and, therefore, a suicidal peace.
There will be beauty and peace at the end of the
journey, in the terms of the fulfillment of the promises, but that will be an earned beauty stemming
from action.

In other words, we have a new contrast here. The
fact of the capacity to stop by the roadside and

contemplate the woods sets man off from the beast, but in so far as such contemplation involves a repudiation of the world of action and obligation it cancels the definition of man which it had seemed to establish. So the poem leaves us with that paradox, and that problem. We can accept neither term of the original contrast, the poem seems to say; we must find a dialectic which will accommodate both terms. We must find a definition of our humanity which will transcend both terms.

This theme is one which appears over and over in Frost's poems—the relation, to state the issue a little differently, between the fact and the dream. In another poem, "Mowing," he puts it this way, "The fact is the sweetest dream that labor knows." That is, the action and the reward cannot be defined separately, man must fulfill himself, in action, and the dream must not violate the real. But the solution is not to sink into the brute—to act like the little horse who knows that the farmhouses mean oats—to sink into nature, into appetite. But at the same time, to accept the other term of the original contrast in our poem, to surrender to the pull of the delicious blackness of the woods, is to forfeit the human definition, to sink into nature by another way, a dangerous way which only the human can achieve. So our poem, which is supposed to celebrate nature, may really be a poem about man defining himself by resisting the pull into nature. There are many poems on this subject in Frost's work. In fact, the first poem in his first book is on this subject and uses the same image of the dark wood with its lethal beauty. It is called "Into My Own."

One of my wishes is that those dark trees,
So old and firm they scarcely show the breeze,
Were not, as 'twere, the merest mask of gloom,
But stretched away until the edge of doom.

I should not be withheld but that some day
Into their vastness I should steal away,

Fearless of ever finding open land,
Or highway where the slow wheel pours the sand.

I do not see why I should e'er turn back,
Or those should not set forth upon my track
To overtake me, who should miss me here
And long to know if still I held them dear.

They would not find me changed from him they
* knew—*
Only more sure of all I thought was true.

Here the man enters the dark wood but manages
to carry his humanity with him; he remains more
sure of all he had thought was true. And thus the
poem becomes a kind of parable of the position of
the artist, the man who is greatly concerned with
the flux of things, with the texture of the world,
with, even, the dark "natural" places of man's
soul. He is greatly concerned with those things, but
he manages to carry over, in terms of those things,
the specifically human.

From "Into My Own" let us turn to a late poem,
which again gives us the man and the dark wood
and the invitation to come into the lethal beauty.
This one is called "Come In."

As I came to the edge of the woods,
Thrush music—hark!
Now if it was dusk outside,
Inside it was dark.

Too dark in the woods for a bird
By sleight of wing
To better its perch for the night,
Though it still could sing.

The last of the light of the sun
That had died in the west
Still lived for one song more
In a thrush's breast.

Far in the pillared dark
Thrush music went—
Almost like a call to come in
To the dark and lament.

But no, I was out for stars:
I would not come in.
I meant not even if asked,
And I hadn't been.

In this woods, too, there is beauty, and an invitation for the man to come in. And, as in "Stopping by Woods on a Snowy Evening," he declines the invitation. Let us develop a little more fully the implications of the contrast between the two poems. The thrush in the woods cannot now do anything to alter its position. Practical achievement is at an end—the sleight of wing (a fine phrase) can do no good. But it still can sing. That is, the darkness can still be conquered in the very lament. In other words, the poet is prepared to grant here that a kind of satisfaction, a kind of conquest, is possible by the fact of expression, for the expression is, in itself, a manifestation of the light which has been withdrawn. Even in terms of the lament, in terms of the surrender to the delicious blackness, a kind of ideal resolution—and one theory of art, for that matter—is possible. (We remember that it was a thing for a man to do and not for a horse to do to stop by the other dark woods.)

But here the man, as before, does not go into the woods. He will not make those terms with his destiny, not, in any case, unless forced to do so. (The thrush cannot do otherwise, but a man can, perhaps, and if he can do otherwise he more fully defines himself as man.) No, the man is out for stars, as he says. Which seems to say that man, by his nature (as distinguished from bird), is not dependent upon the day; he can find in the night other symbols for his aspiration. He will not lament the passing of the day, but will go out for stars.

> *I would not come in.*
> *I meant not even if asked,*
> *And I hadn't been.*

What are we to take as the significance of this last little turn? Is it merely a kind of coyness, a little ironical, wry turn, without content, a mere mannerism? (And in some of Frost's poems we do have the mere mannerism, a kind of self-imitation.) Why had not the man been asked to come in? The thrush's song had seemed to be an invitation. But it had not been an invitation after all. For the bird cannot speak to the man. It has not the language of man. It can speak only in terms of its own world, the world of nature and the dark woods, and not in terms of the man who is waiting for the darkness to define the brilliance of the stars. So here we have again the man-nature contrast (but we must remember that nature is in man, too), the contrast between the two kinds of beauty, and the idea that the reward, the dream, the ideal, stems from action and not from surrender of action.

Let us leave the dark-wood symbol and turn to a poem which, with other materials, treats Frost's basic theme. This is "After Apple-Picking," the poem which I am inclined to think is Frost's masterpiece, it is so poised, so subtle, so poetically coherent in detail.

My long two-pointed ladder's sticking through a tree
Toward heaven still,
And there's a barrel that I didn't fill
Beside it, and there may be two or three
Apples I didn't pick upon some bough.
But I am done with apple-picking now.
Essence of winter sleep is on the night,
The scent of apples: I am drowsing off.
I cannot rub the strangeness from my sight
I got from looking through a pane of glass
I skimmed this morning from the drinking trough
And held against the world of hoary grass.

It melted, and I let it fall and break.
But I was well
Upon my way to sleep before it fell,
And I could tell
What form my dreaming was about to take.
Magnified apples appear and disappear,
Stem end and blossom end,
And every fleck of russet showing clear.
My instep arch not only keeps the ache,
It keeps the pressure of a ladder-round.
I feel the ladder sway as the boughs bend.
And I keep hearing from the cellar bin
The rumbling sound
Of load on load of apples coming in.
For I have had too much
Of apple-picking: I am overtired
Of the great harvest I myself desired.
There were ten thousand thousand fruit to touch,
Cherish in hand, lift down, and not let fall.
For all
That struck the earth,
No matter if not bruised or spiked with stubble,
Went surely to the cider-apple heap
As of no worth.
One can see what will trouble
This sleep of mine, whatever sleep it is.
Were he not gone,
The woodchuck could say whether it's like his
Long sleep, as I describe its coming on,
Or just some human sleep.

The items here—ladder in apple tree, the orchard, drinking trough, pane of ice, woodchuck—
all have their perfectly literal meanings—the echo
of their meaning in actuality. And the poem, for a
while anyway, seems to be commenting on that
actual existence those items have. Now, some
poems make a pretense of living only in terms of
that actuality. For instance, "Stopping by Woods on
a Snowy Evening" is perfectly consistent at the
level of actuality—a man stops by the woods, looks
into the woods, which he finds lovely, dark and

deep, and then goes on, for he has promises to keep. It can be left at that level, if we happen to be that literal-minded, and it will make a sort of sense.

However, "After Apple-Picking" is scarcely consistent at the level of actuality. It starts off with a kind of consistency, but something happens. The hero of the poem says that he is drowsing off— and in broad daylight, too. He says that he has a strangeness in his sight which he drew from the drinking trough. So the literal world dissolves into a kind of dream world—the literal world and the dream world overlapping, as it were, like the two sets of elements in a superimposed photograph. What is the nature of this dream world? And what is its relation to the literal world, the world of real apples and the aching instep arch and the real woodchuck?

The poem opens with a few lines which seem to apply wholeheartedly to the literal world:

My long two-pointed ladder's sticking through a tree
Toward heaven still,
And there's a barrel that I didn't fill
Beside it, and there may be two or three
Apples I didn't pick upon some bough.

It is all literal enough. We even observe the very literal down-to-earth word "sticking" and the casualness of the tone of the whole passage. In fact, it would be hard to say this more simply than it is said. Even the rhymes are unobtrusive, and all the more so because all of the lines except one are run-on lines. But let us, in the light of the rest of the poem, look more closely. The ladder, we observe, has been left sticking "toward heaven still." That is, as we have said, casual and commonplace enough, but we suddenly realize it isn't merely that, when we remember the poem is about the kind of heaven the poet wants, the kind of dream-after-labor he wants—and expects.

So, to break the matter down into crude statement and destroy the quality of the suggestive-in-the-commonplace, we have a kind of preliminary appearance of the theme which concerns the relation of labor and reward, earth and heaven. With our knowledge of the total poem, we can look back, too, at the next several lines and reread them: Maybe I missed something in my life, in my labor, the poet says, but not much, for I tried quite conscientiously to handle carefully every item of my harvest of experience, to touch with proper appreciation everything that came to hand. Maybe I did miss a few things, he seems to say, but I did the best I could, and on the whole did pretty well.

But now the harvest is over, he says, and the "essence of winter sleep is on the night, the scent of apples." He is aware of the conclusion, the successful conclusion of his effort, and in that awareness there is a strangeness in his sight. He is now looking not into the world of effort but the world of dream, of the renewal. It is misty and strange, as seen through the pane of ice, but still it has the familiar objects of the old world of effort, but the objects now become strange in their very familiarity. He is poised here on the frontier between the two worlds, puzzling about their relationship. But he can already tell, he says, what will be the content of the dream world, the world of reward for labor now accomplished.

> *And I could tell*
> *What form my dreaming was about to take.*
> *Magnified apples appear and disappear,*
> *Stem end and blossom end,*
> *And every fleck of russet showing clear.*

The dream will relive the world of effort, even to the ache of the instep arch where the ladder rung was pressed. But is this a cause for regret or for self-congratulation? Is it a good dream or a bad dream? The answer is not to be found in statement, for as far as the statement goes he says:

> *For I have had too much*
> *Of apple-picking: I am overtired*
> *Of the great harvest I myself desired.*

No, we must look for the answer in the temper of the description he gives of the dream—the apples, stem end and blossom end, and every fleck of russet showing clear. The richness and beauty of the harvest—magnified now—is what is dwelt upon. In the dream world every detail is bigger than life, and richer, and can be contemplated in its fullness. And the accent here is on the word contemplated. Further, even as the apple picker recalls the details of labor which made him overtired, he does so in a way which denies the very statement that the recapitulation in dream will "trouble" him. For instance, we have the delicious rhythm of the line,

> I feel the ladder sway as the boughs bend.

It is not the rhythm of nightmare, but of the good dream. Or we find the same temper in the next few lines in which the poet returns to the fact that he, in the real world, the world of effort, had carefully handled and cherished each fruit, and *cherished* is not the word to use if the labor is mere labor, the brutal act. So even though we find the poet saying that his sleep will be troubled, the word *troubled* comes to us colored by the whole temper of the passage, ironically qualified by that temper. For he would not have it otherwise than troubled, in this sense.

To quote again:

> One can see what will trouble
> This sleep of mine, whatever sleep it is.
> Were he not gone,
> The woodchuck could say whether it's like his
> Long sleep, as I describe its coming on,
> Or just some human sleep.

Well, what does the woodchuck have to do with it? How does he enter the poem, and with what credentials? His sleep is contrasted with "just some human sleep." The contrast, we see, is on the basis of the dream. The woodchuck's sleep will be dreamless and untroubled. The woodchuck is simply in

the nature from which man is set apart. The animal's sleep is the sleep of oblivion. But man has a
dream which distinguishes him from the woodchuck. But how is this dream related to the literal
world, the world of the woodchuck and apple har-
vests and daily experience? It is not a dream which
is cut off from that literal world of effort—a heaven
of ease and perpetual rewards, in the sense of rewards as coming after and in consequence of effort.
No, the dream, the heaven, will simply be a reliving of the effort—magnified apples, stem end
and blossom end, and every fleck, every aspect of
experience, showing clear.

We have been considering the literal world and
the dream world as distinct, for that is the mechanism of the poem, the little myth of the poem.
But here it may be well to ask ourselves if the poet
is really talking about immortality and heaven—
if he is really trying to define the heaven he wants
and expects after this mortal life. No, he is only
using that as an image for his meaning, a way to
define his attitude. And that attitude is an attitude
toward the here and now, toward man's conduct of
his life in the literal world. So we must make another transliteration.

This attitude has many implications. And this
leads us to a rather important point about poetry.
When we read a poem merely in terms of a particular application of the attitude involved in it, we
almost always read it as a kind of cramped and
mechanical allegory. A poem defines an attitude, a
basic view, which can have many applications. It
defines, if it is a good poem, a sort of strategic point
for the spirit from which experience of all sorts
may be freshly viewed.

But to return to this poem: What would be some
of the implied applications? First, let us take it in
reference to the question of any sort of ideal which
man sets up for himself, in reference to his dream.
By this application the valid ideal would be that
which stems from and involves the literal world,

which is arrived at in terms of the literal world and not by violation of man's nature as an inhabitant of that literal world. Second, let us take it in reference to man's reward in this literal world. By this application we would arrive at a statement like this: Man must seek his reward in his fulfillment through effort and must not expect reward as something coming at the end of effort, like the oats for the dray horse in the trough at the end of the day's pull. He must cherish each thing in his hand. Third, let us take it in reference to poetry, or the arts. By this application, which is really a variant of the first, we would find that art must stem from the literal world, from the common body of experience, and must be a magnified "dream" of that experience as it has achieved meaning, and not a thing set apart, a mere decoration.

These examples, chosen from among many, are intended merely to point us back into the poem —to the central impulse of the poem itself. But they are all summed up in this line from "Mowing," another of Frost's poems: "The fact is the sweetest dream that labor knows." However, we can step outside of the poems a moment and find a direct statement from the anti-Platonic Frost. He is comparing himself with E. A. Robinson, but we can see the application to the thematic line which has been emerging in the poems we have been considering.

I am not the Platonist Robinson was. By Platonist I mean one who believes what we have here is an imperfect copy of what is in heaven. The woman you have is an imperfect copy of some woman in heaven or in someone else's bed. Many of the world's greatest—maybe all of them—have been ranged on that romantic side. I am philosophically opposed to having one Iseult for my vocation and another for my avocation. . . . Let me not sound the least bit smug. I define a difference with proper humility. A truly gallant Platonist will remain a bachelor as Robinson did from unwillingness to reduce any woman to the condition of being used without being idealized.

Smug or not—and perhaps the poet protests his humility a little too much—the passage does give us a pretty clear indication of Frost's position. And the contrast between "vocation" and "avocation" which he uses leads us to another poem in which the theme appears, "Two Tramps in Mud Time." The last stanza is talking about the relation of "love" and "need" as related to an activity—which may be transliterated into "dream" and "fact" if we wish:

> *But yield who will to their separation,*
> *My object in living is to unite*
> *My avocation and my vocation*
> *As my two eyes make one in sight.*
> *Only where love and need are one,*
> *And the work is play for mortal stakes,*
> *Is the deed ever really done*
> *For Heaven and the future's sakes.*

And we may notice that we have, in line with our earlier poems on the theme, the apparently contrasting terms "mortal stakes" and "Heaven."

In conclusion, I may cite "Desert Places," which is a late and more bleakly stoical version of "Stopping by Woods on a Snowy Evening," and "Birches," which is almost a variant of "After Apple-Picking." Here are the closing lines of "Birches":

So was I once myself a swinger of birches.
And so I dream of going back to be.
It's when I'm weary of considerations,
And life is too much like a pathless wood
Where your face burns and tickles with the cob-
> *webs*
Broken across it, and one eye is weeping
From a twig's having lashed across it open.
I'd like to get away from earth awhile
And then come back to it and begin over.
May no fate willfully misunderstand me
And half grant what I wish and snatch me away
Not to return. Earth's the right place for love:

I don't know where it's likely to go better.
I'd like to go by climbing a birch tree,
And climb black branches up a snow-white trunk
Toward heaven, till the tree could bear no more,
But dipped its top and set me down again.
That would be good both going and coming back.
One could do worse than be a swinger of birches.

For the meaning, in so far as it is abstractly paraphrasable as to theme: Man is set off from nature by the fact that he is capable of the dream, but he is also of nature, and his best dream is the dream of the fact, and the fact is his position of labor and fate in nature though not of her. For the method: The poet has undertaken to define for us both the distinction between and the interpenetration of two worlds, the world of nature and the world of the ideal, the heaven and the earth, the human and the non-human (oppositions which appear in various relationships), by developing images gradually from the literal descriptive level of reference to the symbolic level of reference.

It may be said quite truly in one sense that this interpenetration, this fusion, of the two worlds is inherent in the nature of poetry—that whenever we use a metaphor, even in ordinary conversation, we remark on the interpenetration in so far as our metaphor functions beyond the level of mere mechanical illustration. But the difference between the general fact and these poems is that the interpenetration of the two worlds, in varying ranges of significance, is itself the theme of the poems. We can whimsically say that this does not prove very much. Even the most vindictive Platonist could not do very differently, for in so far as he was bound to state his Platonic theme in words—words, which belong to our world of fact and contingency—he would be unwittingly celebrating the un-Platonic interpenetration of the two worlds.

But there is a practical difference if not an ultimate one. We might get at it this way: The process the poet has employed in all of these poems, but most fully and subtly I think in "After Apple-Pick-ing," is to order his literal materials so that, in looking back upon them as the poem proceeds, the reader suddenly realizes that they have been transmuted. When Shakespeare begins a sonnet with the question, "Shall I compare thee to a summer's day?" and proceeds to develop the compari-son, "Thou art more lovely and more temperate," he is assuming the fact of the transmutation, of the interpenetration of the worlds, from the very start. But in these poems, Frost is trying to indi-cate, as it were, the very process of the transmuta-tion, of the interpenetration. That, and what that implies as an attitude toward all our activities, is the very center of these poems, and of many others among his work.

Irony with a Center:

KATHERINE ANNE PORTER

THE FICTION of Katherine Anne Porter, despite widespread critical adulation, has never found the public which its distinction merits. Many of her stories are unsurpassed in modern fiction, and some are not often equaled. She belongs to the relatively small group of writers—extraordinarily small, when one considers the vast number of stories published every year in English and American magazines—who have done serious, consistent, original, and vital work in the form of short fiction—the group which would include James Joyce, Katherine Mansfield, Sherwood Anderson, and Ernest Hemingway. This list does not include a considerable number of other writers who, though often finding other forms more congenial—the novel or poetry—have scored occasional triumphs in the field of short fiction. Then, of course, there is a very large group of writers who have a great facility, a great mechanical competence, and sometimes moments of real perception, but who work from no fundamental and central conviction.

It was once fashionable to argue complacently that the popular magazine had created the short story—had provided the market and had cultivated an appetite for the product. It is true that the magazine did provide the market, but at the same time, and progressively, the magazine has corrupted the short story. What the magazine encourages is not so much the short story as a conscious or unconscious division of the artistic self of the writer. One can still discover (as in an address delivered by Mr. Frederick Lewis Allen to the American Philosophical Society) a genial self-congratulation in the face of "mass appreciation." But, writes Mr. R. P. Blackmur in reply:

In fact, mass appreciation of the kind which Mr. Allen approves represents the constant danger to the artist of any serious sort: the danger of popularization *before* creation. . . . The difference between great art and popular art is relatively small; but the difference between either and popularized art is radical, and absolute. Popular art is topical and natural, great art is deliberate and thematic. What can be popularized in either is only what can be sold . . . a scheme which requires the constant replacement of the shoddy goods. He (Mr. Allen) does not mean to avow this; he no doubt means the contrary; but there it is. Until American or any other society is educated either up to the level or back to the level of art with standards, whether popular or great, it can be sold nothing but art without standards. . . .

The fact that Miss Porter has not attempted a compromise may account for the relatively small body of her published fiction. There was the collection of stories published in 1931 under the title *Flowering Judas;* an enlarged collection, under the same title in 1935, which includes two novelettes, *The Cracked Looking-Glass* and *Hacienda,* the latter of which had been previously published by Harrison, in Paris; a collection of three novelettes under the title *Pale Horse, Pale Rider,* in 1939; the Modern Library edition of *Flowering Judas;* and a few pieces, not yet in book form, which have appeared in various magazines—for instance, sections of the uncompleted biography of Cotton Mather and the brilliant story "A Day's Work." [1]

Her method of composition does not, in itself, bend readily to the compromise. In many instances, a story or novelette has not been composed straight off. Instead, a section here and a section there have been written—little germinal scenes explored and developed. Or scenes or sketches of character which were never intended to be incorporated in the finished work have been developed in the process of trying to understand the full potentiality of the material. One might guess at an approach something like this: a special, local excitement provoked by the material—character or incident; an attempt to define the nature of that local excitement, as local—to squeeze it and not lose a drop; an attempt to understand the relationships of the local excitements and to define the implications—to arrive at theme; the struggle to reduce theme to pattern. That would seem to be the natural history of the

---

1. Since included in the volume *The Leaning Tower.*

characteristic story. Certainly, it is a method which requires time, scrupulosity, and contemplation.

The method itself is an index to the characteristics of Miss Porter's fiction—the rich surface detail scattered with apparently casual profuseness and the close structure which makes such detail meaningful; the great compression and economy which one discovers upon analysis; the precision of psychology and observation, the texture of the style.

Most reviewers, commenting upon Miss Porter's distinction, refer to her "style"—struck, no doubt, by an exceptional felicity of phrase, a precision in the use of metaphor, and a subtlety of rhythm. It is not only the appreciation of the obviously poetical strain in Miss Porter's work that has tended to give her reputation some flavor of the special and exquisite, but also the appreciation of the exceptional precision of her language. When one eminent critic praises her for an "English of a purity and precision almost unique in contemporary American fiction," he is giving praise richly merited and praise for a most important quality, but this praise, sad to relate as a commentary on our times, is a kind that does encourage the special reputation. This same eminent critic also praises Miss Porter as an artist, which goes to say that he himself knows very well that her language is but one aspect of her creations; but even so, the word *artist* carries its own overtones of exquisiteness.

The heart of the potential reader may have been chilled—and I believe quite rightly—by the praise of "beautiful style." He is put off by a reviewer's easy abstracting of style for comment and praise; his innocence repudiates the fallacy of agreeable style. The famous common reader is not much concerned with English as such, pure or impure, precise or imprecise, and he is no more concerned with the artist as artist. He is concerned with what the English will say to him, and with what the artist will do for him, or to him.

It is, of course, just and proper for us to praise Miss Porter for her English and her artistry, but we should remind ourselves that we prize those things because she uses them to create vivid and significant images of life. All this is not to say that we are taking the easy moralistic, or easy Philistine, view of English or artistry. We know that the vividness and the significance of any literary work exist only in the proper medium, and that only because of a feeling for the medium and an understanding of artistry did the writer succeed, in the first place, in discovering vividness and significance. We hope that we shall never have to remind ourselves of that fact, and now we remind ourselves of the vividness and significance in which Miss Porter's English and artistry eventuate, only because we would balance praise for the special with praise for the general, praise for subtlety with praise for strength, praise for sensibility with praise for intellect.

But let us linger upon the matter of Miss Porter's style in the hope that it can be used as a point of departure. Take, for example, a paragraph from the title story of *Flowering Judas*, the description of Braggioni, the half-Italian, half-Indian revolutionist in Mexico, "a leader of men, skilled revolutionist, and his skin has been punctured in honorable warfare." His followers "warm themselves in his reflected glory and say to each other, 'He has a real nobility, a love of humanity raised above mere personal affections.' The excess of this self-love has flowed out, inconveniently for her, over Laura"—the puzzled American girl who has been lured to Mexico by revolutionary enthusiasm and before whom he sits with his guitar and sings sentimental songs, while his wife weeps at home. But here is the passage.

Braggioni . . . leans forward, balancing his paunch between his spread knees, and sings with tremendous emphasis, weighing his words. He has, the song relates, no father and no mother, nor even a friend to console him; lonely as a wave of the sea he comes and goes, lonely as a wave. His mouth opens round and yearns sideways, his balloon cheeks grow oily with the labor of song. He bulges marvelously in his expensive garments.

Over his lavender collar, crushed upon a purple necktie, held by a diamond hoop: over his ammunition belt of tooled leather worked in silver, buckled cruelly around his gasping middle: over the tops of his glossy yellow shoes Braggioni swells with ominous ripeness, his mauve silk hose stretched taut, his ankles bound with the stout leather thongs of his shoes.

When he stretches his eyelids at Laura she notes again that his eyes are the true tawny yellow cat's eyes. He is rich, not in money, he tells her, but in power, and this power brings with it the blameless ownership of things, and the right to indulge his love of small luxuries. "I have a taste for the elegant refinements," he said once, flourishing a yellow silk handkerchief before her nose. "Smell that? It is Jockey Club, imported from New York." Nonetheless he is wounded by life. He will say so presently. "It is true everything turns to dust in the hand, to gall on the tongue." He sighs and his leather belt creaks like a saddle girth.

The passage is sharp and evocative. Its phrasing embodies a mixture, a fusion, of the shock of surprise and the satisfaction of precision—a resolved tension, which may do much to account for the resonance and vibration of the passage. We have in it the statement, "His mouth opens round and yearns sideways"—and we note the two words *yearns* and *sideways;* in the phrase, "labor of song"; in, "he bulges marvelously"; in, "Braggioni swells with ominous ripeness." But upon inspection it may be discovered that the effect of these details is not merely a local effect. The subtle local evocations really involve us in the center of the scene; we are taken to the core of the meaning of the scene, and thence to the central impulse of the story; and thence, possibly to the germinal idea of all of this author's fiction. All of these filaments cannot be pursued back through the web—the occasion does not permit; but perhaps a few can be traced to the meaning of the scene itself in the story.

What we have here is the revolutionist who loves luxury, who feels that power gives blameless justification to the love of elegant refinements, but whose skin has been punctured in "honorable war-fare"; who is a competent leader of men, but who is vain and indolent; who is sentimental and self-pitying, but, at the same time, ruthless; who be-trays his wife and yet, upon his return home, will weep with his wife as she washes his feet and weeps; who labors for the good of man, but is filled with self-love.

We have here a tissue of contradictions, and the very phraseology takes us to these contradictions. For instance, the word *yearns* involves the senti-mental, blurred emotion, but immediately after-ward the words *sideways* and *oily* remind us of the grossness, the brutality, the physical appetite. So with the implied paradox in the "labor of song." The ammunition belt, we recall, is buckled *cruelly* about his "gasping middle." The ammunition belt reminds us that this indolent, fat, apparently soft, vain man is capable of violent action, is a man of violent profession, and sets the stage for the word *cruelly*, which involves the paradox of the man who loves mankind and is capable of individual cruelties, and which, further, reminds us that he punishes himself out of physical vanity and pun-ishes himself by defining himself in his calling—the only thing that belts in his sprawling, meaning-less animality. He swells with "ominous ripeness" —and we sense the violent threat in the man as contrasted with his softness, a kind of great over-ripe plum as dangerous as a grenade, a feeling of corruption mixed with sentimental sweetness; and specifically we are reminded of the threat to Laura in the situation. We come to the phrase "wounded by life," and we pick up again the motif hinted at in the song and in the lingering rhythms: "He has, the song relates, no father and no mother, nor even a friend to console him; lonely as a wave of the sea he comes and goes, lonely as a wave." In nothing is there to be found a balm—not in revolution, in vanity, in love—for the "vast cureless wound of his self-esteem." Then, after the bit about the wound, we find the sentence: "He sighs and his leather belt creaks like a saddle girth." The defeated, sentimental sigh, the cureless wound, and the bestial creaking of the leather.

If this reading of the passage is acceptable, the passage itself is a rendering of the problem which the character of Braggioni poses to Laura. It is stated, in bare, synoptic form, elsewhere:

The gluttonous bulk of Braggioni has become a symbol of her many disillusions, for a revolutionist should be lean, animated by heroic faith, a vessel of abstract virtues. This is nonsense, she knows it now and is ashamed of it. Revolution must have leaders, and leadership is a career for energetic men. She is, her comrades tell her, full of romantic error, for what she defines as a cynicism is to them merely a developed sense of reality.

What is the moral reality here? This question is, I should say, the theme of the story, which exists in an intricate tissue of paradox, and is posed only in the dream Laura has at the end, a dream which embodies but does not resolve the question.

With all the enchanting glitter of style and all the purity of language and all the flow and flicker of feeling, Miss Porter's imagination, as a matter of fact, is best appreciated if we appreciate its essential austerity, its devotion to the fact drenched in God's direct daylight, its concern with the inwardness of character, and its delight in the rigorous and discriminating deployment of a theme. Let us take another passage from her work, a passage from the novelette *Noon Wine*, the description of Mr. Thompson, a poor dirt-farmer in Texas, busy at his churning, a task that he, in his masculine pride and bitter incompetence, finds contemptible and demeaning:

Mr. Thompson was a tough weather-beaten man with stiff black hair and a week's growth of black whiskers. He was a noisy proud man who held his neck so straight his whole face stood level with his Adam's apple, and the whiskers continued down his neck and disappeared into a black thatch under his open collar. The churn rumbled and swished like the belly of a trotting horse, and Mr. Thompson seemed somehow to be driving a horse with one hand, reining it in and urging it forward; and every now and then he turned halfway around and squirted a tremendous spit of tobacco juice out over the steps. The door stones were brown and gleaming with fresh tobacco juice.

This passage is simple and unpretending, a casual introductory description near the beginning of a story, but it succeeds in having its own kind of glitter and purity and flow. Here those things come, as in so much of Miss Porter's fiction, from the writer's rigorous repudiation of obvious literary resources, resources which, on other occasions, she can use so brilliantly. The things that stir our admiration in the passage from "Flowering Judas" are notably absent here, are notably eschewed. Here the style is of the utmost transparency, and our eye and ear are captivated by the very ordinariness of the ordinary items presented to us, the trotting motion of the churn, the swish of the milk, the tobacco juice glittering on the door stones. Miss Porter has the power of isolating common things, the power that Chekhov or Frost or Ibsen or, sometimes, Pound has, the power to make the common thing glow with an Eden-innocence by the mere fact of the isolation. It is a kind of indicative poetry.

Miss Porter's eye and ear, however, do not seize with merely random and innocent delight on the objects of the world, even though we may take that kind of delight in the objects she so lovingly places before us, transmuted in their ordinariness. If the fact drenched in daylight commands her unfaltering devotion, it is because such facts are in themselves a deep language, or can be made to utter a language of the deepest burden. What are the simple facts saying in the paragraph just quoted?

They are saying something about Mr. Thompson, poor Mr. Thompson who will die of a self-inflicted gunshot wound before many pages have passed, and will die of it because he is all the things we might have surmised of him if we had been able to understand beforehand the language of the simple facts of the scene at the churn. The pridefully stiff neck and the black whiskers, they tell us something. He is the sort of man who ought, or thinks he ought, to be holding the reins of a spanking horse and not the cord of a churn, and his very gesture has a kind of childish play acting. Somewhere in his deepest being, he is reminded of the spanking horse with the belly swishing in the trot, the horse such a fine manly man ought to have under his hand, if luck just weren't so ornery and unreasonable, and so he plays the game with himself. But he can't quite convince himself. It is only a poor old churn, after all, woman's work on a rundown and debt-bit shirt-tail farm, with kids and an ailing wife, and so he spits his tremendous spits of masculine protest against fate, and the brown juice gleams with its silly, innocent assertiveness on the stones the woman's broom has, so many times, swept clean of this and that. In the end, looking back, we can see that the story is the story of a noisy, proud, stiff-necked man whose pride has constantly suffered under failure, who salves his hurt pride by harmless bluster with his wife and children, and who, in the end, stumbles into a situation which takes the last prop of certainty from his life.

Our first glimpse of Mrs. Thompson is in the "front room," where she lies with the green shade down and a wet cloth over her poor weak eyes. But in spite of the weeping eyes, the longing for the cool dark, and all her sad incompetence, on the one hand, and Mr. Thompson's bluster and hurt pride on the other, there is a warm secret life between them:

"Tell *you* the truth, Ellie," said Mr. Thompson, picking his teeth with a fork and leaning back in the best of humors, "I always thought your granma was a ter'ble ole fool. She'd just say the first thing that popped into her head and call it God's wisdom."

"My granma wasn't anybody's fool. Nine times out of

ten she knew what she was talking about. I always say, the first thing you think is the best thing you can say."

"Well," said Mr. Thompson, going into another shout, "you're so re*ef*ined about that goat story, you just try speaking out in mixed comp'ny sometime! You just try it. S'pose you happened to be thinking about a hen and a rooster, hey? I reckon you'd shock the Babtist preacher!" He gave her a good pinch on her thin little rump. "No more meat on you than a rabbit," he said, fondly. "Now I like 'em cornfed."

Mrs. Thompson looked at him open-eyed and blushed. She could see better by lamplight. "Why, Mr. Thompson, sometimes I think you're the evilest-minded man that ever lived." She took a handful of hair on the crown of his head and gave it a good, slow pull. "That's to show you how it feels, pinching so hard when you're supposed to be playing," she said, gently.

This little glimpse of their secret life, Mr. Thompson's masculine, affectionate bragging and bullying and teasing, and Mrs. Thompson's shy and embarrassed playfulness, comes as a surprise in the middle of their drab world, a sudden brightness and warmth. Without this episode we should never get the full force of Mr. Thompson's bafflement and anger when Mr. Hatch, the baleful stranger, misinterprets Mr. Thompson's prideful talk of his wife's ill health and says that he himself would get rid of a puny wife mighty quick. And without this episode we should never sense how that bafflement and anger flow, as one more component, into the moment when Mr. Thompson sees, or thinks he sees, the blade of Mr. Hatch's bowie knife go into the poor Swede's stomach, and he brings his axe down on Hatch's head, as though stunning a beef.

We are, however, getting ahead of ourselves. Let us summarize the apparently simple story. On Mr. Thompson's poverty-bit farm a stranger appears, a Swede, Mr. Helton, who takes work at a low wage, plays the harmonica in his off hours, and seems to inhabit some vague and lonely inner world. But Mr. Helton is a worker, and for the first time the farm begins to pay. Mr. Thompson can give up "woman's work," can do the big important things that become a man, and can bask in the new prosperity. Nine years later, to interrupt the new prosperity, another stranger appears, a Mr. Hatch, who reveals that the Swede is a murderer and a lunatic whom he will arrest and take back North to the asylum. When the Swede appears, Mr. Thompson sees, or thinks he sees, Mr. Hatch's knife going into his stomach. With his axe he kills Mr. Hatch, defending the Swede, defending what, he does not know.

After the deed, there isn't, strangely enough, a scratch on the Swede's stomach. This doesn't bother the jury, and Mr. Thompson is acquitted in no time at all. But it does bother Mr. Thompson. He simply can't understand things, how he could see the knife go in and then find it not true, and all the other things he can't understand. He had never intended to do it, he was just protecting the poor Swede. But we are aware that there had been the slow building up of the mysterious anger against Mr. Hatch, of the fear that Mr. Hatch threatened the new prosperity of the farm. And in the trial Mr. Thompson has been caught in a web of little lies, small distortions of fact, nothing serious, nothing needed to prove he wasn't guilty, just little twists to make everything clearer and simpler.

Is Mr. Thompson innocent or guilty? He doesn't really know. Caught in the mysteriousness of himself, caught in all the impulses which he had never been able to face, caught in all the little lies which had really meant no harm, he can't know the truth about anything. He can't stand the moral uncertainty of this situation, but he does not know what it is that most deeply he can't stand. He can't stand not knowing what he himself really is. His pride can't stand that kind of nothingness. Not knowing what it is he can't stand, he is under the compulsion to go, day after day, around the countryside, explaining himself, explaining how he had not meant to do it, how it was defense of the Swede, how it was self-defense, all the while plunging deeper and deeper into the morass of his fate. Then he finds that his own family have, all along, thought him guilty. So the proud man has to kill himself to prove, in his last pride, that he is really innocent.

That, however, is the one thing that can never be proved, for the story is about the difficult definition of guilt and innocence. Mr. Thompson, not able to trust his own innocence, or understand the nature of whatever guilt is his, has taken refuge in the lie, and the lie, in the end, kills him. The issue here, as in "Flowering Judas," is not to be decided simply. It is, in a sense, left suspended, the terms defined, but the argument left only at a provisional resolution. Poor Mr. Thompson—innocent and yet guilty, and in his pride unable to live by the provisional.

The Cracked Looking-Glass, too, is about guilt and innocence. It is the story of a high-spirited, pleasure-loving Irish girl, married to a much older man, faithful to him, yet needing the society of young fun-provoking men, to whom she takes a motherly or sisterly attitude. She lives a kind of lie —in fact, she can't tell anything without giving it a romantic embroidery. Then she is horrified to discover that her Connecticut neighbors think her a bad woman, suspect her of infidelities. At the end, sitting in her tight kitchen with Old Dennis, "while beyond were far off places full of life and gaiety . . . and beyond everything like a green field with morning sun on it lay youth and Ireland," she leans over and puts her hand on her husband's knee, and asks him, in an ordinary voice: "Whyever did ye marry a woman like me?"

Dennis says mind, she doesn't tip the chair over, and adds that he knew he could never do better. Then:

> She sat up and felt his sleeves carefully. "I want you to wrap up warm this bitter weather, Dennis," she told him. "With two pairs of socks and the chest protector, for if anything happened to you, whatever would become of me in this world?"

"Let's not think of it," said Dennis, shuffling his feet.
"Let's not, then," said Rosaleen. "For I could cry if
you crooked a finger at me."

Again the provisional resolution of the forces of
the story: not a solution which Rosaleen can live
by with surety, but one which she must re-learn
and re-earn every day.

With the theme of *"The Cracked Looking-Glass"*
in mind, let us take another of the novelettes, *Old
Mortality*.

To begin, *Old Mortality* is relatively short, some
twenty thousand words, but it gives an impression
of the mass of a novel. One factor contributing to
this effect is the length of the time span; the novelette falls into three sections, dated 1885–1902,
1904, and 1912. Another factor is the considerable
number of the characters, who, despite the brevity
of the story, are sketched in with great precision;
we know little about them, but that little means
much. Another, and not quite so obvious but perhaps more important, factor is the rich circumstantiality and easy discursiveness, especially in Part I,
which sets the tone of the piece. The author lingers
on anecdote, apparently just to relish the anecdote,
to extract the humor or pathos—but in the end we
discover that there has been no casual self-indul-
gence, or indulgence of the reader; the details of
the easy anecdote, which seemed to exist at the moment for itself alone, have been working busily in
the cellarage of our minds.

Part I, 1885–1902, introduces us to two little
girls, Maria and Miranda, aged twelve and eight,
through whose eyes we see the family. There is the
grandmother, who takes no part in the action of
the story, but whose brief characterization, we discover, is important—the old lady who, "twice a
year compelled in her blood by the change of seasons, would sit nearly all day beside old trunks and
boxes in the lumber room, unfolding layers of garments and small keepsakes . . . unwrapping locks
of hair and dried flowers, crying gently and easily

as if tears were the only pleasure she had left."
(Her piety—stirred by the equinoxes, as unreflect-
ing as tropism—provides the basic contrast for the
end of the story; her piety does not achieve the
form of legend—merely a compulsion of the blood,
the focus of old affections.) There is the father, "a
pleasant everyday sort of man"—who once shot to
protect the family "honor" and had to run to Mexico. There is Cousin Eva, chinless and unbeautiful
amidst the belles, who, when we first meet her,
teaches Latin in a female seminary and tries to interest Maria and Miranda in that study by telling
them the story of John Wilkes Booth, "who, hand-
somely garbed in a long black cloak"—so the story
is recast by the little girls—"had leaped to the stage
after assassinating President Lincoln. 'Sic semper
tyrannis,' he had shouted superbly, in spite of his
broken leg." There is Amy, dead, already a legend,
a beautiful sad family story, the girl who almost
had a duel fought over her in New Orleans, who
drove her suitor, Cousin Gabriel, almost to distrac-
tion before she married him, and who died under
mysterious circumstances a few weeks after her
marriage. There is Gabriel himself, fond of the
races, cut off by his grandfather without a penny,
a victim of the bottle in his bereavement; he marries
Miss Honey, who can never compete with the legend of the dead Amy. In this section, the little girls
attempt to make the people they know and the
stories they have heard fit together, make sense;
and always at the center is the story of Amy.

Part II, in contrast with Part I with its discursiveness, its blurring of time, its anecdotal richness,
gives a single fully developed scene, dated 1904.
The father takes the little girls, on holiday from
their convent school, to the races. There, out of
family piety, they bet their dollar on Uncle Gabriel's horse—a poor hundred-to-one shot. (Piety and
common sense—they know even at their tender
years that a hundred-to-one bet is no bet at all—
are in conflict, and piety wins only because of the
father's pressure.) But Gabriel's horse comes in,

and they see for the first time their romantic Uncle Gabriel—"a shabby fat man with bloodshot blue eyes . . . and a big melancholy laugh like a groan"—now drunk, and after his victory, weeping. But he takes them to meet Miss Honey, Amy's successor, in his shabby apartment, and the little girls know that Miss Honey hates them all.

Part III, 1912, shows us Miranda on a train going to the funeral of Uncle Gabriel, who has died in Lexington, Kentucky, but has been brought home to lie beside Amy—to whom he belongs. On the train Miranda, now a young lady recently married, meets Cousin Eva, whom she has not seen for many years, who has, since the days at the seminary, crusaded for woman suffrage and gone to jail for her convictions. The talk goes back to the family story, to Amy. "Everybody loved Amy," Miranda remarks, but Cousin Eva replies: "Not everybody by a long shot. . . . She had enemies. If she knew she pretended she didn't. . . . She was sweet as honeycomb to everybody. . . . That was the trouble. She went through life like a spoiled darling, doing as she pleased and letting other people suffer for it." Then: "'I never believed for one moment,' says Cousin Eva, putting her mouth close to Miranda's ear and breathing peppermint hotly into it, 'that Amy was an impure woman. Never! But let me tell you there were plenty who did believe it.'" So Cousin Eva begins to reinterpret the past, all the romantic past, the legend of Amy, who, according to Cousin Eva, was not beautiful, just goodlooking, whose illness hadn't been romantic, and who had, she says, committed suicide.

Cousin Eva defines the bitter rivalry under the gaiety of the legend, the vicious competition among the belles. And more:

Cousin Eva wrung her hands. "It was just sex," she said in despair; [The word *despair*, caught in the frustrated and yet victorious old woman's casual gesture, is important—a resonance from her personal story which gives an echo to the theme of the story itself.] "their minds dwelt on nothing else. They didn't call it that, it

was all smothered under pretty names, but that's all it
was, sex."

So Cousin Eva, who has given her life to learning
and a progressive cause, defines all the legend in
terms of economics and biology. "They simply fes-
tered inside," she says of all the Amys, "they fes-
tered."

But Miranda, catching a Baudelairean vision of
"corruption concealed under lace and flowers,"
thinks quite coldly: "Of course, it was not like that.
This is no more true than what I was told before,
it's every bit as romantic." And in revulsion from
Cousin Eva, she wants to get home, though she is
grown and married now, and see her father and sister, who are solid and alive, are not merely "definitions."

But when she arrives her father cannot take
her in, in the old way. He turns to Cousin Eva.
And the two old people, who represent the competing views of the past—love and poetry opposed to
biology and economics—sit down together in a
world, their world of the past, which excludes Miranda. Miranda thinks: "Where are my own people
and my own time?" She thinks, and the thought
concludes the story: "Let them go on explaining
how things happened. I don't care. At least I can
know the truth about what happens to me, she assured herself silently, making a promise to herself,
in her hopefulness, her ignorance."

So much for the action of the story. We see immediately that it is a story about legend, and it is
an easy extension to the symbol for tradition, the
meaning of the past for the present. We gradually
become acquainted with the particular legend
through the little girls, but the little girls themselves, in their innocence, criticize the legend.
Their father, speaking of Amy's slimness, for instance, says: "There were never any fat women in
the family, thank God." But the little girls remember Aunt Keziah, in Kentucky, who was famous
for her heft. (Such an anecdote is developed richly

and humorously, with no obvious pointing to the
theme, beyond the logic of the context.) Such details, in Part I, develop the first criticism of the legend, the criticism by innocent common sense. In
Part II, the contrast between Gabriel as legend and
Gabriel as real extends the same type of criticism,
but more dramatically; but here another, a moral
criticism, enters in, for we have the effect of Amy
on other people's lives, on Gabriel and Miss Honey.
This, however, is not specified; it merely charges
the scene of the meeting between Miranda and
Cousin Eva on the way to Gabriel's funeral. Part III
at first gives us, in Cousin Eva's words, the modern
critical method applied to the legend—as if invok-
ing Marx and Freud.

Up to this point, the line of the story has been
developed fairly directly, though under a complicated surface. The story could end here, a story of
repudiation, and some readers have interpreted it
as such. But—and here comes the first reversal of
the field—Miranda repudiates Cousin Eva's version, as romantic, too, in favor of the "reality" of
her father, whom she is soon to see. But there is
another shift. Miranda discovers that she is cut off
from her father, who turns to Cousin Eva, whose
"myth" contradicts his "myth," but whose world he
can share. Miranda, cut off, determines to leave
them to their own sterile pursuit of trying to understand the past. She will understand herself, the
truth of what happens to her. This would provide
another point of rest for the story—a story about
the brave younger generation, their hope, courage,
and honesty, and some readers have taken it thus.
But—withheld cunningly until the end, until the
last few words—there is a last reversal of the field.
Miranda makes her promise to herself in "her
hopefulness, her ignorance." And those two words,
hopefulness, ignorance, suddenly echo throughout
the story.

Miranda will find *a* truth, as it were, but it, too,
will be a myth, for it will not be translatable, or,
finally, communicable. But it will be the only truth

she can win, and for better or worse she will have to live by it. She must live by her own myth. But she must earn her myth in the process of living. Her myth will be a new myth, different from the mutually competing myths of her father and Cousin Eva, but stemming from that antinomy. Those competing myths will simply provide the terms of her own dialectic of living.

We remember that the heroine's name is Miranda, and we may remember Miranda of Shakespeare's *Tempest*, who exclaims, "O brave new world, that has such people in it!" Perhaps the identity of the name is not an accident. Miranda of *Old Mortality* has passed a step beyond that moment of that exclamation, but she, too, has seen the pageant raised by Prospero's wand—the pageant evoked by her father, the pleasant everyday sort of father, who, however, is a Prospero, though lacking the other Prospero's irony. For *Old Mortality*, like *The Tempest*, is about illusion and reality, and comes to rest upon a perilous irony.

In *Old Mortality* Miss Porter has used very conventional materials; the conventional materials, however, are revitalized by the intellectual scope of the interpretation and the precision and subtlety of structure. But Miss Porter has not committed herself to one type of material. The world of balls and horsemanship and romance is exchanged in *Noon Wine*, as we have seen, for a poverty-ridden Texas farm; in *Pale Horse, Pale Rider*, for a newspaper office and a rooming house at the time of World War I; in "Hacienda," "Flowering Judas" and "María Concepción," for Mexico. We may ask, What is the common denominator of these stories, aside from the obvious similarities of style (though the style itself is very flexible)? What is the central "view," the central intuition?

In these stories, and, as I believe, in many others, there is the same paradoxical problem of definition, the same delicate balancing of rival considerations, the same scrupulous development of

competing claims to attention and action, the same
interplay of the humorous and the serious, the
same refusal to take the straight line, the formula,
through the material at hand. This has implied
for some readers that the underlying attitude is one
of skepticism, negation, refusal to confront the
need for immediate, watertight, foolproof solutions.
The skeptical and ironical bias is, I think, important in Miss Porter's work, and it is true that her
work wears an air of detachment and contemplation. But, I should say, her irony is an irony with a
center, never an irony for irony's sake. It simply
implies, I think, a refusal to accept the formula, the
ready-made solution, the hand-me-down morality,
the word for the spirit. It affirms, rather, the constant need for exercising discrimination, the ardu-
ous obligation of the intellect in the face of conflict-
ing dogmas, the need for a dialectical approach to
matters of definition, the need for exercising as
much of the human faculty as possible.

This basic attitude finds its correlation in her
work, in the delicacy of phrase, the close structure,
the counterpoint of incident and implication. That
is, a story must test its thematic line at every point
against its total circumstantiality; the thematic
considerations must, as it were, be validated in
terms of circumstance and experience, and never
be resolved in the poverty of statement.

In one sense, it is the intellectual rigor and discrimination that gives Miss Porter's work its classic distinction and control—that is, if any one
quality can be said to be uniquely responsible. No,
no single quality can take that credit, but where
many writers have achieved stories of perception,
feeling, sensibility, strength, or charm, few have
been able to achieve stories of a deep philosophic
urgency in the narrow space, and fewer still have
been able to achieve the kind of thematic integration of a body of stories, the mark of the masters,
the thing that makes us think first of the central
significance of a writer rather than of some inci-

dental and individual triumph. For Miss Porter's bright indicative poetry is, at long last, a literally metaphysical poetry, too. The luminosity is from inward.

Love and Separateness
in EUDORA WELTY

He could understand God's giving Separateness first and then giving Love to follow and heal in its wonder; but God had reversed this, and given Love first and then Separateness, as though it did not matter to Him which came first.—"A Still Moment"

IF WE put *The Wide Net*, Eudora Welty's second collection of stories, up against her first collection, *A Curtain of Green*, we can immediately observe a difference: the stories of *The Wide Net* represent a specializing, an intensifying, of one of the many strains which were present in *A Curtain of Green*. All of the stories in *A Curtain of Green* bear the impress of Miss Welty's individual talent, but there is a great variety among them in subject matter and method and, more particularly, mood. It is almost as if the author had gone at each story as a fresh start in the business of writing fiction, as if she had had to take a new angle each time out of a joy in the pure novelty of the perspective. We

find the vindictive farce of "The Petrified Man," the
nightmare of "Clytie," the fantasy and wit of "Old
Mr. Marblehall," the ironic self-revelation of "Why
I Live at the P.O.," the nearly straight realism of
"The Hitch-Hikers," the macabre comedy and pathos of "Keela, the Outcast Indian Maiden." The
material of many of the stories was sad, or violent,
or warped, and even the comedy and wit were not
straight, but if read from one point of view, if
read as a performance, the book was exhilarating,
even gay, as though the author were innocently de-
lighted not only with the variety of the world but
with the variety of ways in which one could look
at the world and the variety of things that stories
could be and still be stories. Behind the innocent
delight of the craftsman, and of the admirer of the
world, there was also a seriousness, a philosophical
cast of mind, which gave coherence to the book,
but on the surface there was the variety, the succession of surprises. In *The Wide Net* we do not
find the surprises. The stories are more nearly cut
to one pattern.

We do not find the surprises. Instead, on the first
page, with the first sentence of the first story,
"First Love," we enter a special world: "Whatever
happened, it happened in extraordinary times, in a
season of dreams . . ." And that is the world in
which we are going to live until we reach the last
sentence of the last story. "Whatever happened,"
the first sentence begins, as though the author cannot be quite sure what did happen, cannot quite
undertake to resolve the meaning of the recorded
event, cannot, in fact, be too sure of recording all
of the event. This is coyness, of course; or a way
of warning the reader that he cannot expect quite
the ordinary direct light on the event. For it is "a
season of dreams"—and the faces and gestures and
events often have something of the grave retardation, the gnomic intensity, the portentous suggestiveness of dreams. The logic of things here is not
quite the logic by which we live, or think we live,
our ordinary daylight lives. In "The Wide Net," for

example, the young husband, who thinks his wife
has jumped into the river, goes out with a party
of friends to dredge for the body, but the sad occasion turns into a saturnalian fish-fry which is interrupted when the great King of the Snakes raises
his hoary head from the surface of the river. But
usually, in *The Wide Net*, the wrenching of logic
is not in terms of events themselves, though "The
Purple Hat" is a fantasy, and "Asphodel" moves in
the direction of fantasy. Usually the events as
events might be given a perfectly realistic treatment (Dreiser could take the events of "The Landing" for a story). But in these cases where the
events and their ordering are "natural" and not supernatural or fantastic, the stories themselves finally belong to the "season of dreams" because of
the special tone and mood, the special perspective,
the special sensibility with which they are rendered.

Some readers, in fact, who are quite aware of
Miss Welty's gifts, have recently reported that they
are disturbed by the recent development of her
work. Diana Trilling, in her valuable and sobering
comments on current fiction, which appear regularly in the *Nation*, says that the author "has developed her technical virtuosity to the point where
it outweighs the uses to which it is put, and her vision of horror to the point of nightmare." There are
two ideas in this indictment, and let us take the
first one first and come to the second much later.
The indictment of the technique is developed along
these lines: Miss Welty has made her style too
fancy—decorative, "falsely poetic" and "untrue,"
"insincere." ("When an author says 'look at me' instead of 'look at it,' there is insincerity. . . .") This
insincerity springs from "the extreme infusion of
subjectivism and private sensibility." But the subjectivism, Mrs. Trilling goes on to say, leads not
only to insincerity and fine writing but to a betrayal
of the story's obligation to narrative and rationality.
Miss Welty's stories take off from a situation, but

"the stories themselves stay with their narrative no more than a dance, say, stays with its argument." That is the summary of the indictment.

The indictment is, no doubt, well worth the close attention of Miss Welty's admirers. There is, in fact, a good deal of the falsely poetic in Miss Welty's present style, metaphors that simply pretend to an underlying logic, and metaphors (and descriptions) that, though good themselves, are irrelevant to the business in hand. And sometimes Miss Welty's refusal to play up the objective action—her attempt to define and refine the response rather than to present the stimulus—does result in a blurred effect. But the indictment treats primarily not of such failures to fulfill the object the artist has set herself but of the nature of that object. The critic denies, in effect, that Miss Welty's present kind of fiction is fiction at all: "It is a book of ballets, not of stories."

Now is it possible that the critic is arguing from some abstract definition of "story," some formalistic conception which does not accommodate the present exhibit, and is not concerning herself with the question of whether or not the present exhibit is doing the special job which it proposes for itself, and, finally, the job which we demand of all literature? Perhaps we should look at a new work first in terms of its effect and not in terms of a definition of type, because every new work is in some degree, however modest, wrenching our definition, straining its seams, driving us back from the formalistic definition to the principles on which the definition was based. Can we say this, therefore, of our expectation concerning a piece of literature, new or old: That it should intensify our awareness of the world (and of ourselves in relation to the world) in terms of an idea, a "view." This leads us to what is perhaps the key statement by Diana Trilling concerning *The Wide Net*: she grants that the volume "has tremendous emotional impact, despite its obscurity." In other words, she says, unless

I misinterpret her, that the book does intensify the reader's awareness—but *not* in terms of a presiding idea.

This has led me to reread Miss Welty's two volumes of stories in the attempt to discover the issues which are involved in the "season of dreams." To begin with, almost all of the stories deal with people who, in one way or another, are cut off, alienated, isolated from the world. There is the girl in "Why I Live at the P.O."—isolated from her family by her arrogance, meanness, and sense of persecution; the half-witted Lily Daw, who, despite the efforts of "good" ladies, wants to live like other people; the deaf-mutes of "The Key," and the deaf-mute of "First Love"; the people of "The Whistle" and "A Piece of News," who are physically isolated from the world and who make their pathetic efforts to re-establish something lost; the traveling salesman and the hitch-hikers of "The Hitch-Hikers," who, for their different reasons, are alone, and the traveling salesman of "Death of a Traveling Salesman" who, in the physically and socially isolated backwoods cabin, discovers that he is the one who is truly isolated; Clytie, isolated in family pride and madness and sexual frustration, and Jennie of "At the Landing," and Mrs. Larkin of "A Curtain of Green," the old women of "A Visit of Charity" and the old Negro woman of "A Worn Path"; the murderer of "Flowers for Marjorie," who is cut off by an economic situation and the pressure of a great city; Mr. Marblehall in his secret life; Livvie, who, married to an old man and trapped in his respectable house, is cut off from the life appropriate to her years; Lorenzo, Murrell, and Audubon in "A Still Moment," each alone in his dream, his obsession; the old maids of "Asphodel," who tell the story of Miss Sabina and then are confronted by the naked man and pursued by the flock of goats. In some of the cases, the matter is more indirectly presented. For instance, in "Keela, the Outcast Indian Maiden," we find, as in *The Ancient Mariner,* the story of a man who, having committed a crime, must try to re-establish his connection with humanity; or in the title story of *The Wide Net,* William Wallace, because he thinks his wife has drowned herself, is at the start of the story cut off from the world of natural joy in which he had lived.

We can observe that the nature of the isolation may be different from case to case, but the fact of isolation, whatever its nature, provides the basic situation of Miss Welty's fiction. The drama which develops from this basic situation is of either of two kinds: first, the attempt of the isolated person to escape into the world; or second, the discovery by the isolated person, or by the reader, of the nature of the predicament.

As an example of the first type, we can remember Clytie's obsessed inspection of faces ("Was it possible to comprehend the eyes and the mouth of other people, which concealed she knew not what, and secretly asked for still another unknown thing?") and her attempt to escape, and to solve the mystery, when she lays her finger on the face of the terrified barber who has come to the ruinous old house to shave her father. Or there is Jennie, of "At the Landing," or Livvie, or the man of "Keela." As an example of the second type, there is the new awareness on the part of the salesman in "The Hitch-Hikers," or the new awareness on the part of the other salesman in the back-country cabin.

Even in "A Still Moment" we have this pattern, though in triplicate. The evangelist Lorenzo, the outlaw Murrell, and the naturalist and artist Audubon stand for a still moment and watch a white heron feeding. Lorenzo sees a beauty greater than he can account for (he had earlier "accounted for" the beauty by thinking, "Praise God, His love has come visible"), and with the sweat of rapture pouring down from his forehead, shouts into the marshes, "Tempter!" He has not been able to escape from his own obsession, or in other words, to make his definition of the world accommodate the white heron and the "natural" rapture which takes him. Murrell, looking at the bird, sees "only whiteness ensconced in darkness," and thinks that "if it would look at him a dream penetration would fill and gratify his heart"—the heart which Audubon has already defined as belonging to the flinty darkness of a cave. Neither Lorenzo nor Murrell can "love" the bird, and so escape from their own curse as did, again, the Ancient Mariner. But there remains the case of Audubon himself, who does "love" the bird, who can innocently accept nature. There is, however, an irony here. To paint the bird he must "know" the bird as well as "love" it, he must know it feather by feather, he must have it in his hand. And so he must kill it. But having killed the bird, he knows that the best he can make of it now in a painting would be a dead thing, "never the essence, only a sum of parts," and that "it would always meet with a stranger's sight, and never be one with beauty in any other man's head in the world." Here, too, the fact of the isolation is realized: as artist and lover of nature he had aspired to a communication, a communion, with other men in terms of the bird, but now "he saw his long labor most revealingly at the point where it met its limit" and he is forced back upon himself.

"A Still Moment," however, may lead us beyond the discussion of the characteristic situation, drama, and realization in Miss Welty's stories. It may lead us to a theme which seems to underlie the stories. For convenience, though at the risk of incompleteness, or even distortion, we may call it Innocence and Experience. Let us take Audubon in relation to the heron. He loves the bird, innocently, in its fullness of being. But he must subject this love to knowledge; he must kill the bird if he is to commemorate its beauty, if he is to establish his communion with other men in terms of the bird's beauty. There is in the situation an irony of limit and contamination.

Let us look at this theme in relation to other stories. "A Memory," in *A Curtain of Green,* gives a simple example. Here we have a young girl lying on a beach and looking out at the scene through a frame made by her fingers, for the girl can say of herself, "To watch everything about me I regarded grimly and possessively as a need." (As does Audubon, in "A Still Moment.") And further: "It did not matter to me what I looked at; from any observation I would conclude that a secret of life had been nearly revealed to me. . . ." Now the girl is cherishing a secret love, a love for a boy at school about whom she knows nothing, to whom she has never even spoken, but whose wrist her hand had once accidentally brushed. The secret love had made her watching of the world more austere, had sharpened her demand that the world conform to her own ideas, and had created a sense of fear. This fear had seemed to be realized one day when, in the middle of a class, the boy had a fit of nosebleed. But that is in the past. This morning she suddenly sees between the frame of her fingers a group of coarse, fat, stupid, and brutal people disporting themselves on the sand with a maniacal, aimless vigor which comes to climax when the fat woman, into the front of whose bathing suit the man had poured sand, bends over and pulls down the cloth so that the lumps of mashed and folded sand empty out. "I felt a peak of horror, as though her breasts themselves had turned to sand, as though they were of no importance at all and she did not care." Over against this defilement (a defilement which implies that the body, the breasts which turn to sand, has no meaning), there is the refuge of the dream, "the undefined austerity of my love."

"A Memory" presents the moment of the discovery of the two poles—the dream and the world; the idea and nature; innocence and experience; individuality and the anonymous, devouring life-flux; meaning and force; love and knowledge. It presents the contrast in terms of horror (as do "The Petrified Man" and "Why I Live at the P.O." when taken in the context of Miss Welty's work) and with the issue left in suspension, but other stories present it with different emphases and tonalities.

For instance, when William Wallace, in "The

Wide Net," goes out to dredge the river, he is presumably driven by the fear that his wife has jumped in, but the fear is absorbed into the world of the river, and in a saturnalian revel he prances about with a great catfish hung on his belt, like a river-god laughing and leaping. But he had also dived deep down into the water: "Had he suspected down there, like some secret, the real true trouble that Hazel had fallen into, about which words in a letter could not speak . . . how (who knew?) she had been filled to the brim with that elation that they all remembered, like their own secret, the elation that comes of great hopes and changes, sometimes simply of the harvest time, that comes with a little course of its own like a tune to run in the head, and there was nothing she could do about it, they knew —and so it had turned into this? It could be nothing but the old trouble that William Wallace was finding out, reaching and turning in the gloom of such depths."

This passage comes clear when we recall that Hazel, the wife who is supposed to have committed suicide by drowning, is pregnant: she had sunk herself in the devouring life-flux, has lost her individuality there, just as the men hunting for the body have lost the meaning of their mission. For the river is simply force, which does not have its own definition; in it are the lost string of beads to wind around the little Negro boy's head, the catfish for the feast, the baby alligator that looks "like the oldest and worst lizard," and the great King of the Snakes. As Doc, the wise old man who owns the net, says: "The outside world is full of endurance." And he also says: "The excursion is the same when you go looking for your sorrow as when you go looking for your joy." Man has the definition, the dream, but when he plunges into the river he runs the risk of having it washed away. But it is important to notice that in this story, there is not horror at the basic contrast, but a kind of gay acceptance of the issue: when William Wallace gets home he finds that his wife had fooled him, and spanks her, and then she lies smiling in the crook of his arm. "It was the same as any other chase in the end."

As "The Wide Net," unlike "A Memory," does more than merely present the terms of contrast, so do such stories as "Livvie" and "At the Landing." Livvie, who lives in the house of wisdom (her infirm husband's name is Solomon) and respectability (the dream, the idea, which has withered) and Time (there is the gift of the silver watch), finally crosses into the other world, the world of the black buck, the field hand, in his Easter clothes—another god, not a river-god but a field god. Just after Solomon's death, the field hand in his gorgeous Easter clothes takes Livvie in his arms, and she drops the watch which Solomon had given her, while outside "the redbirds were flying and crisscrossing, the sun was in all the bottles on the prisoned trees, and the young peach was shining in the middle of them with the bursting light of spring."

If Livvie's crossing into the world of the field god is joyous, the escape of Jennie, in "At the Landing," is rendered in a different tonality. This story assimilates into a new pattern many of the elements found in "A Memory," "The Wide Net," "Livvie," and "Clytie." As in the case of Clytie, Jennie is caught in the house of pride, tradition, history, and as in the case of Livvie, in a house of death. The horror which appears in "A Memory," in "Clytie," reappears here. The basic symbolism of "Livvie" and of "The Wide Net" is again called into play. The river, as in "The Wide Net," is the symbol of that world from which Jennie is cut off. The grandfather's dream at the very beginning sets up the symbolism which is developed in the action:

"The river has come back. That Floyd came to tell me. The sun was shining full on the face of the church, and that Floyd came around it with his wrist hung with a great long catfish. . . . That Floyd's catfish has gone loose and free. . . . And all of a sudden, my dears— my dears, it took its river life back, and shining so brightly swam through the belfry of the church, and downstream."

Floyd, the untamed creature of uncertain origin, is like William Wallace, the river-god dancing with the great catfish at his belt. But he is also, like the buck in "Livvie," a field god, riding the red horse in a pasture full of butterflies. He is free and beautiful, and Jennie is drawn after him, for "she knew that he lived apart in delight." But she also sees him scuffling playfully with the hideous old Mag: the god does not make nice distinctions. When the flood comes over the Landing (upsetting the ordered lives, leaving slime in the houses), Floyd takes her in his boat to a hill (significantly the cemetery hill where her people are buried), violates her, feeds her wild meat and fish (field and river), and when the flood is down, leaves her. She has not been able to talk to him, and when she does say, "I wish you and I could be far away. I wish for a little house," he only stares into the fire as though he hasn't heard a word. But after he has gone she cannot live longer in the Landing; she must find him.

Her quest leads her into the dark woods (which are like an underwater depth) and to the camp of the wild river people, where the men are throwing knives at a tree. She asks for Floyd, but he is not there. The men put her in a grounded houseboat and come in to her. "A rude laugh covered her cry, and somehow both the harsh human sounds could easily have been heard as rejoicing, going out over the river in the dark night." Jennie has crossed into the other world to find violence and contamination, but there is not merely the horror as in "Clytie" and "A Memory." Jennie has acted out a necessary role: she has moved from the house of death, like Livvie, and there is "gain" as well as "loss." We must not forget the old woman who looks into the dark houseboat, at the very end of the story, and understands when she is told that the strange girl is "waiting for Billy Floyd." The old woman nods "out to the flowing river, with the firelight following her face and showing its dignity."

If this general line of interpretation is correct,

we find that the stories represent variations on the same basic theme, on the contrasts already enumerated. It is not that there is a standard resolution for the contrasts which is repeated from story to story; rather, the contrasts, being basic, are not susceptible of a single standard resolution, and there is an implicit irony in Miss Welty's work. But if we once realize this, we can recognize that the contrasts are understood not in mechanical but in vital terms: the contrasts provide the terms of human effort, for the dream must be carried to, submitted to, the world, innocence to experience, love to knowledge, knowledge to fact, individuality to communion. What resolution is possible is, if I read the stories with understanding, in terms of the vital effort. The effort is a "mystery," because it is in terms of the effort, doomed to failure but essential, that the human manifests itself as human. Again and again, in different forms, we find what we find in Joel of "First Love": "Joel would never know now the true course, or the true outcome of any dream: this was all he felt. But he walked on, in the frozen path into the wilderness, on and on. He did not see how he could ever go back and still be the boot-boy at the Inn."

It is possible that, in trying to define the basic issue and theme of Miss Welty's stories, I have made them appear too systematic, too mechanical. I do not mean to imply that her stories should be read as allegories, with a neat point-to-point equating of image and idea. It is true that a few of her stories, such as "The Wide Net," do approach the limit of allegory, but even in such cases we find rather than the system of allegory a tissue of symbols which emerge from, and disappear into, a world of scene and action which, once we discount the author's special perspective, is recognizable in realistic terms. The method is similar to the method of much modern poetry, and to that of much modern fiction and drama, but at the same time it is a method as old as fable, myth, and parable. It is a method by which the items of fiction (scene, action, character, etc.) are presented not as document but as comment, not as a report but as a thing made, not as history but as idea. Even in the most realistic and reportorial fiction, the social picture, the psychological analysis, and the pattern of action do not rest at the level of mere report; they finally operate as expressive symbols as well.

Fiction may be said to have two poles, history and idea, and the emphasis may be shifted very far in either direction. In the present collection the emphasis has been shifted very far in the direction of idea, but at the same time there remains a sense of the vividness of the actual world: the picnic of "The Wide Net" is a real picnic as well as a "journey," Cash of "Livvie" is a real field hand in his Easter clothes as well as a field god. In fact, it may be said that when the vividness of the actual world is best maintained, when we get the sense of one picture superimposed upon another, different and yet somehow the same, the stories are most successful.

The stories which fail are stories like "The Purple Hat" and "Asphodel," in which the material seems to be manipulated in terms of an idea, in which the relation between the image and the vision has become mechanical, in which there is a strain, in which we do find the kind of hocus-pocus deplored by Diana Trilling.

And this brings us back to the criticism that the volume "has tremendous emotional impact, despite its obscurity," that the "fear" it engenders is "in inverse ratio to its rational content." Now it seems to me that this description does violence to my own experience of literature, that we do not get any considerable emotional impact unless we sense, at the same time, some principle of organization, some view, some meaning. This does not go to say that we have to give an abstract formulation to that principle or view or meaning before we can experience the impact of the work, but it does go to say that it is implicit in the work and is having its effect upon us in immediate aesthetic terms. Furthermore, in regard to the particular work in question, I do not feel that it is obscure. If anything, the dreamlike effect in many of the stories seems to result from the author's undertaking to squeeze meaning from the item which, in ordinary realistic fiction, would be passed over with a casual glance. Hence the portentousness, the retardation, the otherworldliness. For Miss Welty is like the girl in "A Memory":

. . . from any observation I would conclude that a secret of life had been nearly revealed to me, and from the smallest gesture of a stranger I would wrest what was to me a communication or a presentiment.

In many cases, as a matter of fact, Miss Welty has heavily editorialized her fiction. She wants us to get that smallest gesture, to participate in her vision of things as intensely meaningful. And so there is almost always a gloss to the fable.

One more word: It is quite possible that Miss Welty has pushed her method to its most extreme limit. It is also possible that the method, if pursued much farther, would lead to monotony and self-imitation and merely decorative elaboration. Perhaps we shall get a fuller drama when her vision is submitted more daringly to fact, when the definition is plunged into the devouring river. But meanwhile Miss Welty has given us stories of brilliance and intensity; and as for the future, Miss Welty is a writer of great resourcefulness, sensitivity, and intelligence, and can probably fend for herself.

A Note on the Han...

of THOMAS W...

THOMAS WOLFE owns an enormous ta...
chooses to exercise it on an enormous s...
talent was recognized promptly enoug...
years ago when his first novel, *Look H*...
Angel, came from the press to overwhel...
percentage of the critics. Nor was this se...
success for a first novel undeserved, ev...
book was not, as Hugh Walpole suggested,
perfect as a novel can be." Now Mr. Wo...
ond novel, *Of Time and the River,* appears,
enthusiasm of the reception of the first w...
ably be repeated; though not, I venture to
on a scale scarcely so magnificent. That
to be seen; but it may not be too early to
a definition of the special excellence and
cial limitations of the enormous talent t...
produced two big books and threatens to
others in the near future.

If Mr. Wolfe's talent is enormous, his e...
are more enormous, and fortunately so. A bi...
is forbidding, but at the same time it carries
lenge in its very pretension. It seems to say,
is a serious project and demands serious att...
from serious minds." There is, of course, the
bery of the three-decker. Mr. Wolfe is prolifi...
publishers assure the public that he has w...
in the neighborhood of two million words.
scheme of six novels, two are now published
Homeward, Angel, 1884–1920, and *Of Time*
the River, 1920–1925); two more are already

ten (*The October Fair,* 1925–1928, and *The Hills Beyond Pentland,* 1838–1926); and two more are projected (*The Death of the Enemy,* 1928–1933, and *Pacific End,* 1791–1884). Presumably, the novels unpublished and unwritten will extend forward and backward the ramifications of the fortunes of the Gant and Pentland families.

Look Homeward, Angel and the present volume are essentially two parts of an autobiography; the pretense of fiction is so thin and slovenly that Mr. Wolfe in referring to the hero writes indifferently "Eugene Gant" or "I" and "me." There may be many modifications, omissions, and additions in character and event, but the impulse and material are fundamentally personal. The story begins in *Look Homeward, Angel* in the latter part of the nineteenth century with the arrival of Gant, the father of the hero, in Altamont, in the state of Catawba, which is Asheville, North Carolina. It continues with the marriage to Eliza Pentland, the birth of the various children, the debaucheries and repentances of old Gant, the growth of the village into a flourishing resort, the profitable real-estate speculations of Eliza, her boarding house, the education of Eugene Gant in Altamont and at the State University, the collapse of old Gant's health, and the departure of Eugene for Harvard. *Of Time and the River* resumes on the station platform as Eugene leaves for Harvard, sees him through three years there in the drama school under "Professor Thatcher," presents in full horror of detail the death of old Gant from cancer of the prostate, treats the period in New York when Eugene teaches the Jews in a college there, and takes the hero to Europe, where he reads, writes, and dissipates tremendously. He is left at the point of embarking for America. During this time he is serving his apprenticeship as a writer and trying to come to terms with his own spirit and with America. So much for the bare materials of the two books.

The root of Mr. Wolfe's talent is his ability at portraiture. The figures of Eliza Gant and old Gant, of Ben and Helen, in *Look Homeward, Angel,* are permanent properties of the reader's imagination. Mr. Wolfe has managed to convey the great central vitality of the old man, for whom fires would roar up the chimney and plants would grow, who stormed into his house in the evening laden with food, and whose quality is perpetually heroic, mythical, and symbolic. It is the same with Eliza, with her flair for business; her almost animal stupidity; her great, but sometimes aimless, energies; her almost sardonic and defensive love for her son, whom she does not understand; her avarice and her sporadic squandering of money. These two figures dominate both books; even after old Gant is dead the force of his personality, or rather the force of the symbol into which that personality has been elevated, is an active agent, and a point of reference for interpretation.

These two characters, and Ben and Helen in a lesser degree, are triumphs of poetic conception. The uncle in *Of Time and the River,* Bascom Pentland, shares some of their qualities. He exhibits the family lineaments, the family vitality, and something of the symbolic aspect of the other characters; but the method of presentation is more conventional and straightforward, and the result more static and anecdotal.

Mr. Wolfe's method in presenting these characters, and the special kind of symbolism he manages to derive from them, is subject to certain special limitations. Obviously it would not serve as a routine process for the treatment of character, at least not on the scale on which it is here rendered. The reader of a novel demands something more realistic, less lyrical; he demands an interplay of characters on another and more specific level, a method less dependent on the direct intrusion of the novelist's personal sensibility. As I have said, the figures of the Gant family are powerful and overwhelming as symbols, as an emotional focus for the novel, and as a point of reference. But the method collapses completely when applied to Starwick, a character of equal importance in Mr. Wolfe's scheme.

We amass a great fund of information concerning Francis Starwick. He was born in a town in the Middle West and early rebelled against the crudities and ugliness of his background. At Harvard he assists Professor Thatcher in the drama school and leads the life of a mannered and affected aesthete, foppish in dress, artificial in speech, oversensitive, and sometimes cruel. At Harvard, he becomes Eugene's best friend. Later he appears in Europe in company with two young women of Boston families, somewhat older than he, who are in love with him and who are willing to pay, with their reputations and their purses, for the pleasure of his conversation. With these three Eugene enters a period of debauchery in Paris. Finally he discovers that Starwick is homosexual, and in his undefinable resentment beats him into unconsciousness.

But this body of information is not all that the writer intends. F. Scott Fitzgerald and Ernest Hemingway have been able to use effectively such characters as Starwick and to extract their meaning, because as novelists they were willing to work strictly in terms of character. But in *Of Time and the River* the writer is forever straining to convince the reader of some value in Starwick that is not perceptible, that the writer himself cannot define; he tries, since he is writing an autobiography, to make Starwick a symbol, a kind of alter ego, for a certain period of his own experience. The strain is tremendous; and without conviction. The writing about Starwick, as the climax of the relationship approaches, sinks into a slush of poetical bathos. And here is the end of the long scene of parting:

"You are my mortal enemy. Goodbye."

"Goodbye, Eugene," said Starwick sadly. "But let me tell you this before I go. Whatever it was I took from you, it was something that I did not want or wish to take. And I would give it back again if I could."

"Oh, fortunate and favored Starwick," the other

jeered. "To be so rich—to have such gifts and not to know he has them—to be forever victorious, and to be so meek and mild."

"And I will tell you this as well," Starwick continued. "Whatever anguish and suffering this mad hunger, this impossible desire, has caused you, however fortunate or favored you may think I am, I would give my whole life if I could change places with you for an hour—know for an hour an atom of your anguish and your hunger and your hope. . . . Oh, to feel so, suffer so, and live so!—however mistaken you may be! . . . To have come lusty, young, and living into this world. . . . not to have come like me, still-born from your mother's womb —never to know the dead heart and the passionless passion—the cold brain and the cold hopelessness of hope—to be wild, mad, furious, and tormented—but to have belief, to live in anguish, but to live—and not to die." . . . He turned and opened the door. "I would give all I have and all you think I have, for just one hour of it. You call me fortunate and happy. *You* are the most fortunate and happy man I ever knew. Goodbye, Eugene."

"Goodbye, Frank. Goodbye, my enemy."

"And goodbye, my friend," said Starwick. He went out, and the door closed behind him.

The dialogue, the very rhythms of the sentences, and the scene itself, scream the unreality.

The potency of the figures from the family and the failure with Starwick may derive from the autobiographical nature of Mr. Wolfe's work. Eliza and old Gant come from a more primary level of experience, figures of motherhood and fatherhood that gradually, as the book progresses, assume a wider significance and become at the same time a reference for the hero's personal experience. And the author, knowing them first on that level, has a way of knowing them more intimately and profoundly as people than he ever knows Starwick. Starwick is more artificial, because he is at the same time a social symbol and a symbol for a purely private confusion of which the roots are never clear.

Most of the other characters are treated directly.
Mr. Wolfe has an appetite for people and occasionally a faculty of very acute perception. The portrait of Abe Jones, the Jewish student at the college
in New York, and those of the people at the Coulson
household in Oxford, are evidence enough of this
capacity. But his method or, rather, methods of
presentation are various and not unvaryingly successful. There are long stretches of stenographic
dialogue that has little focus, or no focus whatsoever; for instance, the first part of the conversation
of the businessmen in the Pullman in Book I, of the
residents of the hotel in Book IV, of the artistic
hangers-on at the Cambridge tea parties, or even of
Eugene and his companions in the Paris cafés.
Some of this reporting is very scrupulous, and good
as reporting, but in its mass, its formlessness, and
its lack of direction it is frequently dull; the momentary interest of recognition is not enough to
sustain it, and it bears no precise relation to the intention of the novel. It is conversation for conversation's sake, a loquacity and documentation that
testify to the author's talent but not to his intelligence as an artist. Generally this type of presentation is imitative of Sinclair Lewis's realistic dialogue, but it lacks the meticulous, cautious, and
selective quality of the best of Lewis, the controlled
malice; it is too random, and in an incidental
sense, too heavily pointed.

Further, there are tremendous masses of description and characters. Mr. Wolfe has the habit
of developing his own clichés for description of
character, and of then exhibiting them at irregular
intervals. It is as if he realized the bulk of the novel
and the difficulty a reader might experience in recognizing a character on reappearance, and so determined to prevent this, if possible, by repetition and
insistence. For instance, Starwick and Ann, one of
the young women from Boston who is in love with
Starwick, have a complete set of tags and labels
that are affixed to them time after time during the
novel. Mr. Wolfe underrates the memory of the

reader; or this may be but another instance of the lack of control that impairs his work.

Only in the section dealing with the Coulson episode does Mr. Wolfe seem to have all his resources for character presentation under control. The men who room in the house, the jaunty Captain Nicholl with his blasted arm and the other two young men from the motor-car factory—these with the Coulsons themselves are very precise to the imagination, and are sketched in with an economy usually foreign to Mr. Wolfe. The Coulson girl, accepting the mysterious ruin that presides over the household, is best drawn and dominates the group. Here Mr. Wolfe has managed to convey an atmosphere and to convince the reader of the reality of his characters without any of his habitual exaggerations of method and style. This section, with slight alterations, originally appeared as a short story; it possesses what is rare enough in *Of Time and the River,* a constant focus.

I have remarked that some of Mr. Wolfe's material is not subordinated to the intention of the book. What is his intention? On what is the mass of material focused? What is to give it form? His novels are obviously autobiographical. This means that the binding factor should be, at least in part, the personality of the narrator, or, since Mr. Wolfe adopts a disguise, of the hero, Eugene Gant. The two books are, in short, an account of the development of a sensibility; obviously something more is intended than the looseness and irresponsibility of pure memoirs or observations. The work demands comparison with such works as Joyce's *Portrait of the Artist as a Young Man* or Lawrence's *Sons and Lovers;* it may even demand comparison with proper autobiographies, such as Rousseau's *Confessions* or *The Education of Henry Adams.* But the comparison with these books is not to the advantage of Mr. Wolfe's performance. It has not the artistry of the first two, the constant and dramatic relation of incident to a developing consciousness of the world, nor has it the historical importance of

the third, or the philosophical and intellectual interest of the last.

The hero of *Look Homeward, Angel,* though a
child and adolescent, is essentially more interesting
than the Eugene of *Of Time and the River.* He is
more comprehensible, because there is a real (and
necessarily conventional) pattern to his developing
awareness of the world around him. Further, the
life of the Gant household, and even of the community, is patterned with a certain amount of
strictness in relation to Eugene: the impress of the
vast vitality of old Gant, the lack of understanding
on the part of the mother and the perpetual emotional drag of resentment and affection she exerts
on her son, the quarrels with Steve, the confusion
and pathos of the sexual experiences, the profound
attachment between Ben and Eugene, and the cli-
mactic and daring scene with Ben's spirit. There is
a progress toward maturity, a fairly precise psychological interest. The novel contains much pure
baggage and much material that is out of tone,
usually in the form of an ironic commentary that
violates the point of view; but the book is more of
a unit, and is, for that reason perhaps, more exciting and forceful.

In *Of Time and the River,* as Eugene in his Pullman rides at night across Virginia, going "north-
ward, worldward, towards the secret borders of Virginia, towards the great world cities of his hope,
the fable of his childhood legendry," the following
passage is interpolated:

Who has seen fury riding in the mountains? Who has
known fury striding in the storm? Who has been mad
with fury in his youth, given no rest or peace or certitude by fury, driven on across the earth by fury, until
the great vine of his heart was broke, the sinews
wrenched, the little tenement of bone, blood, marrow,
brain, and feeling in which great fury raged, was
twisted, wrung, depleted, worn out, and exhausted by
the fury which it could not lose or put away? Who has
known fury, how it came?

How have we breathed him, drunk him, eaten fury to

the core, until we have him in us now and cannot lose
him anywhere we go? It is a strange and subtle worm
that will . . .

The furious Eugene is scarcely made comprehensible. The reader amasses a large body of facts
about him, as about Starwick, but with something
of the same result. He knows that Eugene is big;
that he is a creature of enormous appetites of which
he is rather proud; that he has the habit of walking
much at night; that he is fascinated by the health
and urbanity of his friend Joel and by the personality of Starwick; that he ceases to like Shelley after
spending an afternoon in a jail cell; that he reads
twenty thousand books in ten years; that he is obsessed by the idea of devouring all of life. Then, the
reader knows the facts of Eugene's comings and go-
ings, and knows the people he meets and what
they say. But the Eugene susceptible of such definition is not the hero of the book, or at least does
not function adequately as such. The hero is really
that nameless fury that drives Eugene. The book
is an effort to name that fury, and perhaps by
naming it, to tame it. But the fury goes unnamed
and untamed. Since the book is formless otherwise,
only a proper emotional reference to such a center
could give it form. Instead, at the center there is
this chaos that steams and bubbles in rhetoric
and apocalyptic apostrophe, sometimes grand and
sometimes febrile and empty; the center is a mael-
strom, perhaps artificially generated at times; and
the other, tangible items are the flotsam and jet-
sam and dead wood spewed up, iridescent or soggy,
as the case may be.

It may be objected that other works of literary
art, and very great ones at that, have heroes who
defy definition and who are merely centers of
"fury." For instance, there is Hamlet, or Lear. But
a difference may be observed. Those characters
may defy the attempt at central definition, but the
play hangs together in each case as a structure
without such definition; that is, there has been no

confusion between the sensibility that produced a play, as an object of art, and the sensibility of a hero in a play. (And the mere fact that *Hamlet* and *Lear* employ verse as a vehicle adds further to the impression of discipline, focus, and control.)

There are two other factors in the character of Eugene that may deserve mention. The hero feels a sense of destiny and direction, the sense of being "chosen" in the midst of a world of defeated, aimless, snobbish, vulgar, depleted, or suicidal people. (This is, apparently, the source of much of the interpolated irony in both books, an irony almost regularly derivative and mechanical.) In real life this conviction of a high calling may be enough to make a "hero" feel that life does have form and meaning; but the mere fact that a hero in a novel professes the high calling and is contrasted in his social contacts with an inferior breed does not, in itself, give the novel form and meaning. The transference of the matter from the actuality of life to the actuality of art cannot be accomplished so easily. Second, at the very end of the novel, Eugene, about to embark for America, sees a woman who, according to the somewhat extended lyrical epilogue, makes him "lose" self and so be "found":

After all the blind, tormented wanderings of youth, that woman would become his heart's centre and the target of his life, the image of immortal one-ness that again collected him to one, and hurled the whole collected passion, power, and might of his one life into the blazing certitude, the immortal governance and unity, of love.

Certainly this is what we call fine writing; it may or may not be good writing. And probably, falling in love may make a man "find himself"; but this epilogue scarcely makes the novel find itself.

It is possible sometimes that a novel possessing no structure in the ordinary sense of the word, or not properly dominated by its hero's personality or fortunes, may be given a focus by the concrete incorporation of an idea, or related ideas. Now, *Of*

Time and the River has such a leading idea, but an idea insufficient in its operation. The leading symbol of the father, old Gant, gradually assumes another aspect, not purely personal; he becomes, in other words, a kind of symbol of the fatherland, the source, the land of violence, drunkenness, fecundity, beauty, and vigor, on which the hero occasionally reflects during his wanderings and to which in the end he returns. But this symbol is not the total expression of the idea, which is worked out more explicitly and at length. There are long series of cinematic flashes of "phases of American life": locomotive drivers, gangsters, pioneers, little towns with the squares deserted at night, evangelists, housewives, rich and suicidal young men, whores on subways, drunk college boys. Or there are more lyrical passages, less effective in pictorial detail, such as the following:

It was the wild, sweet, casual, savage, and incredibly lovely earth of America, and of the wilderness, and it haunted them like legends, and pierced them like a sword, and filled them with a wild and swelling prescience of joy that was like sorrow and delight.

This kind of material alternates with the more sedate or realistic progress of the chronicle, a kind of running commentary of patriotic mysticism on the more tangible events and perceptions. For Mr. Wolfe has the mysticism of the American idea that we find in Whitman, Sandburg, Masters, Crane, and Benét. He pants for the Word, the union that will clarify all the disparate and confused elements which he enumerates and many of which fill him with revulsion and disgust. He, apparently, has experienced the visionary moment he proclaims, but, like other mystics, he suffers some difficulty when he attempts to prepare it for consumption by the ordinary citizens of the Republic. He must wreak some indignity on the chastity of the vision. This indignity is speech: but he burns, perversely, to speak.

The other promulgators of the American vision

have been poets. Mr. Wolfe, in addition to being a
poet in instinct, is, as well, the owner on a large
scale of many of the gifts of the novelist. He attempts to bolster, or as it were, to prove, the mystical and poetic vision by fusing it with a body of
everyday experience of which the novelist ordinarily treats. But there is scarcely a fusion or a correlation; rather, an oscillation. On the tangible side,
the hero flees from America, where his somewhat
quivering sensibilities are frequently tortured, and
goes to Europe; in the end, worn out by drinking
and late hours, disgusted with his friends, unac-
quainted with the English or the French, and suffering homesickness, he returns to America. But
Mr. Wolfe, more than most novelists, is concerned
with the intangible; not so much with the psychological process and interrelation as with the visionary "truth."

The other poets, at least Whitman and Crane,
have a certain advantage over the poet in Mr.
Wolfe. They overtly consented to be poets; Mr.
Wolfe has not consented. Therefore their vision is
purer, the illusion of communication (*illusion,* for
it is doubtful that they have really communicated
the central vision) is more readily palatable, because they never made a serious pretense of proving it autobiographically or otherwise; they were
content with the hortatory moment, the fleeting
symbol, and the affirmation. (Benét, of course, did
attempt in *John Brown's Body* such a validation,
but with a degree of success that does not demand
comment here.) It may simply be that the poets
were content to be lyric poets, and therefore could
more readily attempt the discipline of selection and
concentration; in those respects, even Whitman
shows more of an instinct for form than does Mr.
Wolfe. Mr. Wolfe is astonishingly diffuse, astonishingly loose in his rhetoric—qualities that, for the
moment, may provoke more praise than blame.
That rhetoric is sometimes grand, but probably
more often tedious and tinged with hysteria. Because he is officially writing prose and not poetry,

he has no caution of the clichés of phrase or
rhythm, and no compunction about pilfering from
other poets.

His vocabulary itself is worth comment. If the
reader will inspect the few passages quoted in the
course of this essay he will observe a constant quality of strain, a fancy for the violent word or phrase
(but often conventionally poetic as well as violent):
"wild, sweet, casual, savage . . . ," "haunted them
like legends," "no rest or peace or certitude of fury,"
"target of his life," "blazing certitude, the immortal governance and unity, of love." Mr. Wolfe often
shows very powerfully the poetic instinct, and the
praise given by a number of critics to his "sen-
suousness" and "gusto" is not without justification
in the fact; but even more often his prose simply
shows the poetic instinct unbuckled on a kind of
week-end debauch. He sometimes wants it both
ways: the structural irresponsibility of prose and
the emotional intensity of poetry. He may overlook
the fact that the intensity is rarely to be achieved
without a certain rigor in selection and structure.

Further, Mr. Wolfe, we understand from blurbs
and reviewers, is attempting a kind of prose epic.
American literature has produced one, *Moby Dick*.
There is much in common between *Moby Dick* and
Of Time and the River, but there is one major
difference. Melville had a powerful fable, a myth
of human destiny, which saved his work from the
centrifugal impulses of his genius, and which gave
it structure and climax. Its dignity is inherent in
the fable itself. No such dignity is inherent in Mr.
Wolfe's scheme, if it can properly be termed a
scheme. The nearest approach to it is in the character of old Gant, but that is scarcely adequate. And
Mr. Wolfe has not been able to compensate for the
lack of a fable by all his well-directed and misdirected attempts to endow his subject with a proper
dignity, by all his rhetorical insistence, all the
clarity and justice of his incidental poetic perceptions, all the hysteria or magnificent hypnosis.

Probably all of these defects, or most of them,

are inherent in fiction which derives so innocently
from the autobiographical impulse. In the first
place, all the impurities and baggage in the novel
must strike the author as of peculiar and necessary
value because they were observed or actually occurred. But he is not writing a strict autobiography
in which all observations or experiences, however
vague, might conceivably find a justification. He is
trying, and this in the second place, to erect the
autobiographical material into an epical and symbolic importance, to make of it a fable, a "Legend
of Man's Hunger in His Youth." This much is declared by the subtitle.

Mr. Wolfe promises to write some historical novels, and they may well be crucial in the definition
of his genius, because he may be required to reorder the use of his powers. What, thus far, he has
produced is fine fragments, several brilliant pieces
of portraiture, and many sharp observations on
men and nature: in other words, these books are
really voluminous notes from which a fine novel,
or several fine novels, might be written. If he
never writes these novels, it may yet be that his
books will retain a value as documents of some
historical importance and as confused records of
an unusual personality. Meanwhile, despite his
admirable energies and his powerful literary en-
dowments, his work illustrates once more the
limitations, perhaps the necessary limitations, of an
attempt to exploit directly and naïvely the personal
experience and the self-defined personality in art.

And meanwhile it may be well to recollect that
Shakespeare merely wrote *Hamlet;* he was *not*
Hamlet.

MELVILLE the Poet

F. O. MATTHIESSEN has undertaken to give in twenty-two pages [1] a cross section of the rather large body of the poetry of Herman Melville. If he had intended to give merely a little gathering of his poet's best blossoms, his task would have been relatively easy. But he has also undertaken, as he says in his brief but instructive preface, to "take advantage of all the various interests attaching to any part of Melville's work." So some items appear because they present the basic symbols which are found in the prose or because they "serve to light up facets of Melville's mind as it developed in the years after his great creative period."

In one sense all one can do is to say that Mr. Matthiessen, with the space permitted by the series to which this book belongs ("The Poets of the Year"), has carried out his plan with the taste and discernment which could have been predicted by any reader of his discussion of Melville's poetry in the *American Renaissance*. But I shall take this occasion to offer a few remarks supplementary to the preface and to point out other poems and passages in Melville's work which I hope Mr. Matthiessen admires or finds interesting but which could have no place in his arbitrarily limited collection.

First, I wish to comment on Melville's style. It is ordinarily said that he did not master the craft of verse. Few of his poems are finished. Fine lines, exciting images, and bursts of eloquence often appear, but they appear side by side with limping lines, inexpressive images, and passages of bom-

1. *Selected Poems of Herman Melville.*

bast. In a way, he is a poet of shreds and patches. I
do not wish to deny the statement that he did not
master his craft, but I do feel that it needs some
special interpretation.

If, for example, we examine the poems under the
title "Fruit of Travel Long Ago," in the *Timoleon*
volume of 1891, we see that the verse here is
fluent and competent. In his belated poetic apprenticeship, he was capable of writing verse which is
respectable by the conventional standards of the
time. But the effects which he could achieve within
this verse did not satisfy him. Let us look at the
poem called "In a Bye-Canal." The first section gives
us verse that is conventionally competent:

> *A swoon of noon, a trance of tide,*
> *The hushed siesta brooding wide*
> * Like calms far off Peru;*
> *No floating wayfarer in sight,*
> *Dumb noon, and haunted like the night*
> * When Jael the wiled one slew.*
> *A languid impulse from the car*
> *Plied by my indolent gondolier*
> *Tinkles against a palace hoar,*
> * And hark, response I hear!*
> *A lattice clicks; and lo, I see*
> *Between the slats, mute summoning me,*
> *What loveliest eyes of scintillation,*
> *What basilisk glance of conjuration!*

But the next eight lines are very different. The metrical pattern is sorely tried and wrenched.

> *Fronted I have, part taken the span*
> *Of portent in nature and peril in man.*
> *I have swum—I have been*
> *'Twixt the whale's black fluke and the white shark's*
> * fin;*
> *The enemy's desert have wandered in,*
> *And there have turned, have turned and scanned,*
> *Following me how noiselessly,*
> *Envy and Slander, lepers hand in hand.*

Then the poem returns to its normal movement and
tone:

> All this. But at the latticed eye—
> "Hey, Gondolier, you sleep, my man;
> Wake up!" And shooting by, we ran;
> The while I mused, This surely now,
> Confutes the Naturalists, allow!
> Sirens, true sirens verily be,
> Sirens, waylayers in the sea.
> Well, wooed by these same deadly misses,
> Is it shame to run?
> No! Flee them did divine Ulysses,
> Brave, wise, and Venus' son.

The poem breaks up. The central section simply
does not go with the rest. It is as though we have
here a statement of the poet's conviction that the
verse which belonged to the world of respectability
could not accommodate the rendering of the experience undergone " 'Twixt the whale's black fluke
and the white shark's fin." [2] Perhaps the violences,
the distortions, the wrenchings in the versification
of some of the poems are to be interpreted as the
result not of mere ineptitude but of a conscious
effort to develop a nervous, dramatic, masculine
style. (In this connection, the effort at a familiar
style in *John Marr and Other Sailors*, especially in
"Jack Roy," is interesting.) That Melville was conscious of the relation of the mechanics of style to
fundamental intentions is ably argued by William
Ellery Sedgwick in *Herman Melville: The Tragedy
of Mind* in connection with the verse of *Clarel*. Mr.
Sedgwick argues that the choice of short, four-beat
lines, usually rhyming in couplets, a form the very
opposite to what would have been expected, was
dictated by a desire to confirm himself in his new
perspective. "The form of *Clarel* was prop or sup-

---

2. Can this be an echo of the "wolf's black jaw" and the
"dull ass' hoof" in Ben Jonson's "An Ode to Himself"
(*Underwoods*)? In both Jonson and Melville, the content is
the same: the affirmation of independence in the face of a
bad and envious age.

port to his new state of consciousness, in which his spontaneous ego or self-consciousness no longer played an all-commanding role." I would merely extend the application of the principle beyond *Clarel,* without arguing, as Mr. Sedgwick argues in the case of *Clarel,* that Melville did develop a satisfactory solution for his problem.

If we return to "In a Bye-Canal," we may observe that the poem is broken not only by a shift in rhythm but also by a shift in tone. The temper of the poem is very mixed. For instance, the lines

> *Dumb noon, and haunted like the night*
> *When Jael the wiled one slew*

introduce a peculiarly weighted, serious reference into the casual first section which concludes with the playful *scintillation-conjuration* rhyme. Then we have the grand section of the whale and the shark. Then the realistic admonition to the gondolier. Then the conclusion, with its classical allusion, at the level of *vers de société.* Probably no one would argue that the disparate elements in this poem have been assimilated, as they have, for example, in Marvell's "To His Coy Mistress." But I think that one may be well entitled to argue that the confusions of temper in this poem are not merely the result of ineptitude but are the result of an attempt to create a poetry of some vibrancy, range of reference, and richness of tone.

In another form we find the same effort much more successfully realized in "Jack Roy" in the difference between the two following stanzas:

Sang Larry o' the Cannakin, smuggler o' the wine,
At mess between guns, lad in jovial recline:

"In Limbo our Jack he would chirrup up a cheer,
The martinet there find a chaffing mutineer;
From a thousand fathoms down under hatches o'
    your Hades
He'd ascend in love-ditty, kissing fingers to your
    ladies!"

Never relishing the knave, though allowing for the
    menial,
Nor overmuch the king, Jack, nor prodigally genial.
Ashore on liberty, he flashed in escapade,
Vaulting over life in its levelness of grade,
Like the dolphin off Africa in rainbow a-sweeping—
Arch iridescent shot from seas languid sleeping.

Or we find the same fusion of disparate elements in
"The March into Virginia," one of Melville's best
poems:

Did all the lets and bars appear
To every just or larger end,
Whence should come the trust and cheer?
Youth must its ignorant impulse lend—
Age finds place in the rear.
All wars are boyish, and are fought by boys,
The champions and enthusiasts of the state:

. . . . .

No berrying party, pleasure-wooed,
No picnic party in the May,
Ever went less loath than they
Into that leafy neighborhood.
In Bacchic glee they file toward Fate,
Moloch's uninitiate;

. . . . .

But some who this blithe mood present,
As on in lightsome files they fare,
Shall die experienced ere three days are spent—
Perish, enlightened by the volleyed glare; [3]
Or shame survive, and, like to adamant,
The throe of Second Manassas share.

On a smaller scale, Melville's effort to get range
and depth into his poetry is illustrated by the occasional boldness of his comparisons. For example,
in "The Portent," the beard of John Brown protrud-
ing from the hangman's cap is like the trail of a
comet or meteor presaging doom.

---

3. Melville's double use of the word *enlightened* here is interesting and effective. The poem "Shiloh, a Requiem" echoes the metaphorical sense of the word in the line, "What
like a bullet can undeceive?"

> *Hidden in the cap*
> *Is the anguish none can draw;*
> *So your future veils its face,*
> *Shenandoah!*
> *But the streaming beard is shown*
> *(Weird John Brown),*[4]
> *The meteor of the war.*

Or in one of the early poems, "In a Church of Padua," we find the confessional compared to a div-ing-bell:

> *Dread diving-bell! In thee inurned*
> *What hollows the priest must sound,*
> *Descending into consciences*
> *Where more is hid than found.*

It must be admitted that Melville did not learn his craft. But the point is that the craft he did not learn was not the same craft which some of his more highly advertised contemporaries did learn with such glibness of tongue and complacency of spirit. Even behind some of Melville's failures we can catch the shadow of the poem which might have been. And if his poetry is, on the whole, a po-etry of shreds and patches, many of the patches are of a massy and kingly fabric—no product of the local cotton mills.

But to turn to another line of thought: Both Mr. Matthiessen and Mr. Sedgwick have been aware of the importance of the short poems in relation to Melville's general development. Mr. Sedgwick does give a fairly detailed analysis of the relation of *Battle-Pieces* to *Clarel*. "Even in the *Battle-Pieces*," he says, "we feel the reservations of this (religious) consciousness set against the easy and partial affir-mations of patriotism and partisan conflict." And he quotes, as Mr. Matthiessen has quoted in the preface to the present collection and in the *Ameri-can Renaissance,* an extremely significant sentence from the prose essay which Melville appended to

---

4. The depth and precision of the word *weird* is worthy of notice.

the *Battle-Pieces:* "Let us pray that the terrible historic tragedy of our time may not have been enacted without instructing our whole beloved country through pity and terror." And Mr. Sedgwick refers to one of the paradoxes of "The Conflict of Convictions," that the victory of the Civil War may betray the cause for which the North was fighting:

> *Power unanointed may come—*
> *Dominion (unsought by the free)*
> *And the Iron Dome*
> *Stronger for stress and strain,*
> *Fling her huge shadow athwart the main;*
> *But the Founders' dream shall flee. . . .*

But even in this poem there are other ideas which relate to Melville's concern with the fundamental ironical dualities of existence: will against necessity, action against ideas, youth against age, the changelessness of man's heart against the concept of moral progress, the bad doer against the good deed, the bad result against the good act, ignorance against fate, etc. These ideas appear again and again, as in "The March into Virginia":

> *Did all the lets and bars appear*
> *To every just or larger end,*
> *Whence should come the trust and cheer?*
> *Youth must the ignorant impulse lend—*
> *Age finds place in the rear.*
> *All wars are boyish, and are fought by boys,*
> *The champions and enthusiasts of the state.*

Or in "On the Slain Collegians":

> *Youth is the time when hearts are large,*
> *And stirring wars*
> *Appeal to the spirit which appeals in turn*
> *To the blade it draws.*
> *If woman incite, and duty show*
> *(Though made the mask of Cain),*
> *Or whether it be Truth's sacred cause,*
> *Who can aloof remain*
> *That shares youth's ardour, uncooled by the snow*
> *Of wisdom or sordid gain?*

Youth, action, will, ignorance—all appear in heroic
and dynamic form as manifestations of what Mr.
Sedgwick has called Melville's "radical Protestantism," the spirit which had informed *Moby Dick*.
But in these poems the commitment is nicely balanced, and even as we find the praise of the dynamic and heroic we find them cast against the
backdrop of age, idea, necessity, wisdom, fate. Duty
may be made the "mask of Cain" and "lavish
hearts" are but, as the poem on the Collegians
puts it, "swept by the winds of their place and
time." All bear their "fated" parts. All move toward
death or toward the moment of wisdom when they
will stand, as "The March into Virginia" puts it,
"enlightened by the volleyed glare."

Man may wish to act for Truth and Right, but
the problem of definitions is a difficult one and solution may be achieved only in terms of his own
exercise of will and his appetite for action. That
is, his "truth" and the Truth may be very different
things in the end. "On the Slain Collegians" sums
the matter up:

> *What could they else—North or South?*
> *Each went forth with blessings given*
> *By priests and mothers in the name of Heaven;*
>   *And honour in both was chief.*
> *Warred one for Right, and one for Wrong?*
> *So be it; but they both were young—*
> *Each grape to his cluster clung,*
> *All their elegies are sung.*

Or there is "The College Colonel," the young officer
who returns from the war, a crutch by his saddle,
to receive the welcome of the crowd and especially,
as "Boy," the salute of age. But to him comes "al-
loy."

> *It is not that a leg is lost*
> *It is not that an arm is maimed.*
> *It is not that the fever has racked—*
> *Self he has long disclaimed.*

But all through the Seven Days' Fight,
And deep in the Wilderness grim,
And in the field-hospital tent,
And Petersburg crater, and dim
Lean brooding in Libby, there came—
Ah heaven!—what truth *to him.*

The official truth and the official celebration are equally meaningless to him who has been "enlightened by the volleyed glare"—who has known pity and terror.

The event, the act, is never simple. Duty may be made the mask of Cain. In "The Conflict of Convictions," it is asked:

Dashed aims, at which Christ's martyrs pale,
Shall Mammon's slaves fulfill?

And in the same poem, in the passage which Mr. Sedgwick quotes, Melville conjectures that the Iron Dome, stronger for stress and strain, may fling its huge, imperial shadow across the main; but at the expense of the "Founders' dream." But other dire effects of the convulsion, even if it involves Right, may be possible. Hate on one side and Phariseeism on the other may breed a greater wrong than the one corrected by the conflict. The "gulfs" may bare "their slimed foundations," as it is phrased in the same poem in an image which is repeated in "America." The allegorical female figure, America, is shown sleeping:

But in that sleep contortion showed
The terror of the vision there—
A silent vision unavowed,
Revealing earth's foundations bare,
And Gorgon in her hiding place.
It was a thing of fear to see
So foul a dream upon so fair a face,
And the dreamer lying in that starry shroud.

Even if the victory is attained, there is no cause for innocent rejoicing. As, in "The College Colonel," the hero looks beyond the cheering crowd to his

"truth," so in "Commemorative of a Naval Victory,"
the hero must look beyond his "festal fame":

But seldom the laurel wreath is seen
Unmixed with pensive pansies dark;
There's a light and shadow on every man
Who at last attains his lifted mark—
Nursing through night the ethereal spark.
Elate he never can be;
He feels that spirits which glad had hailed his
  worth,
Sleep in oblivion. —The shark
Glides white through the phosphorous sea.

There is more involved here than the sadness over
the loss of comrades. The shark comes as too violent and extravagant an image for that. The white
shark belongs to the world of the "slimed foundations" which are exposed by the convulsion. It is
between the whale's black fluke and the white
shark's fin that wisdom is learned. He is the Maldive shark, which appears in the poem by that
name, the "Gorgonian head" (the "Gorgon in her
hiding place" appears too in the bared foundations
of earth glimpsed in the dream of "America"), the
"pale ravener of horrible meat," the Fate symbol.

We may ask what resolution of these dualities
and dubieties may be found in Melville's work. For
there is an effort at a resolution. The effort manifests itself in three different terms: nature, history,
and religion.

In reference to the first term, we find the simple
treatment of "Shiloh":

> *Foemen at morn, but friends at eve—*
> *Fame or country least their care:*
> *(What like a bullet can undeceive!)*
> *But now they lie low,*
> *While over them the swallows skim*
> *And all is hushed at Shiloh.*

Mortal passion and mortal definition dissolve in
the natural process, as in "Malvern Hill":

> *We elms of Malvern Hill*
> *Remember everything;*
> *But sap the twig will fill:*
> *Wag the world how it will,*
> *Leaves must be green in Spring.*

The focal image at the end of "A Requiem for Soldiers Lost in Ocean Transports" repeats the same effect:

> *Nor heed they now the lone bird's flight*
> *Round the lone spar where mid-sea surges pour.*

There is, however, a step beyond this elegiac calm of the great natural process which absorbs the human effort and agony. There is also the historical process. It is possible, as Melville puts it in "The Conflict of Convictions," that the "throes of ages" may rear the "final empire and the happier world." The Negro woman in "Formerly a Slave" looks

> *Far down the depth of thousand years,*
> *And marks the revel shine;*
> *Her dusky face is lit with sober light,*
> *Sibylline, yet benign.*

In "America," the last poem of *Battle-Pieces*, the contorted expression on the face of the sleeping woman as she dreams the foul dream of earth's bared foundations, is replaced, when she rises, by a "clear calm look."

> *. . . It spake of pain,*
> *But such a purifier from stain—*
> *Sharp pangs that never come again—*
> *And triumph repressed by knowledge meet,*
> *And youth matured for age's seat—*
> *Law on her brow and empire in her eyes.*
> *So she, with graver air and lifted flag;*
> *While the shadow, chased by light,*
> *Fled along the far-drawn height,*
> *And left her on the crag.*

"Secession, like Slavery, is against Destiny," Melville wrote in the prose Supplement to *Battle-*

Pieces. For to him, if history was fate (the "foulest crime" was inherited and was fixed by geographical accident upon its perpetrators), it might also prove to be redemption. In *Mardi,* in a passage which Mr. Sedgwick quotes in reference to the slaves of Vivenza, Melville exclaims: "Time—all-healing Time—Time, great philanthropist! Time must befriend these thralls." Melville, like Hardy, whom he resembles in so many respects and with whose war poems his own war poems share so much in tone and attitude, proclaimed that he was neither an optimist nor a pessimist, and in some of his own work we find a kind of guarded meliorism, like Hardy's, which manifests itself in the terms of destiny, fate, time, that is, in the historical process.

The historical process, however, does not appear always as this mechanism of meliorism. Sometimes the resolution it offers is of another sort, a sort similar to the elegiac calm of the natural process: the act is always poised on the verge of history, the passion, even at the moment of greatest intensity, is always about to become legend, the moral issue is always about to disappear into time and leave only the human figures, shadowy now, fixed in attitudes of the struggle. In "Battle of Stone River, Tennessee," we find the stanzas which best express this.

> *With Tewksbury and Barnet heath,*
> *In days to come the field shall blend,*
> *The story dim and date obscure;*
> *In legend all shall end.*
> *Even now, involved in forest shade*
> *A Druid-dream the strife appears,*
> *The fray of yesterday assumes*
> *The haziness of years.*
>> *In North and South still beats the vein*
>> *Of Yorkist and Lancastrian.*
>
> .   .   .   .   .
>
> *But Rosecrans in the cedarn glade*
> *And, deep in denser cypress gloom,*

> *Dark Breckinridge, shall fade away*
> *Or thinly loom.*
> *The pale throngs who in forest cowed*
> *Before the spell of battle's pause,*
> *Forefelt the stillness that shall dwell*
> *On them and their wars.*
> > *North and South shall join the train*
> > *Of Yorkist and Lancastrian.*

In "The March into Virginia" the young men laughing and chatting on the road to Manassas are "Moloch's uninitiate" who "file toward Fate."

> *All they feel is this: 'tis glory,*
> *A rapture sharp, though transitory*
> *Yet lasting in belaurelled story.*

The glory of the act ends in legend, in the perspective of history, which is fate. Human action enters the realm where it is, to take a line from "The Coming Storm,"

> *Steeped in fable, steeped in fate.*

Nature and history proved the chief terms of resolution in *Battle-Pieces*. Only rarely appears the third term, religion, and then in a conventional form. For instance, there is "The Swamp-Angel," which deals with the bombardment of Charleston:

> *Who weeps for the woeful City*
> *Let him weep for our guilty kind;*
> *Who joys at her wild despairing—*
> *Christ, the Forgiver, convert his mind.*

It is actually in the terms of nature and history that the attitude which characterizes *Clarel* first begins to make itself felt. Mr. Sedgwick has defined Melville's attitude as the result of a "religious conversion to life." In it he renounced the quest for the "uncreated good," the individualistic idealism of *Moby Dick*, the "radical Protestantism." Mr. Sedgwick continues: "Behind *Clarel* lies the recognition that for ripeness, there must be receptivity; that from the point of view of the total consciousness it is not more blessed to give than to receive. One receives in order to be received into life and fulfilled by life. . . . Melville's act was toward humanity, not away from it. He renounced all the prerogatives of individuality in order to enter into the destiny which binds all human beings in one great spiritual and emotional organism. He abdicated his independence so as to be incorporated into the mystical body of humanity." There is the affirmation at the end of *Clarel:*

But through such strange illusions have they passed
Who in life's pilgrimage have baffled striven—
Even death may prove unreal at the last,
And stoics be astounded into heaven.

Then keep thy heart, though yet but ill-resigned—
Clarel, thy heart, the issues there but mind;
That like the crocus budding through the snow—
That like a swimmer rising from the deep—
That like a burning secret which doth go
Even from the bosom that would hoard and keep;
Emerge thou mayst from the last whelming sea,
And prove that death but routs life into victory.

Or we find the same attitude expressed by the comforting spirit which appears at the end of "The Lake":

She ceased and nearer slid, and hung
In dewy guise; then softlier sung:
"Since light and shade are equal set,
And all revolves, nor more ye know;
Ah, why should tears the pale cheek fret
For aught that waneth here below.
Let go, let go!"

With that, her warm lips thrilled me through,
She kissed me while her chaplet cold
Its rootlets brushed against my brow
With all their humid clinging mould.
She vanished, leaving fragrant breath
And warmth and chill of wedded life and death.

And when, in the light of these poems we look back upon "The Maldive Shark" we see its deeper significance. As the pilot fish may find a haven in the serrated teeth of the shark, so man, if he learns the last wisdom, may find an "asylum in the jaws of the Fates."

This end product of Melville's experience has, in the passage which I have already quoted from Mr. Sedgwick, been amply defined. What I wish to emphasize is the fact that there is an astonishing continuity between the early poems, especially *Battle-Pieces*, and *Clarel*. Under the terms of nature and history, the religious attitude of *Clarel* and "The Lake" is already being defined.

A Poem of Pure

Imagination:

an Experiment in Reading

THE DISCUSSION OF *The Ancient Mariner* always begins with reference to Mrs. Barbauld, that lady of "fine taste, correct understanding, as well as pure integrity," as Crabb Robinson called her. I suppose

it is only reasonable to begin the discussion with
Mrs. Barbauld, for if that "best specimen of female
Presbyterian society in the country" is long since
dust, her children, male and female, are legion
and vocal. The famous remark to which her fine
taste and correct understanding gave utterance had
to do with a poem which, upon its appearance, had
given offense to the judicious. A long time after the
appearance of the poem itself, the poet, now a
weak and lisping old man, recorded Mrs. Barbauld's
remark, if we can believe the report in *Table Talk,*
and his own comment upon it:

Mrs. Barbauld once told me that she admired *The Ancient Mariner* very much, but that there were two faults
in it—it was improbable, and had no moral. As for the
probability, I owned that that might admit some question; but as to the want of a moral, I told her that in
my own judgment the poem had too much; and that the
only, or chief fault, if I might say so, was the obtrusion
of the moral sentiment so openly on the reader as a
principle or cause of action in a work of such pure
imagination. It ought to have had no more moral than
the *Arabian Nights* tale of the merchant's sitting down
to eat dates by the side of a well, and throwing the
shells aside, and lo! a genie starts up, and says he *must*
kill the aforesaid merchant, *because* one of the date
shells had, it seems, put out the eye of the genie's son.

This passage, to which I shall return, gives Mrs.
Barbauld her uneasy immortality.

I do not quote it, however, to pay the wonted
tribute of a sneer. In fact, I am inclined to sympathize with the lady's desire that poetry have some
significant relation to the world, some meaning.
True, the kind of meaning prized by her female
Presbyterian sensibility leaves something to be desired in the way of subtlety, if we are to judge from
her own poems—from, for example, "An Inventory
of the Furniture of Dr. Priestley's Study," "In-
scription for an Ice-house," "Address to the Deity,"
or "To Mr. S. T. Coleridge, 1797," in which she
advises the "youth beloved of Science—of the Muse

beloved," to shun the "maze of metaphysic lore,"
where Indolence "fixes her turf-built seat." But it is
easy to sympathize with her general point of view.
The instinctive demand for significance is healthy,
and one can especially sympathize with it after en-
countering a brand of hyperaesthetical criticism of
our poem. This brand of criticism does not, to my
knowledge, occur in the purlieus of bohemianism
or in the shimmering pages of the *fin de siècle*, but
rather, it flourishes in the very citadels of academic
respectability, and in the works of some of the
most eminent and sober students of Coleridge.

For example, one such critic, after stating that
the passage concerning Mrs. Barbauld makes it
forever clear that there was "no intention to give
the poem a moral meaning," goes on to say: "Obviously, only the reader who cannot enjoy this
journey into the realm of the supernatural finds it
necessary to seek out a moral." [1]

There are two questions involved here: First,
what did Coleridge mean in the passage from the
Table Talk? Second, what does Earl Leslie Griggs,
the critic referred to above, mean by his remark?
It so happens that Griggs has misread his text
when he takes it as evidence that there is no "moral
intention" in the poem. For Coleridge, according to
his young kinsman Henry Nelson Coleridge, who
recorded the *Table Talk*, did not say that the poem
as it exists has no moral, but said that it suffers
from the "obtrusion of the moral sentiment so
openly." Nor did he say or even imply that the poem
would be better if there were *no* moral. He merely
said that the "obtrusion of the moral sentiment" is
too "open." If the passage affirms anything, it affirms that Coleridge intended the poem to have a
"moral sentiment," but felt that he had been a trifle
unsubtle in fulfilling his intention. So all the critics
who take this passage to argue that Coleridge intended *The Ancient Mariner* to be a poem without
a theme, without relevance to life, have, like Griggs,

1. The notes to this essay begin on p. 272.

reversed the undebatable sense of the text of the
Table Talk.

Now, at the risk of a digression, I shall turn to
the second question: what does Griggs mean by the
word *moral* when he says that the poem has no
"moral intention"? I take it that Griggs uses the
word *moral* in a broad, general sense, equating it
with theme understood as comment on human conduct and values. If he means something more specific, he has not given any indication of it. And if
this broad, general sense is what he means, he is
saying that the poem has no theme.

Presumably Griggs' remark is based on some
theory of "pure poetry"—some notion that a poem
should not "mean" but "be," and that the "be-ing" of
a poem does not "mean." The actual statement
he makes, however, does not concern his own, but
Coleridge's theory of poetry: Coleridge, he says, had
no "moral intention" and the poem has no theme.
It may be that Griggs has stated his views a little
unclearly and holds that special variant of the general theory of pure poetry which says that poetry
(which is pure realization—however that may be
interpreted) does make comments on life but that
the truths it offers us are not worth listening to.
But even that is a very different thing from assert-
ing that a poet, Coleridge in this case, is not even
undertaking to deliver an utterance about life. His
theme may be a statement of error, but it is a statement. My first purpose in this essay is to establish
that *The Ancient Mariner* does embody a statement,
and to define the nature of that statement, the
theme, as nearly as I can.

It may be objected that Griggs does not, however, wish the word *moral* read in the broad, general sense which I have here provisionally adopted
—that he intends such a narrow sense that room
is left for all sorts of themes and meanings, just so
long as they are not too painfully reminiscent of
Sunday School. If that be objected, I can only appeal to the context of his statement. Why does he
give us the simple alternatives of a "moral inten-

tion" and an enjoyable "journey into the realm of the supernatural"? And why does he dismiss so airily what he calls the "various efforts at interpretation," and specifically S. F. Gingerich's theory that the poem symbolizes the doctrine of necessitarianism? But I have dwelt on this matter only because it represents a point of view, about both *The Ancient Mariner* and poetry in general, which one frequently encounters. And certainly I do not wish to appear ungrateful to Griggs, to whom all admirers of Coleridge owe a great debt.

Nor do I wish to appear ungrateful to John Livingston Lowes,[2] whose views on this point will next engage us. Lowes seems to accept a very different premise from that of Griggs, for he says that "some interest deeply human, anchored in the familiar frame of things," was fundamental to Coleridge's plan. This "interest deeply human" turns out to be the idea of transgression and absolution, and of the train of consequence which persists even after absolution as what the Gloss terms "the penance of life." "You repent," says Lowes, "and a load is lifted from your soul. But you have not thereby escaped your deed. . . . It is the inexorable law of life."

This much, in itself, would seem to constitute a theme for the poem, a comment on human conduct and values. But Lowes now proceeds to reverse the direction of his argument—or if he does not do precisely that, he limits his reading of the function of the theme so that it is to be understood as having no relevance to actual life. The law of life appears in the poem, he says, merely to unify and "credibilize" the poem, because "we accept illusion only when in some fashion it bears the semblance of truth." He demands: "Has it still another end, to wit, edification?" He quickly adds that he is well aware of Coleridge's homiletical propensity, but he denies "edification" as being the poet's intention: "Nevertheless, to interpret the drift of 'The Ancient Mariner' as didactic in its intention is to stultify both Coleridge and one's self. For such an inter-

pretation shatters the world of illusion which is the
very essence of the poem."

The argument here is so vaguely put that it is
difficult to understand precisely what the critic does
mean. In one sense, it is quite true that the "intention" of the poet is not to "edify" the reader but
to make a poem. In that sense, Lowes may be understood. But we must remember that in so far as
the poem is truly the poet's, in so far as it ultimately expresses him, it involves his own view of
the world, his own values. Therefore the poem will,
for better or worse, have relevance, by implication
at least, to the world outside the poem, and is not
merely a device for creating an illusion. But this is
precisely what Lowes proceeds to deny. The poem
has, he says, no reference to reality: "And through
the very completeness of their incorporation with
the text of 'The Ancient Mariner,' the truths of experience which run in sequence through it have
lost, so far as any inculcation of a moral through
the poem is concerned, all didactic value." He sup-
ports this view by saying that "the 'moral' of the
poem, *outside the poem,* will not hold water," because "consequence and cause, *in terms of the
world of reality* are ridiculously incommensurable," and "punishment . . . palpably does not fit
the crime."

What this amounts to seems to be this: (1) Coleridge introduces a theme into his poem merely as
a structural device—he did not intend for it to be
taken seriously. (2) We would not take it seriously
anyway because it violates our moral sense—a man
should not have to suffer so much just for shooting
a bird.

These pronouncements lead me to a further
statement concerning my purpose here: I shall try
to establish that the statement which the poem
does ultimately embody is thoroughly consistent
with Coleridge's basic theological and philosophical
views as given to us in sober prose, and that, without regard to the question of the degree of self-

consciousness on the part of the poet at any given moment of composition, the theme is therefore "intended." [3] I shall also try to establish that the particular ground given by Lowes for the rejection of the relevance of the "moral" is based on a misreading of the poem—a reading which insists on a literal rather than a symbolic interpretation. In the end, I shall be attacking, in new terms, the position held by Griggs, for just as Griggs defines the poem as a journey into the supernatural for the sake of the journey, so Lowes defines it as an illusion for the sake of illusion. For them both, the poem is nothing more than a pleasant but meaningless dream.

The poem's "inconsequence is the dream's irrelevance," says the author of *The Road to Xanadu,* and thereby summarizes the view held by a large body of critics, who, either by way of praise or blame, have commented on the dreamlike quality of the poem. For such critics, as for Swinburne, Coleridge is one of the " 'footless birds of Paradise,' who have only wings to sustain them, and live their lives out in a perpetual flight through the clearest air of heaven." For these critics, *The Ancient Mariner* has no contact with reality. To support this view, that the poem is no more than a dream, they appeal to the report, in De Quincey's *Literary and Lake Reminiscences,* of Coleridge's remark that "before meeting a fable in which to embody his ideas, he had meditated a poem on delirium, confounding its own dream-scenery with external things, and connected with the imagery of high latitudes."

Let us examine the nature of this evidence. Coleridge presumably did connect his poem with dreams, just as he referred to his poem "The Raven," if we are to take Lamb's word, as a dream.[4] And we can well believe that a good deal of the *material* for the poem may have come from the poet's opium dreams. But the fact that Coleridge himself made this association between the poem and dreams does little to support the view that he thought of the poem as having no theme with a ref-

erence to reality. Coleridge's notion concerning
dreams forbids that interpretation. "Dreams," he
puts it in the *Table Talk,* "have nothing in them
which is absurd and nonsensical." And again:
"You will observe that even in dreams nothing is
fancied without an antecedent *quasi* cause. It could
not be otherwise." And in connection with speculations on the significance of dreams and visions:
". . . Who shall determine to what extent the re-
productive imagination, unsophisticated by the will,
and undistracted by intrusions from the sense, may
or may not be concentred and sublimed into fore-
sight and presentiment?"

There is no reason, however, for us to go
to Coleridge's theory of dreams. De Quincey's sentence, in fact, betrays the critics who would use it
to prove that Coleridge intended *The Ancient Mariner* to have no theme with a reference to reality,
for the sentence says quite flatly that Coleridge's
"ideas" preceded the "fable." In other words, at
least according to De Quincey, there had been a
general idea, a theme, in the poet's mind which finally found its appropriate medium of expression
in the story of the "old navigator." And if the idea
had an independent existence before an appropriate fable was hit upon, the idea must have had for
the poet more than the structural importance assigned to it by Lowes. An idea can scarcely be said
to function merely to unify and credibilize if nothing exists for it to unify and credibilize.

So much for one piece of evidence offered to support the view that the poem's "inconsequence is the
dream's irrelevance." But there is another piece of
evidence usually offered for this view—the passage
from the *Table Talk* already quoted. I have pointed
out how Griggs misreads one part of that famous
passage. Let us look at it more closely. In it Coleridge refers to his poem as a work of "pure imagination," and it is this phrase which is most often
offered to support the view held by Griggs, Lowes,
and their school of readers. I am inclined to believe that they take the word imagination here at

their own convenience and not in Coleridge's context and usage. They take it, as a matter of fact, in the casual and vulgar sense, as equivalent to meaninglessness or illusion; or if they don't take it in the casual and vulgar sense, they take it in terms of a poetic theory of illusion for illusion's sake which, as stated, denies significance to the word as fully as does the casual and vulgar sense.

Actually, a little reflection instructs us that the word was for Coleridge freighted with a burden of speculation and technical meaning. His theory of the imagination, upon which his whole art-philosophy hinges, "was primarily the vindication of a particular attitude to life and reality." And it would be strange if Coleridge, with his lifelong passion for accuracy of terminology and subtlety of distinction, had tossed away that sacred word which stood for the vindication of his most fundamental beliefs as irresponsibly as the merchant in the story of *The Arabian Nights* tosses away the "date shell."

To return to our argument, we must ask what is the burden of technical meaning with which Coleridge had freighted the word *imagination*? At the moment we shall not be concerned with a detailed exposition of Coleridge's theory, and certainly not with an account of the stages of its growth and clarification. We shall be, instead, concerned to see how Coleridge's concept would redeem works of pure imagination from the charge, amiable or otherwise, of being in themselves meaningless and nothing but refined and ingenious toys for an idle hour.

The key passage for this purpose is the famous one from the *Biographia Literaria,* but we shall group around it other passages drawn from various sources. Here is the key passage:

The Imagination then I consider either as primary or secondary. The primary Imagination I hold to be the living power and prime agent of all human perception, and as a repetition in the finite mind of the eternal act of creation in the infinite I Am. The secondary Imagination I consider as an echo of the former, coexisting with the conscious will, yet still as identical with the primary in the kind of its agency, and differing only in degree and in the mode of its operation. It dissolves, diffuses, dissipates in order to recreate: or where this process is rendered impossible, yet still at all events it struggles to idealize and to unify.

It is the primary imagination which creates our world, for nothing of which we are aware is given to the passive mind. By it we know the world, but for Coleridge knowing is making, for, "To know is in its very essence a verb active." We know by creating, and one of the things we create is the Self, for a subject is that which "becomes a subject by the act of constructing itself objectively to itself; but which never is an object except for itself, and only so far as by the very same act it becomes a subject." It is irrelevant here whether we accept Coleridge's theory or regard all this, as did the vindictive Carlyle on his visit to the old sage, as a dreary, adenoidal mumbo-jumbo of "om-ject" and "sum-ject," a "mooning singsong" of "theosophico-metaphysical monotony" in a "Kantean haze-world" populated by "dim-melting ghosts and shadows." The point, for present purposes, is that Coleridge attributes to imagination this fundamental significance.

We have been speaking only of what he calls primary imagination, the perception which produces our ordinary world of the senses. Even here we can observe that when "the imagination is conceived as recognizing the inherent interdependence of subject and object (or complementary aspects of a single reality), its dignity is immeasurably raised." But when we turn to his interpretation of the secondary imagination, that dignity is further enhanced. For here we leave creation at the unconscious and instinctive level and define it as coexisting with, and in terms of, the conscious will; here it operates as a function of that freedom which is the essential attribute of spirit.

Does Coleridge imply, however, that the poet in composing his poem acts according to a fully developed and objectively statable plan, that he has a blueprint of intention in such an absolute sense? To this question the answer is *no*. Several texts can be adduced on this point, for example in "On Poesy": "There is in genius itself an unconscious activity; nay, that is the genius in the man of genius." But how can this be made to square with the key statement about the secondary imagination as "coexisting with the conscious will"?

Perhaps the answer could be found in an application of Coleridge's discussion of the Self, Will, and Motive. The common idea of will, he says, is the power to respond to a motive conceived of as acting upon it from the outside. But what is motive? Not a thing, but the thought of a thing. But all thoughts are not motives. Therefore motive is a determining thought. But what is a thought? A thing or an individual? Where does it begin or end? "Far more readily could we apply these questions to an ocean billow. . . . As by a billow we mean no more than a particular movement of the sea, so neither by a thought can we mean more than the mind thinking in some one direction. Consequently a motive is neither more nor less than the act of an intelligent being determining itself . . ." [5] But will "is an abiding faculty or habit or fixed disposition to certain objects," and rather than motive originating will, it itself is originated in terms of that predisposition or permanent will.

It seems clear that the secondary imagination does operate as a function of that permanent will, and in terms of the basic concerns by which that will fulfills itself, but the particular plan or intention for a particular poem may be actually developed in the course of composition in terms of that "unconscious activity," which is the "genius in the man of genius," and may result from a long process of trial and error. "The organic form is innate," Coleridge writes in "Shakespeare, a Poet Generally"; "it shapes, as it develops, itself from within, and the fulness of its development is one and the same with the perfection of its outward form."

Again, he says that the artist will not be successful
unless he is impelled by a "mighty inward force,"
but he distinguishes this force, by implication at
least, from plan or intention, for he goes on to say
that the "obscure impulse" must "gradually become a bright and clear and burning Idea." [6] In
other words, the plan and meaning of the work
may be discovered in the process of creation. But
it is to be remembered that this process is a function of the permanent will which constantly moves
to fulfill itself in consciousness.[7]

It is possible that we have in Coleridge's theory
of poetic creation a transposition into psychological terms of Plotinus' doctrine of creation:

Consider the universe . . . are we, now, to imagine
that its maker first thought it out in detail . . . and
that having thus appointed every item beforehand, he
then set about the execution?. . . All things must exist
in something else; of that prior—since there is no
obstacle, all being continuous within the realm of
reality—there has suddenly appeared a sign, an image,
whether given forth directly or through the ministry of
soul or of some phase of soul, matters nothing for the
moment: thus the later aggregate of existence springs
from the divine world in greater beauty. There because
There unmingled but mingled here. From the beginning
to end all is gripped by the Forms of the Intellectual
Realm: Matter itself is held by the Ideas of the elements
and to those Ideas are added other Ideas and others
again, so that it is hard to work down to crude Matter
beneath all that sheathing of Idea. Indeed since Matter
itself, in its degree, is an Idea—the lowest—all the universe is Idea and there is nothing that is not Idea as
the archetype was. And all is made silently since nothing had part in the making but Being and Idea—a further reason why creation went on without toil. . . .
Thus nothing stood in the way of the Idea . . . the creation is not hindered on its way even now; it stands firm
in virtue of being All. To me, moreover, it seems that if
we ourselves were archetypes, Ideas, veritable Being,
and the Idea with which we construct here were our
veritable Essence, then our creative power too would
toillessly effect its purpose: as man now stands, he does

not produce in his work a true image of himself: become man, he has ceased to be All. . .[8]

However it works in poetic creation, the secondary imagination gives us more than poetry. The secondary imagination, as I. A. Richards puts it, "gives us not only poetry—in the limited sense in which literary critics concern themselves with it— but every aspect of the routine world in which it is invested with other values than those necessary for our bare continuance as living beings: all objects for which we can feel love, awe, admiration; every quality beyond the account of physics, chemistry, and the physiology of sense-perception, nutrition, reproduction, and locomotion; every awareness for which a civilized life is preferred by us to an uncivilized." But Richards, the child of the materialistic Bentham, with whom Coleridge, according to John Stuart Mill, had to divide the intellectual kingship of his age, is here casting into psychological terms what in Coleridge's thought appears often in theological and metaphysical terms;[9] and though Coleridge himself was constantly fascinated by what he called the "facts of mind" and defended the use of the word *psychological,* he was not content to leave the doctrine of the creativity of mind at the psychological level. There is a God, and the creativity of the human mind, both in terms of the primary and in terms of the secondary imagination, is an analogue of Divine creation and a proof that man is created in God's image. Furthermore, the world of Nature is to be read by the mind as a symbol of Divinity, a symbol characterized by the "translucence of the eternal through and in the temporal," which "always partakes of the reality which it renders intelligible; and while it enunciates the whole, abides itself as a living part in that unity of which it is representative." Reason, as opposed to the understanding, is, in Coleridge's system, the organ whereby man achieves the "intuition and spiritual consciousness of God," and the imagination operates to read Nature in the

light of that consciousness, to read it as a symbol
of God. It might be said that reason shows us
God, and imagination shows us how Nature participates in God.

So, if we look at the phrase, a work of "pure imagination," in the light of Coleridge's theory of the
imagination, we see that such a work would be one
which not only, to borrow from Coleridge's portrait
of the ideal poet, "brings the whole soul of man
into activity, with the subordination of its faculties
to each other according to their relative worth and
dignity," and makes of the reader himself a "creative being" in the image of God, but also gives us
a revelation, for "all truth is a species of Revelation." And so that phrase "pure imagination" as applied to *The Ancient Mariner* gives us little excuse
to read the poem as an agreeable but scarcely
meaningful effusion. Not only when Coleridge is
theorizing does he insist upon "truth," upon "meaning." He often does so even in casual remarks upon
particular poems or poets. For instance: "Not
twenty lines of Scott's poetry will ever reach poster-
ity; it has relation to nothing." Or: "How shall he
fully enjoy Wordsworth, who has never meditated
on the truths which Wordsworth has wedded to immortal verse?"

At this point I wish to anticipate a possible objection. It may be said that I am basing an argument for a certain interpretation of the poem on
two passages, one from De Quincey and one from
Henry Nelson Coleridge, which have only the status
of hearsay testimony and are therefore without
legal standing. It is true that we cannot know exactly what Coleridge said on either occasion, but
it is not true that I am basing an argument upon
these passages. I should be better pleased to leave
them out of the discussion altogether and treat
only of the poem itself and other material of in-
disputable authorship. Though I shall not base my
own argument upon these passages, I am forced,
however, to consider them in detail because they
have been used now and again, for more than a

hundred years, to support an interpretation of the poem which I consider fallacious. All I wish to put at stake here is this: If these passages of hearsay testimony are to be used at all, they will support my general contention.

II

If *The Ancient Mariner* has a meaning, what is that meaning?

It is true that a poem may mean a number of different things. By this I do not intend to say that a poem means different things to different readers. This is, of course, true in one sense, but true, first, only in so far as the poet fails, as fail he must in some degree, in the exercise of his creative control, and second, in so far as each reader must, as a result of his own history and nature, bring to the poem a different mass of experience, strength of intellect, and intensity of feeling. In this second sense we may say that the reader does not interpret the poem but the poem interprets the reader. We may say that the poem is the light and not the thing seen by the light. The poem is the light by which the reader may view and review all the areas of experience with which he is acquainted.

I do not intend to say merely that a poem has different meanings for different readers, but that it may have different meanings for the same reader. For present purposes we may discriminate two senses in which this is true.

First, it is clear that a poem has different meanings when placed in different perspectives of interest. We may look at it as a document in the history of a language, in the history of literary forms, in the history of political ideas, or in a thousand other different perspectives, and in each of them discover a different kind of meaning. The significant factor in determining the difference among meanings in this sense is that the reader, from outside the poem, prescribes the particular perspective in which the poem is to be placed.

Second, a poem may have different meanings ac-

cording to the different perspectives which are inherent in the poem itself and are not proposed from
outside. But it may be objected that the difference
between the *extrinsic* and *intrinsic* perspectives may
not, in practice, really subsist. An illustration may
clarify the distinction proposed. In the play *Julius
Caesar* the topic of the transition from the Republic to the Empire appears. The same topic may be
regarded in either the extrinsic or the intrinsic perspective. The decisive factor is this: If we regard it
in the extrinsic perspective, we relate it to a body
of facts and ideas many of which have not the
slightest relation to the play. For instance, many of
the facts pertinent to this perspective have been
discovered and many of the ideas have been formulated since the date of composition of the play. If
we regard the topic, however, in the intrinsic perspective, we relate the pattern which the topic receives in the play to other patterns in the play. For
instance, the political theme (as we may call the
topic as patterned in the play, as viewed in the intrinsic perspective) is related to the other themes,
for instance, to the philosophical theme, which is
here, I take it, primarily concerned with the question of free will and determinism. In other words,
the various extrinsic perspectives disintegrate the
play for their own special purposes; the various intrinsic perspectives merely define the themes
which, it is assumed, the play unifies and makes
mutually interpretive. Any substantial work will operate at more than one thematic level, and this is
what makes it so difficult to define *the* theme of a
profound creation; the root-idea will have many
possible formulations and many of them will appear, or be suggested, in the work.

In *The Ancient Mariner* I wish to distinguish two
basic themes, both of them very rich and provocative, and I shall, in the course of my discussion, attempt to establish their interrelation.

One theme I shall call *primary*, the other *secondary*. I do not mean to imply that one is more important than the other. But the one which I shall

call primary is more obviously presented to us, is, as it were, at the threshold of the poem. The primary theme may be defined as the issue of the fable (or of the situation or discourse if we are applying this kind of analysis to a poem which does not present a fable). The primary theme does not necessarily receive a full statement. In fact, in *The Ancient Mariner* it receives only a kind of coy and dramatically naïve understatement which serves merely as a clue—"He prayeth best, etc." But the theme thus hinted at is the outcome of the fable taken at its face value as a story of crime and punishment and reconciliation. I shall label the primary theme in this poem as the theme of sacramental vision, or the theme of the "One Life." The operation of this theme in the poem I shall presently explore.

As the primary theme may be taken as the issue of the fable, so the secondary theme may be taken as concerned with the context of values in which the fable is presented and which the fable may be found ultimately to embody, just as more obviously it embodies the primary theme. I shall label the secondary theme in this poem as the theme of the imagination. After having explored the operation of the theme of sacramental unity in the poem, I shall explore the operation of the theme of the imagination, and shall then attempt to define the significance of their final symbolic fusion in the poem.

Before proceeding to the investigation of these themes in the poem, I wish, however, to distinguish them from another type of theme which is sometimes emphasized in the discussion of this work. This type is the personal theme; it is concerned with those internal conflicts of the poet which may find expression in the poem. We have an example of this type of theme defined by Hugh I'Anson Fausset when he writes that the poem is "an involuntary but inevitable projection into imagery of his [Coleridge's] own inner discord. The Mariner's sin against Nature in shooting the Albatross im-

aged his own morbid divorce from the physical.
. . ." Or we find more elaborately developed examples in Kenneth Burke's treatment, in *The Philosophy of Literary Form,* of the sexual and opium
motives.

Without question there is an important relationship between such personal motivations and the
poem finally created. The poem may very well represent, in one sense, an attempt to resolve such
conflicts. The poem, read in this light, may give us
a poignant chapter of biography, and as an image
of human suffering and aspiration may move us
deeply. But we may remember that the poem,
even regarded in this light, is not an attempt
merely to present the personal problem but an attempt to transcend the personal problem, to objectify and universalize it. And it is because of the attempt to objectify and universalize, that we can
distinguish the themes inherent in the poem as
such from the personal theme or themes which remain irrevocably tied to the man. The personal
experience may provide motivations and materials,
but in so far as it remains purely personal it does
not concern us in the present context. Burke puts
the matter very sensibly concerning his own studies
of the personal themes of *The Ancient Mariner:*

I am not saying that we need to know of Coleridge's
marital troubles and sufferings from drug addiction in
order to appreciate "The Ancient Mariner" and other poems wherein the same themes figure. I am saying that,
in trying to understand the psychology of the poetic act,
we may introduce such knowledge, where it is available,
to give us material necessary for discussing the full
nature of this act. Many of the things that a poet's work
does for *him* are not things that the same work does for
us (i.e., there is a difference in act between the poem as
being-written and the poem as being-read).

For example, Coleridge's drug addiction may have
given him the psychological pattern underlying the
crime of the Mariner and his sufferings in the

poem; we do not have to be drug addicts ourselves, or to know that the poet was one, to respond to that psychological pattern.

It is necessary to emphasize this distinction between the personal and the objective themes, since the present poem, more than most, has suffered from critics who have confused them in dealing with it. Burke's sensible attitude has not been shared by, for instance, Irving Babbitt or John Mackinnon Robertson, who says that Coleridge's work is "an abnormal product of an abnormal nature under abnormal conditions." Robertson's attitude toward the poem, in so far as his reasoning would equate special aspects of the poet's experience with the details of the poem itself, would seem to be the equivalent of the fallacy of *argumentum ad hominem* in logic, and of the fallacy in aesthetics of assuming identity of the material and the thing created from the material, for it overlooks the universalizing and normalizing process always inherent in the creative act.

To return to the matter of the objective themes: That more than one theme should be involved, that the poem should operate on more than one level, would be perfectly consistent with Coleridge's emphasis on diversity within unity, and would be but one example of the principle which Coleridge approves when he quotes the remark "of the late Dr. Whitbread's that no man ever does anything from a single motive." The failure to realize this fact about Coleridge's theory of composition has led a number of critics to try to read *The Ancient Mariner* in terms of a two-dimensional allegory, the sort of reading which gives us such absurdities as the point-to-point equating of the Pilot with the Church and the Pilot's boy with the clergy, or of the Hermit with the "idea of an enlightened religion which is acquainted with the life of the spirit and aware of the difficulties which beset it."

Coleridge's not infrequent remarks on allegory should have warned the critics. The method of allegory—if by allegory we understand a fixed sys-

tem of point-to-point equations—is foreign to his
conception of the role of the imagination. "A poet's
heart and intellect should be *combined*," he says,
"intimately combined and unified with the great
appearances of nature, and not merely held in solution and loose mixture with them, in the shape of
formal similes." But a passage of greater significance on this point deals with the contrast between
false and true religion:

It is among the miseries of the present age that it recognizes no medium between literal and metaphorical.
Faith is either to be buried in the dead letter, or its
name and honors usurped by a counterfeit product of
the mechanical understanding, which in the blindness
of self-complacency confounds symbols with allegories.
Now an allegory is but a translation of abstract notions
into a picture-language, which is itself nothing but an
abstraction from objects of sense. . . . On the other
hand a symbol . . . is characterized by a translucence
of the special in the individual, or of the general in the
special, or of the universal in the general; above all by
the translucence of the eternal through and in the temporal. It always partakes of the reality which it renders
intelligible; and while it enunciates the whole, abides
itself as a living part in that unity of which it is the
representative.[10]

Allegory is, to adopt Coleridge's terms, the product
of the understanding, symbol of the imagination.

Now, these statements by Coleridge raise the
most profound and vexing aesthetic and, for that
matter, epistemological questions, questions which
I do not have the temerity to profess to settle. But
we are committed to try to arrive at some interpretation, even provisional, of these statements, as applicable to his poetic practice. In trying to do this,
we must, for the moment, accept Coleridge's terms
as he uses them. For instance, it is not generally
held that the "metaphorical" mode is mechanical—
is a "translation of abstract notions into a picture-
language." Rather, it is generally held that metaphor is the result of a vital and creative activity—
that, as Susanne Langer puts it, "genuinely new

ideas . . . have to break in upon the mind through some great and bewildering metaphor." But Coleridge is using the word *metaphor* really to mean bad metaphor, i.e., a construction which has the form but not the function of metaphor. For the construction which exercises the proper function he reserves the word *symbol*.

Let us try to define some of the qualities which for him a symbol exhibits.

The symbol serves to *combine*—and he italicizes the word—the "poet's heart and intellect." A symbol involves an idea (or ideas) as part of its potential, but it also involves the special complex of feelings associated with that idea, the attitude toward that idea. The symbol affirms the unity of mind in the welter of experience; it is a device for making that welter of experience manageable for the mind —graspable. It represents a focus of being and is not a mere sign, a "picture-language." [11]

The symbol, then, is massive in the above sense. But it is massive in another sense, too. It has what psychoanalysts call condensation. It does not "stand for" a single idea, and a system of symbols is not to be taken as a mere translation of a discursive sequence. Rather, a symbol implies a body of ideas which may be said to be fused in it. This means that the symbol itself may be developed into a discursive sequence as we intellectually explore its potential. To state the matter in another way, a way perhaps more applicable to the problem of interpreting the present poem, a symbol may be the condensation of several themes and not a sign for one.

The symbol is focal and massive, but Coleridge introduces another quality into his description. He says that it is not mechanical (like allegory) and that it "partakes of the reality which it renders intelligible." The same thing is said here in two ways. What is said is that the symbol is not arbitrary— not a mere sign—but contains within itself the appeal which makes it serviceable as a symbol. Perhaps a distinction may help us here. A symbol may avoid being arbitrary in two ways: by necessity and by congruence.

By a symbol of necessity I mean the kind of symbol which is rooted in our universal natural experience. The wind in *The Ancient Mariner* is such a symbol. All phallic symbols, for example, are of this order. When Coleridge speaks of the poet's heart and intellect being intimately combined with the "great appearances of nature," he may be hinting at the idea of necessity. It is true, of course, that he takes these great appearances of nature to be revelatory of a supersensuous reality. For him Nature symbolizes God, though, as a matter of fact, there is also in Coleridge's thought the idea of a projective symbolism in Nature by which man realizes not God but himself. The problem of these two separate and perhaps contradictory ideas in Coleridge's thought on the symbolism of Nature need not concern us here. What does concern us here is that he apparently has some notion that the great appearances of Nature as symbols carry in themselves a constant, rich meaningfulness; in other words, he has some notion of the symbol of necessity. This would seem to be what is implied, too, by his statement that the symbol "partakes of the reality which it renders intelligible."

I would distinguish, tentatively, the symbol of congruence from the symbol of necessity by saying that the former does not come to us bearing within itself the reason for its appeal to us but is validated by the manipulation of the artist in a special context. For instance, Byzantium is a symbol in the poetry of William Butler Yeats, but without the special context which he creates and the special manipulation which he makes of Byzantium it would never be a symbol for us. This does not mean that he could take any city—ancient Athens or modern Detroit—and make a symbol of it for the same purpose. Byzantium does offer him certain qualities which he can manipulate for the purpose in hand and fit into his special context: the naturalistic art of Athens, to take one aspect of his symbolic purpose, would not give him the forms he aspires to take when "once out of nature," nor would Detroit and the creations of Henry Ford afford the appropriate congruence. Byzantium offers him the congruence, but it is a congruence which he must discover for himself and validate for us.

In any case, the symbol, whether of necessity or of congruence, cannot be arbitrary—it has to participate in the unity of which it is representative. And this means that the symbol has a deeper relation to the total structure of meaning than its mechanical place in plot, situation, or discourse.

To summarize: The symbol is distinguished by being focal, massive, and not arbitrary. Allegory, in the special use of the term by Coleridge, is not focal or massive and is arbitrary. The distinction which Coleridge sets up may be a little clarified by comparison with the distinction stated more recently by C. S. Lewis, in *The Allegory of Love*.

On the one hand you can start with an immaterial fact, such as the passions which you actually experience, and can then invent *visibilia* to express them. . . . This is allegory. . . . But there is another way of using the equivalence which is almost the opposite of allegory, and which I would call sacramentalism or symbolism. If our passions, being immaterial, can be copied by material inventions, then it is possible that our material world in its turn is the copy of an invisible world. . . . The attempt to read that something else through its sensible imitations, to see the archetype in the copy, is what I mean by symbolism or sacramentalism.

Coleridge and Lewis, as we learn from other discussions by Lewis, differ profoundly in their estimates of the artistic worth of allegory, but that is not relevant to the point here. The point here is that Lewis indicates, though he does not stress, the massive significance of symbol and the fact that it is not "invented" but discovered or read. And he goes on to make the interesting comment that the poetry of symbolism finds its greatest expression in the time of the Romantics. If this is true—and I think it is—it is strange that some critics should persist in reading the masterpiece of the Romantic poet who gives us most fully a theory of symbolism as though his poem were a simple, two-dimensional allegory. (I say "two-dimensional" here to avoid, if possible, a quibble about terms. If a reader should wish to maintain that allegory can be a system of focal and massive symbols, I would not quarrel with him. I would simply say that I am talking about "bad" allegory.)

What relevance does all this have for the reading of the poem? If we take the poem as a symbolic poem, we are not permitted to read it in the way which Coleridge called allegorical. We cannot, for instance, say that the Pilot equals the Church, or that the Hermit equals the "idea of an enlightened religion which is acquainted with the life of the spirit." The first of these readings is purely arbitrary. The second, though less arbitrary, simply ignores the massive quality of the episode involving the Hermit—considerations such as the Hermit's relation to nature, the function in returning the Mariner to human society, etc., and chiefly the tenor of the whole episode. This allegorical kind of reading makes the poem into a system of equivalents in a discursive sequence. But, as a matter of fact, we must read it as massive, as operating on more than one thematic level, as embodying a complex of feelings and ideas not to be differentiated except in so far as we discursively explore the poem itself. To take another example, we cannot blandly pass by such a crucial event as the shooting of the Albatross with merely a literal reading, the kind of reading which Lowes, among others, gives it—the kind of reading which makes the bird but a bird; the bird has a symbolic role in a symbolic pattern. Nor can we take the act of shooting the bird as merely wanton—or if wanton, in one sense, on the part of the Mariner, it is not to be taken as wanton on the part of the poet, and the nature of the act must participate in the truth of which it is a symbol.[12]

III

In the preceding section I have tried to indicate some reasons inherent in Coleridge's aesthetic theory for believing that *The Ancient Mariner* is to be read at more than one level, that it has more than one "meaning." In this section, I shall look at the poem in terms of what I have called the primary perspective or primary theme—the theme which is the issue of the fable.

The fable, in broadest and simplest terms, is a story of crime and punishment and repentance and reconciliation (I have refrained from using the word *sin,* because one school of interpretation would scarcely accept the full burden of the implications of the word). It is an example, to adopt for the moment Maud Bodkin's term, without necessarily adopting the full implications of her theory, of the archetypal story of Rebirth or the Night Journey. The Mariner shoots the bird; suffers various pains, the greatest of which is loneliness and spiritual anguish; upon recognizing the beauty of the foul sea snakes, experiences a gush of love for them and is able to pray; is returned miraculously to his home port, where he discovers the joy of human communion in God, and utters the moral, "He prayeth best who loveth best, etc." We arrive at the notion of a universal charity, which even Babbitt admits to be "unexceptionable" in itself, the sense of the "One Life" in which all creation participates and which Coleridge perhaps derived from his neo-Platonic studies and which he had already celebrated, and was to celebrate, in other and more discursive poems.

Such an account as the above, however, leaves certain questions unanswered, and perhaps the best way to get at those questions is to consider the nature of the Mariner's transgression. Many critics, even Lowes, for example, dismiss the matter with such words as *wanton, trivial,* or *unthinking.* They are concerned with the act at the literal level only. In substance, they ask: Did the Mariner as a man have a good practical reason for killing the bird? This literal-mindedness leads to the view that there is a monstrous and illogical discrepancy between the crime and the punishment, a view shared by persons as diverse in critical principles as Lowes with his aestheticism and Babbitt with his neo-humanistic moralism. But we have to ask ourselves what is the symbolic reading of the act. In asking ourselves this question, we have to remember that the symbol, in Coleridge's view, is not arbitrary, but *must contain in itself, literally considered, the seeds of the logic of its extension—that is, it must participate in the unity of which it is representative.* And, more importantly, in asking ourselves this question, we must be prepared to answer quite candidly to ourselves what our own experience of poetry, and life, tells us about the nature of symbolic import; and we must be prepared to abide the risks of the answer. It would be nicer, in fact, if we could forget Coleridge's own theory and stick simply to our own innocent experience. But that, at this date, is scarcely possible.

This question—what is the nature of the Mariner's act?—has received one answer in the theory advanced by Gingerich that the Mariner does not act but is constantly acted upon, that "he is pursued by a dark and sinister fate" after having done the deed "impulsively and wantonly" and presumably under necessity. For Gingerich's theory is that the poem is a reflection of the doctrine of necessity which much occupied Coleridge's speculations during the years immediately leading up to the composition of *The Ancient Mariner*: "I am a complete necessitarian, and I understand the subject almost as well as Hartley himself, but I go farther than Hartley, and believe the corporeality of *thought,* namely that it is motion." So the first problem we must consider is to what extent Coleridge was actually a necessitarian, at least in the poem.

It would seem that Gingerich has vastly oversimplified the whole matter, by choosing texts on one side of the question only, and sometimes by ignoring the context of a text chosen. He ignores, for example, the fact that even during the period when Coleridge professed devotion to Hartley he was under the powerful influence of his mystical studies (in Plato, Plotinus, Bruno, Boehme, etc.), and that looking back, in the *Biographia*, on his period of error he could say: "The writings of these mystics acted in no slight degree to prevent my mind from being imprisoned within the outline of any single dogmatic system. They contributed to keep alive the *heart* in the *head;* gave me an indistinct, yet stirring and working presentiment, that all the products of the mere *reflective* faculty partook of Death." And in the sentence quoted by Gingerich in which Coleridge proclaims himself a complete necessitarian, the context has been neglected: Coleridge proceeds to make a joke of the thrashing which "a certain uncouth automaton," Dr. Boyer, had visited upon one of his charges, a joke which indicates an awareness that the acceptance of the doctrine of necessity and materialism doesn't take the pain out of the offended buttocks. But to be more serious, it is possible to reach into another letter of the same general period, a letter to John Thelwall, in December, 1796, and find Coleridge saying flatly, "I am a Berkleyan." And this occurs in a long and passionate letter, really an essay, which is devoted to the attempt to convert Thelwall to Christianity; and in the course of the letter there is a fervid discussion of sin and repentance, concepts which Gingerich, extending certain texts from "Religious Musings" and other poems as a complete and tidy doctrine, denies to Coleridge. Gingerich even goes so far in his ardor to support his cause as to say that in "The Eolian Harp" (1795) Coleridge "conceives universal life as automatous," and proceeds to quote a few lines which in themselves might bear that interpretation. But he simply ignores the rest of the poem. The concluding stanza, which I shall present, follows immediately upon his chosen passage:

But thy more serious eye a mild reproof
Darts, O beloved Woman! nor such thoughts
Dim and unhallowed dost thou not reject,
And biddest me walk humbly with my God.
Meek daughter in the family of Christ!
Well hast thou said and holily disprais'd
These shapings of the unregenerate mind;
Bubbles that glitter as they rise and break
On vain Philosophy's aye-bubbling spring.
For never guiltless may I speak of him,
The Incomprehensible! save when with awe
I praise him, and with Faith that inly feels;
Who with his saving mercies healed me,
A sinful and most miserable man,
Wilder'd and dark, and gave me to possess
Peace, and this Cot, and thee, heart-honour'd Maid!

Here the conclusion of the poem repudiates as "shapings of the unregenerate mind" the very statements by which Gingerich would argue for a relatively systematic necessitarianism. And we may note further in this passage that we find quite positively stated the idea of sin, a thing which, according to Gingerich, is not in the necessitarian system or in Coleridge's thought. But we can go to a direct, non-poetic statement in his letters, made just after the completion of *The Ancient Mariner:* ". . . I believe most steadfastly in original sin; that from our mothers' wombs our understandings are darkened; and even where our understandings are in the light, that our organization is depraved and our volitions imperfect. . . ." [13]

The point I wish to make is this: We cannot argue that Coleridge was a systematic necessitarian and that therefore the killing of the Albatross is merely the result of the necessary pattern of things and is not to be taken as sinful *per se* or in extension. The fact seems to be that Coleridge was early moving toward his later views, that he was not, as he says, committed to any dogmatic system, and that, as Shawcross points out, the poems themselves "are sufficient to show us that his professed adherence to the necessitarian doctrines of his day was by no means the genuine conviction of his whole being." As early as 1794, he was, we may add, thinking of the mind as an active thing, the "shaping mind"; and if, in one sense, we grant the power of mind we have broken the iron chain of necessity and the individual becomes a responsible agent and not the patient which Babbitt and Gingerich assume the Mariner to be. What A. E. Powell, in *The Romantic Theory of Poetry*, says of Wordsworth, that he lived his philosophy long before he phrased it, is equally true of Coleridge, and in addition to his living into a transcendental philosophy through the practice and love of poetry, he lived into the guilt of opium long before the Mariner shot the Albatross: he knew what guilt is, and if he longed for a view of the universe which would absolve him of responsibility and would comfort him with the thought of participation in the universal salvation promised by Hartley and Priestley, there was still the obdurate fact of his own experience.

We have in these years, it seems, a tortured churning around of the various interpretations of the fact, and the necessitarian philosophy is only one possible philosophy in suspension in that agitated brew. And we even have some evidence that in the period just before the composition of *The Ancient Mariner*—before he had struck upon that fable to embody his idea—the poet was meditating a long poem on the theme of the origin of evil. Early in 1797 Lamb wrote him: "I have a dim recollection that, when in town, you were talking of the Origin of Evil as a most prolific subject for a long poem." [14] As a matter of fact, Coleridge never did "solve" his problem: he found peace simply by accepting the idea of Original Sin as a mystery.

In the *Table Talk* he says: "A Fall of some sort or other—the creation, as it were, of the nonabsolute—is the fundamental postulate of the moral history of Man. Without this hypothesis, Man is unintelligible; with it every phenomenon is explicable. The mystery itself is too profound for human insight."

In his more elaborate and systematic treatment of the subject Coleridge adds another point which is of significance for the poem. Original Sin is not hereditary sin; it is original with the sinner and is of his will. There is no previous determination of the will, because the will exists outside the chain of cause and effect, which is of Nature and not of Spirit. And as for the time of this act of sin, he says that the "subject stands in no relation to time, can neither be in time nor out of time." [15] The bolt whizzes from the crossbow and the bird falls and all comment that the Mariner has no proper dramatic motive or is the child of necessity or is innocent of everything except a little wantonness is completely irrelevant, for we are confronting the mystery of the corruption of the will, the mystery which is the beginning of the "moral history of Man."

The fact that the act is unmotivated in any practical sense, that it appears merely perverse, has offended literalists and Aristotelians alike, and, for that matter, Wordsworth, who held that the Mariner had no "character" (and we may elaborate by saying that having no character he could exhibit no motive) and did not act but was acted upon. The lack of motivation, the perversity, which flies in the face of the Aristotelian doctrine of *hamartia*, is exactly the significant thing about the Mariner's act. The act re-enacts the Fall, and the Fall has two qualities important here: it is a condition of will, as Coleridge says, "out of time," and it is the result of no single human motive.

One more comment, even though I have belabored this point. What is the nature of this sin, what is its content? Though the act which re-enacts the mystery of the Fall is appropriately without motive, the sin of the will must be the appropriate expression of the essence of the will. And we shall turn to a passage in *The Statesman's Manual*. Having just said that, in its "state of immanence or indwelling in reason and religion," the will appears indifferently as wisdom or love, Coleridge proceeds: "But in its utmost abstraction and consequent state of reprobation, the will becomes Satanic pride and rebellious self-idolatry in the relations of the spirit to itself, and remorseless despotism relatively to others . . . by the fearful resolve to find in itself alone the one absolute motive of action." [16] Then he sketches the portrait of the will in abstraction, concluding with the observation that "these are the marks, that have characterized the masters of mischief, the liberticides, the mighty hunters of mankind, from Nimrod to Bonaparte."

We may observe a peculiar phrase, the "mighty hunters of mankind, from Nimrod to Bonaparte," and in this blending of the hunting of beasts and the hunting of man—for Nimrod was himself both the mighty hunter and the founder of the first military state—we have an identification that takes us straight to the crime of the Mariner. The Mariner did not kill a man but a bird, and the literal-minded readers have echoed Mrs. Barbauld and Leslie Stephen: what a lot of pother about a bird. But they forget that this bird is more than a bird. I do not intend, however, to rest my case on the phrase just quoted from *The Statesman's Manual*, for the phrase itself I take to be but an echo from the poem at the time when the author was revising and reliving his favorite poem. Let us go to the poem itself to learn the significance of the bird.

In the poem itself the same identification occurs: the hunting of the bird becomes the hunting of man. When the bird first appears,

> *As if it had been a Christian soul,*
> *We hailed it in God's name.*

It ate food "it ne'er had eat," and every day "came to the mariner's hollo," and then later perched on the mast or shroud for "vespers nine." It partakes of the human food and pleasure and devotions. To make matters more explicit, Coleridge adds in the Gloss the statement that the bird was received with "hospitality" and adds, after the crime, that the Mariner "inhospitably killeth the pious bird of good omen." The crime is, symbolically, a murder, and a particularly heinous murder, for it involves the violation of hospitality and of gratitude (*pious* equals *faithful* and the bird is "of good omen") and of sanctity (the religious connotations of *pious,* etc.). This factor of betrayal in the crime is re-emphasized in Part V when one of the Spirits says that the bird had "loved the man" who killed it.

But why did the poet not give us a literal murder in the first place? By way of answering this question, we must remember that the crime, to maintain its symbolic reference to the Fall, must be motiveless. But the motiveless murder of a man would truly raise the issue of probability. Further-more, the literal shock of such an act, especially if perverse and unmotivated, would be so great that it would distract from the symbolic significance. The poet's problem, then, was to provide an act which, on one hand, would not accent the issue of probability or shockingly distract from the sym-bolic significance, but which, on the other hand, would be adequately criminal to justify the conse-quences. And the necessary criminality is estab-lished, we have seen, in two ways: (1) by making the gravity of the act depend on the state of the will which prompts it, and (2) by symbolically defining the bird as a "Christian soul," as "pious," etc.

There is, however, a third way in which the criminality is established. We can get at it by con-sidering the observation that if a man had been killed, we could not have the "lesson of humani-tarianism," which some critics have taken to be the point of the poem. But we must remember that the humanitarianism itself is a manifestation of a deeper concern, a sacramental conception of the universe, for the bird is hailed "in God's name," both literally and symbolically, and in the end we have, therefore, in the crime against Nature a crime against God. If a man had been killed, the secular nature of the crime—a crime then against man—

would have overshadowed the ultimate religious significance involved. The idea of the crime against God rather than man is further emphasized by the fact that the cross is removed from the Mariner's neck to make place for the dead bird, and here we get a symbolic transference from Christ to the Albatross, from the slain Son of God to the slain creature of God. And the death of the creature of God, like the death of the Son of God, will, in its own way, work for vision and salvation.

It may be instructive to see how another writer has treated these questions in presenting a similar story of the crime against a brute. I refer to Poe's "The Black Cat." In this story precisely the same issues appear, but where Coleridge leaves the issues in fluid suspension and leaves the nature of the crime defined only in the general symbolic tissue of the poem, Poe gives an elaborate analysis of the motivation and meaning of the act:

And then came, as if to my final and irrevocable overthrow, the spirit of Perverseness. Of this spirit philosophy takes no account. Yet I am not more sure that my soul lives, than I am that perverseness is one of the primitive impulses of the human heart—one of the indivisible primary faculties, or sentiments, which give direction to the character of man. Who has not, a hundred times, found himself committing a vile or a stupid action, for no other reason than because he knows he should *not*? Have we not a perpetual inclination, in the teeth of our best judgment, to violate that which is *Law*, merely because we understand it to be such? This spirit of perverseness, I say, came to my final overthrow. It was this unfathomable longing of the soul *to vex itself*—to offer violence to its own nature—to do wrong for the wrong's sake only—that urged me to continue and finally to consummate the injury I had inflicted upon the unoffending brute. One morning, in cold blood, I slipped a noose about its neck and hung it to the limb of a tree—hung it with the tears streaming from my eyes, and with the bitterest remorse at my heart—hung it *because* I knew that it had loved me, and *because* I felt it had given me no reason of offense—hung it *because* I knew that in so doing I was committing a sin—

a deadly sin that would so jeopardize my immortal soul as to place it—if such a thing were possible—even beyond the reach of the infinite mercy of the Most Merciful and Most Terrible God.

All we have to do is to read Original Sin for Perverseness; and Poe himself carries us from the psychological treatment under Perverseness to the theological treatment under Sin.

There is another interesting parallel of treatment: the identification, in the crime, of the brute with the human. In the poem the identification is achieved symbolically, as we have seen. But in the story we must have more than this: the police are to arrest the hero and they will not arrest him for killing a cat, even if the killing is symbolically and spiritually equivalent to a murder. But Poe makes the symbolic transference, too. There are two cats, the first is hanged outright. The second cat, which takes the place of the first to plague the conscience of the hero and to frighten him with the white gallows mark on the breast, trips the hero on the stair to the cellar. The man then aims a blow with an axe at this cat, but his wife stays his hand. The blow intended for the brute is then delivered on the woman. The symbolic transference is made but is made in terms of psychological treatment.[17]

To return to the problems raised by the poem: We have not yet done with the matter of crime and punishment. There is the question of the fellow mariners, who suffer death. Here we encounter not infrequently the objection that they do not merit their fate. The tragic *hamartia,* we are told, is not adequate. The Gloss, however, flatly defines the nature of the crime of the fellow mariners: they have made themselves "accomplices." But apparently the Gloss needs a gloss. The fellow mariners have, in a kind of structural counterpoint (and such a counterpoint is, as we shall see, a characteristic of the poem), duplicated the Mariner's own crime of pride, of "will in abstraction." That is, they make their desire the measure of the act: they first condemn the act, when they think the bird had brought the favorable breeze; then applaud the act when the fog clears and the breeze springs back up, now saying that the bird had brought the fog; then in the dead calm, again condemn the act. Their crime has another aspect: they have violated the sacramental conception of the universe, by making man's convenience the measure of an act, by isolating him from Nature and the "One Life." This point is picked up later in Part IV:

> *The many men, so beautiful!*
> *And they all dead did lie:*
> *And a thousand thousand slimy things*
> *Lived on; and so did I.*

The stanza is important for the reading of the poem. The usual statement for the poem is that the Mariner moves from love of the sea snakes to a love of men (and in the broad sense this is true), but here we see that long before he blesses the snakes he is aware, in his guilt, of the beauty of the dead men, and protests against the fact that the slimy things should live while the beautiful men lie dead. In other words, we have here, even in his remorse, a repetition of the original crime against the sacramental view of the universe: man is still set over, in pride, against Nature. The Gloss points to the important thing here: "He despiseth the creatures of the calm."

There is one other aspect of the guilt of the fellow mariners worthy of notice. They judge the moral content of an act by its consequence; in other words, they would make good disciples of Bishop Paley, who, according to Coleridge, in *Aids to Reflection,* was no moralist because he would judge the morality of an act by consequence and not "contemplate the same in its original spiritual source," the state of the will. The will of the fellow mariners is corrupt. And this re-emphasizes the fact that what is at stake throughout is not the objective magnitude of the act performed—the bird is, literally, a trivial creature—but the spirit in

which the act is performed, the condition of the
will.

So much for the crime of the Mariner and the
crime of his fellows. And we know the sequel, the
regeneration of the Mariner.[18] In the end, he accepts the sacramental view of the universe, and his
will is released from its state of "utmost abstraction" and gains the state of "immanence" in wisdom and love. We shall observe the stages whereby
this process is consummated—this primary theme
of the "One Life" is developed—as we investigate
the secondary theme, the theme of the imagination.

IV

If in the poem one follows the obvious theme of
the "One Life" as presented by the Mariner's crime,
punishment, and reconciliation, one is struck by
the fact that large areas of the poem seem to be
irrelevant to this business: for instance, the special
atmosphere of the poem, and certain images which,
because of the insistence with which they are presented, seem to be endowed with a special import.
Perhaps the best approach to the problem of the
secondary theme is to consider the importance of
light, or rather, of the different kinds of light.

There is a constant contrast between moonlight
and sunlight, and the main events of the poem can
be sorted out according to the kinds of light in
which they occur. Coleridge underscores the importance of the distinction between the two kinds
of light by introducing the poem by the motto
from Burnet, added in the last revision of 1817
(in fact, the general significance of the motto has,
so far as I know, never been explored). The motto
ends: "But meanwhile we must earnestly seek after
truth, maintaining measure, that we may distinguish things certain from those uncertain, day
from night." The motto ends on the day-night contrast, and points to this contrast as a central fact
of the poem. We may get some clue to the content
of the distinction by remembering that in the poem
the good events take place under the aegis of the

moon, the bad events under that of the sun. This, it may be objected, reverses the order of Burnet, who obviously wishes to equate the "certain" or the good with day and the "uncertain" or bad with night. Coleridge's reversal is, I take it, quite deliberate—an ironical reversal which, in effect, says that the rational and conventional view expressed by Burnet seeks truth by the wrong light. In other words, Burnet becomes the spokesman of what we shall presently find Coleridge calling the "mere reflective faculty" which partakes of "Death."

Before we pursue this symbolism in the poem, let us look at moonlight in the larger context of Coleridge's work. Perhaps we shall find that it is serving, not only in *The Ancient Mariner* but elsewhere, the function defined by I. A. Richards: "When a writer has found a theme or image which fixes a point of relative stability in the drift of experience, it is not to be expected that he will avoid it. Such themes are a means of orientation."

As for the moonlight, more than one critic has noted its pervasive presence in Coleridge's work. Swinburne calls Coleridge's genius "moonstruck." And even Irving Babbitt goes so far as to say: "A special study might be made of the role of the moon in Chateaubriand and Coleridge—even if one is not prepared like Carlyle to dismiss Coleridge's philosophy as 'bottled moonshine.'" For the moon is everywhere, from the "Sonnet to the Autumnal Moon" of 1788 on through most of the poems, or many of them, trivial or great, sometimes with a specifically symbolic content, sometimes as the source of a transfiguring light which bathes the scene of *Christabel* or *The Ancient Mariner* or "The Wanderings of Cain" or "Dejection: An Ode" or "The Nightingale" of 1798 or the deep, romantic chasm of "Kubla Khan," and always she is the "Mother of wildly-working visions," as she is called in the sonnet mentioned, or the "Mother of wildly-working dreams," as she is called in "Songs of the Pixies" (1796). And in both the prose and verse, frequently when it is not the moon in this role it is some cloudy luminescence, the "luminous gloom of Plato," or "the slant beams of the sinking orb" of "This Lime-Tree Bower," or the glitter of the sun-lit sea seen through half-closed eyelids in "The Eolian Harp."

We have, without question, a key image in Cole-ridge's moon, or Coleridge's half-light, and Cole-ridge himself has given us, in sober prose, a clue to its significance. Years later, looking back on the brief period of creative joy and the communion of minds which marked the years 1797 and 1798, he recalled the origin of the *Lyrical Ballads:*

During the first year that Mr. Wordsworth and I were neighbours, our conversation turned frequently on the two cardinal points of poetry, the power of exciting the sympathy of the reader by a faithful adherence to the truth of nature, and the power of giving the interest of novelty by the modifying colours of the imagination. The sudden charm, which accidents of light and shade, which moon-light or sun-set, diffused over a known and familiar landscape, appeared to represent the practic-ability of combining both. These are the poetry of nature.

Here the moonlight, or the dimming light of sun-set, changes the familiar world to make it poetry; the moonlight equates with the "modifying colours of the imagination." To support this we have also the account given by Wordsworth in the *Prelude* of the night walk up Mount Snowden in the moon-light:

When into air had partially dissolved
That vision, given to spirits of the night
And three chance human wanderers, in calm thought
Reflected, it appeared to me the type
Of a majestic intellect, its acts
And its possessions, what it has and craves,
What in itself it is, and would become.
There I beheld the emblem of a mind
That feeds upon infinity, that broods
Over the dark abyss, intent to hear
Its voices issuing forth to silent light

In one continuous stream; a mind sustained
By recognitions of transcendent power,
In sense conducting to ideal form,
In soul of more than mortal privilege.
One function, above all, of such a mind
Had Nature shadowed there, by putting forth,
'Mid circumstances awful and sublime,
That mutual domination which she loves
To exert upon the face of outward things,
So moulded, joined, abstracted, so endowed
With interchangeable supremacy,
That men, least sensitive, see, hear, perceive,
And cannot choose but feel. . . .

But to return to Coleridge's own testimony, not rarely we can find the moon appearing in the prose. For instance, we may glance at this passage in *Anima Poetiae* on symbolism: "In looking at objects of Nature while I am thinking, as at yonder moon dim-glimmering through the dewy windowpane, I seem rather to be seeking, as it were *asking* for, a symbolic language for something within me that always and forever exists, than observing anything new." How easily the moon, dim-glimmering, enters the conversation when his mind turns to the imaginative relation of man and Nature.

Let us see how this symbol functions in the poem, in connection with the theme of the imagination. We must remember, however, that here by the imagination we mean the imagination in its value-creating capacity, what Coleridge was later to call the secondary imagination.

We shall not go far into the poem before we realize that the light symbolism is not the only symbolism operating upon us. For instance, we shall encounter winds and storms at various important moments. Our problem, then, is not only to define particular symbolisms, but to establish the relationships among them—to establish the general import.

At the threshold of the poem, however, another consideration intrudes itself upon us. Certain im-

ages are first presented to us, and sometimes may
appear later, at what seems to be merely a natural
level. This question, then, will arise in the minds
of certain readers: How far are we to interpret, as
we look back at the poem, such apparently natural manifestations which at other times, at the
great key moments of the poem, are obviously
freighted with significance? In presenting the poem
here I shall undertake the full rather than the restricted interpretation. My reasoning is this: Once
the import of an image is established for our minds,
that image cannot in its workings upon us elsewhere in the poem be disencumbered, whether or
not we are consciously defining it. The criterion for
such full rather than restricted interpretation is
consistency with the central symbolic import and,
in so far as it is possible to establish the fact, with
the poet's basic views as drawn from external
sources. We can derive no criterion from the poet's
conscious intention *at any given moment in the
poem,* and this question is, in this narrow sense, irrelevant. (In its broader sense, it will be discussed
later in this essay.) In any case, though here I shall
undertake a full interpretation, if a reader should
wish to interpret the poem in a restricted sense, I
would not feel that my basic thesis was impaired.
There is always bound to be some margin for debate in such matters.

The problem of the fullness of interpretation
presents itself to us at the very outset of the poem.
The voyage begins merrily under the aegis of the
sun. Is our sun here merely the natural sun, or is
it also the symbolic sun? But the question is more
acute a stanza or two on, when the storm strikes
and drives the ship south, the behavior of the ship
being described in the powerfully developed image
of flight from a pursuing enemy. Is this a merely
natural storm, or a symbolic one as well? Let us
linger on this question.

Later in the poem we shall find wind and storm
appearing as the symbol of vitality and creative
force. A storm, we recall, strikes as a conse-

quence of the Mariner's redemption and brings him
the life-giving rain. Is the first storm, then, to be
taken with the same force, even though it is presented here in the imagery of a terrible enemy? I
do not find the import here inconsistent with that
of the storm at the Mariner's redemption. The storm
at the redemption, though a "good" storm, is also
presented in imagery of terror and power. The am-
bivalence of the storm is an important feature
which is extended and developed later in the poem.
But for the present, merely glancing forward to
that final interpretation of the wind and storm, we
can say that the first storm is an "enemy" because
to the man living in the world of comfortable familiarity, complacent in himself and under the aegis
of the sun, the creative urge, the great vital up-
heaval, this "bottomwind," [19] is inimical.

When the storm has driven the ship south, we
reach the second stage of the Mariner's adventure,
the land of ice. This land is both beautiful and terrible, as is proper for the spot where the acquaintance with the imagination is to be made. Like the
storm which drives the ship south, it shakes man
from his routine of life. Man finds the land un-
comfortable; he loses his complacency when he
confronts the loneliness:

> *Nor shapes of men nor beasts we ken—*
> *The ice was all between.*

But out of this awe-inspiring manifestation of Nature, which seems at first to be indifferent to man,
comes the first response to man—the Albatross—
to receive the glad "natural" recognition of the mariners.

I have already indicated how the bird-man fusion
is set up, how the bird is hailed in God's name,
etc., how, in other words, the theme of the "One
Life" and the sacramental vision is presented. Now
as a moment of great significance in the poem, I
wish to indicate how the primary theme of the sacramental vision is for the first time assimilated to
the secondary theme of the imagination. The Alba-

tross, the sacramental bird, is also, as it were, a
moon-bird. For here, with the bird, the moon first
enters the poem, and the two are intimately associated:

> *In mist or cloud, on mast or shroud,*
> *It perched for vespers nine;*
> *Whiles all the night, through fog-smoke white,*
> *Glimmered the white Moon-shine.*

The sun is kept entirely out of the matter. The light-
ing is always indirect, for even in the day we have
only "mist or cloud"—the luminous haze, the symbolic equivalent of moonlight. Not only is the
moon associated with the bird, but the wind also.
Upon the bird's advent a "good south wind sprung
up behind." And so we have the creative wind,
the friendly bird, the moonlight of imagination, all
together in one symbolic cluster.

As soon as the cluster is established, the crime,
with shocking suddenness, is announced. We have
seen how the crime is to be read at the level of the
primary theme. At the level of the secondary theme
it is, of course, a crime against the imagination.
Here, in the crime, the two themes are fused. (As
a sidelight on this fact, we may recall that in "Dejection: An Ode," Coleridge gives us the same fusion of the moral and the aesthetic. In bewailing
his own loss of creative power he hints, at the same
time, at a moral taint. The "Pure of heart" do not
lose the imaginative power, "this strong music in
the soul.")

With the announcement of the crime, comes one
of the most effective turns in the poem. As the Wedding Guest recoils from his glittering eye, the Mariner announces:

> *. . . With my cross-bow*
> *I shot the Albatross.*

And then the next line of the poem:

> *The Sun now rose upon the right.*

The crime, as it were, brings the sun. Ostensibly, the line simply describes a change in the ship's direction, but it suddenly, with dramatic violence, supplants moon with sun in association with the unexpected revelation of the crime, and with the fact indicates not only the change of the direction of the ship but the change of the direction of the Mariner's life. The same device is repeated with the second murder of the Albatross—the acceptance of the crime by the fellow mariners. They first condemn the Mariner for having killed the bird "that made the breeze to blow," but immediately upon the rising of the sun, they accept the crime:

> *Nor dim nor red, like God's own head,*
> *The glorious Sun uprist:*
> *Then all averred, I had killed the bird*
> *That brought the fog and mist.*

As has been pointed out earlier, the mariners act in the arrogance of their own convenience. So even their condemnation of the crime has been based on error: they have not understood the nature of the breeze they think the bird had brought. But here we must observe a peculiar and cunningly contrived circumstance: the mariners do not accept the crime until the sun rises, and rises gloriously "like God's own head." The sun is, symbolically speaking, the cause of their acceptance of the crime—they read God as justifying the act on the ground of practical consequence, just as, shall we say, Bishop Paley would have done. They justify the crime because the bird had, they say, brought the fog and mist. In other words, they repudiate the luminous haze, the other light, and consider it an evil, though we know that the fog and mist are associated with the moon in the wind-bird-moon cluster at the end of Part I.

At this point where the sun has been introduced into the poem, it is time to ask how we shall regard it. It is the light which shows the familiar as familiar, it is the light of practical convenience, it is the light in which pride preens itself, it is, to adopt

Coleridge's later terminology, the light of the "understanding," it is the light of that "mere reflective faculty" that "partook of Death." And within a few lines, its acceptance by the mariners has taken them to the sea of death, wherein the sun itself, which had risen so promisingly and so gloriously like "God's own head," is suddenly the "bloody sun," the sun of death—as though we had implied here a fable of the Enlightenment and the Age of Reason, whose fair promises had wound up in the bloodbath of the end of the century.

In the poem, however, at this point where the agony begins, we find an instructive stanza:

> *And some in dreams assuréd were*
> *Of the Spirit that plagued us so;*
> *Nine fathom deep he had followed us*
> *From the land of mist and snow.*

This Polar Spirit, as the Gloss will call him later, is of the land of mist and snow, which we have found to be adjuncts of the wind-bird-moon cluster; hence he, too, belongs to the same group and partakes of its significance. Two facts stand out about the present "carrier" of the imagination: his presence is known by dreams and his errand is one of vengeance. The first fact tells us that the imagination, though denied or unrecognized, still operates with dire intimations at a level below the "understanding"; "understanding" cannot exorcise it and its subconscious work goes on. The second fact tells us that, if violated and despised, the faculty which should naturally be a blessing to man will in its perverted form exact a terrible vengeance.

The fellow mariners do not, of course, comprehend the nature of the Spirit whose presence has been revealed to them in dreams. They have learned, by this time, that a crime has been committed and that vengeance is imminent. But they do not know the nature of the crime or their own share in the guilt. So in their ignorance they hang the Albatross about the Mariner's neck. Thus the second major stage of the poem concludes.

Part III consists of two scenes, one of the sun, one of the moon, in even balance. The first is the appearance of the specter-bark, which is in close association with the sun. There is the elaborate description of the sun, but in addition there is the constant repetition of the word, five times within twelve lines:

1. Rested the broad bright Sun
2. Betwixt us and the Sun
3. And straight the Sun was flecked with bars
4. Are those *her* sails that glance in the Sun
5. Are those *her* ribs through which the Sun.[20]

The whole passage, by means of the iteration, is devoted to the emotional equating of the sun and the death-bark.[21]

Then the "Sun's rim dips," and we have the full and beautiful description of the rising of the "star-dogged Moon." But the moon does not bring relief; instead "At the rising of the Moon," as specified by the placement of the Gloss,

> *Fear at my heart, as at a cup,*
> *My life-blood seemed to sip!*

And immediately after, in the moonlight, the fellow mariners curse the Mariner with a look, and, one after another, fall down dead. The fact of these unhappy events under the aegis of the supposedly beneficent moon raises a question: Does this violate the symbolism of the moon? I do not feel that the poem is inconsistent here. First, if we accept the interpretation that the Polar Spirit belongs to the imagination cluster and yet exacts vengeance, then the fact that horror comes in the moonlight here is simply an extension of the same principle: violated and despised, the imagination yet persists and exacts vengeance. Second, we find a substantial piece of evidence supporting this view, in the parallel scene in Part VI, another scene of the curse by the eye in moonlight:

> *All fixed on me their stony eyes,*
> *That in the Moon did glitter.*

But this parallelism gives us a repetition with a difference. This event occurs after the Mariner has had his change of heart, and so now when the curse by the eye is placed upon him in moonlight, it does not avail; in moonlight now "this spell was snapt," and the creative wind rose again to breathe on the Mariner. In other words, the passage in Part VI interprets by contrast that in Part III. The moonlight, when the heart is unregenerate, shows horror; when the heart has changed, it shows joy.

In Part IV the penance of loneliness and horror, both associated with the crime against the imagination (loneliness by denial of the imagination, horror by the perversion of it), is aggravated with the despising of the creatures of the calm and with the curse in the eyes of the dead. Then, suddenly, we have the second moonrise:

> *The moving Moon went up the sky,*
> *And no where did abide:*
> *Softly she was going up,*
> *And a star or two beside—*

The Gloss here tells us all we need to know, defining the Mariner's relation to the Moon:

> In his loneliness and fixedness he yearneth towards the journeying Moon, and the stars that still sojourn, yet still move onward; and every where the blue sky belongs to them, and is their appointed rest, and their native country and their own natural homes, which they enter unannounced, as lords that are certainly expected and yet there is a silent joy at their arrival.

Life, order, universal communion and process, joy —all these things from which the Mariner is alienated are involved here in the description of the moon and stars. And immediately the description of the water snakes picks up and extends the sense of the stars. The snakes become creatures of light to give us another symbolic cluster:

> *They moved in tracks of shining white,*
> *And when they reared, the elfish light*
> *Fell off in hoary flakes.*

For the Gloss says here: "By the light of the Moon he beholdeth God's creatures of the great calm." And in the light of the moon we have the stages of the redeeming process: first, the recognition of happiness and beauty; second, love; third, the blessing of the creatures; fourth, freedom from the spell. The sequence is important, and we shall return to it. In it the theme of the sacramental vision and the theme of imagination are fused.

Part V, in carrying forward the next period of development consequent upon the Mariner's restored imaginative view of the world, continues, in new combinations, the sun-moon contrast, but here we move toward it by the refreshing rain and then the storm. In the Mariner's dream, which comes in the first heaven-sent sleep, we have the presentiment of the rain and storm, a dream which corresponds to the dream of the Polar Spirit which had hinted to the fellow mariners the nature of the crime: in both cases, at this instinctive, subrational level, the truth is darkly shadowed forth before it is realized in the waking world. In the Mariner's dream, before the real rain comes, the "silly buckets" [22] are filled with dew. Upon waking and drinking the rain, the Mariner, in his light and blessed condition, hears a roaring wind; then, as the Gloss puts it, there are "strange sights and commotions in the sky and the elements," presided over by the moon, which hangs at the edge of the black cloud. The moon of imagination and the storm of creative vitality here join triumphantly to celebrate the Mariner's salvation.

But here let us pause to observe a peculiar fact. The wind does not reach the ship, and the Polar Spirit, who had originally set forth on an errand of vengeance, provides the power of locomotion for the ship. Though he has been functioning as the sinister aspect of the imagination, he, too, is now drawn, in "obedience to the angelic troop," into the new beneficent activity. Not that he is to lose entirely his sinister aspect; we shall see that his vengeance persists, for the Mariner, in his role

as the *poète maudit,* will show that the imagination
is a curse as well as a blessing. But for the moment,
though grudgingly, the Spirit joins the forces of
salvation.

What now, we may ask, is the logic of this situation? If the wind were to drive the ship, the
action would not be adapted to show the role of
the Polar Spirit. Furthermore, if the wind were to
drive the ship, the fusion of the natural and the
supernatural in the terrible and festal activity below and above the sea would not be exhibited. And
this is important, for here we have another moment
of fusion of the primary and secondary themes:
wind, moon, and Polar Spirit belong to the secondary theme of the imagination, but the "angelic
troop," in obedience to which the Spirit acts, belongs properly to the primary theme, the theme of
the "One Life" and the sacramental vision.

I have said that the angelic troop here serves to
introduce the primary theme into the episode.
Certainly, in the reanimation of the bodies of the
fellow mariners, there is implicit the idea of regeneration and resurrection, and in this way the
participation in the general meaning of the episode
becomes clear. But the behavior of the reinspirited
bodies, taken in itself, offers a difficulty. Taken at
the natural level, the manipulating of the sails and
ropes serves no purpose. Taken at the symbolic
level, this activity is activity without content, a
"lag" in the poem, a "meaningless marvel." And the
spirits in the bodies give us an added difficulty.
When day comes, they desert the bodies and as
sweet sounds dart to the sun. The sun, under whose
aegis the bad events of the poem occur, here appears in a "good" association.

Our problem of interpreting these "good" associations is parallel to that of dealing with
the moon when it appears in "bad" association. I
shall treat it analogously, by looking at it in the
special context and not in isolation. This redemption of the sun—for we may call it that—comes
as part of the general rejoicing when the proper

order has been re-established in the universe. The "understanding," shall we say, no longer exists in abstraction, no longer partakes of death, but has its proper role in the texture of things and partakes of the general blessedness. It is, for the moment, "spiritualized." I say for the moment, for at noon, the hour when the sun is in its highest power and is most likely to assert itself in "abstraction," the sun resumes briefly its inimical role and prevents the happy forward motion of the ship:

> *The Sun, right up above the mast,*
> *Had fixed her to the ocean.*

As the Gloss explains here, this event takes place when the Polar Spirit, after having obediently conveyed the ship to the Line, still "requireth vengeance." In other words, the inimical force of the sun is felt at the moment when the power of imagination seems to be turning away vengefully from the Mariner. But this crisis is passed, for after all the Mariner has been redeemed, and the ship plunges forward again with such suddenness that the Mariner is thrown into a "swound."

In his swound the Mariner receives a fuller revelation of his situation and of the nature of the forces operating about him. He learns these things, it is important to notice, in the dream—just as the fellow mariners had received the first intimation of the presence of the Polar Spirit through dreams. And the significance of this fact is the same: the dream is not at the level of the "understanding," but is the appropriate mode by which the special kind of knowledge of the imagination should be revealed.

It is in this dream that the Mariner for the first time receives an explicit statement of the relation of the Albatross and the Polar Spirit. Meanwhile the Gloss tells us that the Polar Spirit, having been assured that the Mariner will continue to do penance (as the Mariner himself learns from the Second Voice), returns southward. But the ship, which had been propelled by the Polar Spirit, continues on its

way by another means, as the Second Voice describes. Do we have here an "unmeaning marvel," or
is there some content to this business? An interpretation at this point probably demands more forcing
than at any other, but there is, perhaps, a possible
one consistent with the rest of the poem. The angelic troop and the Polar Spirit (the first associated
with the primary theme, the second with the secondary theme) are both "supernatural"—as the
Gloss somewhat superfluously remarks. But the
Second Voice gives the Mariner, and us, a scientific, i.e., "natural," explanation of the progress of
the ship. So we have here the supernatural powers
(of the two orders) acting by the agency of the
natural mechanism of the world—the supernatural
and the natural conspiring together on the Mariner's behalf after his redemption.

There is, however, an additional item to be considered in the vision, the description of the moon
and the ocean given by the Second Voice:

> 'Still as a slave before his lord,
> The ocean hath no blast;
> His great bright eye most silently
> Up to the Moon is cast—
>
> If he may know which way to go;
> For she guides him smooth or grim.
> See, brother, see! how graciously
> She looketh down on him.'

This is a fairly obvious definition of the role of the
moon—the adored, the guiding, the presiding
power.

After this definition in dream of the role of the
moon, the Mariner wakes to find it shining and the
dead men standing about with their moon-struck
eyes fixing a curse upon him. This scene recalls
two previous scenes of the poem. First, it recalls
the other scene of the curse by the eye in moonlight before the redemption of the Mariner. Second,
it recalls the main redemption scene when the Mariner blesses the snakes in the moonlight. With the

first we have here a parallelism developing a contrast, and with the second a parallelism developing
a repetition. For in this, we have a second redemption scene—the relief from the curse, which, the
Gloss says, is "finally expiated." But as the spell is
snapped, there is a moment in which the Mariner
is fearfully bemused like one who knows

> . . . *a frightful fiend*
> *Doth close behind him tread.*

This last hint of the curse disappears with the
rising of the strange breeze. It is not a "natural"
breeze, for it does not ripple the water—it blows
only upon the Mariner. The ship moves, but not by
the breeze (presumably by the angelic troop, as before). It is the creative wind again, blowing only
upon the Mariner, fanning his cheek, but also
mingling "strangely" with his "fears"—a hint of
the ambiguous power of the imagination. The rising of the breeze now, after this second redemption
scene, corresponds to the rising of the great storm
after the first redemption scene—a storm which,
we must remember, was both terrible and festal
in its aspect. The rising of the breeze now also recalls the first storm which drove the ship south in
Part I—a parallelism by contrast, for the first storm
was all "enemy" while the present breeze, though
it mingles strangely with the Mariner's fears, is a
sweet breeze.

Suddenly, under the sweet breeze, the Mariner
descries the home port. Appropriately, it is
drenched in the magnificent moonlight. But now
we are to have another kind of light, too, By every
corpse on deck stands a seraph-man with a body
all of light as a signal to the land. So here, in the
two kinds of light by which the return is accomplished, the men of light (associated with the primary theme) and the moon (associated with the
secondary theme), we have a final fusion of the
imagination and the sacramental vision.[23] We may,
as it were, take them to be aspects of the same reality.

This fusion, with the beginning of Part VII, is restated by means of the figure of the Hermit, who is both priest of God and priest of Nature. We may look at the matter in this way: The theme of the "One Life," of the sacramental vision, is essentially religious—it presents us with the world, as the crew of the ship are presented with the Albatross, in "God's name." As we have seen, the poem is shot through with religious associations. On the other hand, the theme of imagination is essentially aesthetic—it presents us with the "great forms" of nature, but those forms as actively seized upon by the human mind and loved *not merely as vehicles for transcendental meaning but in themselves as participating in the reality which they "render intelligible."* The theme is essentially aesthetic, but it is also "natural" in the sense just defined as contrasted with the sense in which nature is regarded as the neutral material worked on by the mere "understanding." The Hermit, who kneels in the woods, embodies both views, both themes.

The Hermit, however, has another aspect. He is also the priest of Society, for it is by the Hermit, who urges the Pilot on despite his fears, that the Mariner is received back into the world of men. This rejoining of the world of men is not, we observe, accomplished simply by the welcoming committee. There is the terrific sound which sinks the ship and flings the stunned Mariner into the Pilot's boat. In the logic of the symbolic structure this would be, I presume, a repetition of the wind or storm motif: the creative storm has a part in re-establishing the Mariner's relation to other men.[24] Even if the destruction of the ship is regarded, as some readers regard it, as a final act of the Polar Spirit, to show, as it were, what he could do if he had a mind to, the symbolic import is not altered, for the Spirit belongs to the cluster of imagination which has the terrifying and cataclysmic as well as benign aspect. As a matter of fact, since the Gloss has earlier dismissed the Polar Spirit at the end of Part V, saying that he "returneth southward," it seems more reasonable to me to interpret the destruction of the ship as the work of the angelic troop, whose capacity to work marvels has already been amply demonstrated. And this reading gives us a fuller symbolic burden, too, and is consistent with the final fusion of themes which we observe in this general episode. At the level of the primary theme, the angelic troop wipe out the crime (i.e., the "criminal" ship and the dead bodies); at the level of the secondary theme, they do so by means of the "storm," which belongs to the symbolic cluster of the imagination.

V

By this reading of the poem the central and crucial fact is the fusion of the primary and secondary themes. And this means that the poem suddenly takes its place as a document of the very central and crucial issue of the period: the problem of truth and poetry. I do not mean to imply that this problem was first recognized by the Romantics. It had had a statement at least as early as the Platonic dialogue *Ion*. But with the English Romantics it was not only a constant topic for criticism, but was, directly or indirectly, an obsessive theme for poetry itself.

We have something of a parallel to this effort at making a marriage of poetry with truth, in the effort of the eighteenth century to establish a "holy alliance between science and religion," an effort which resulted in such works as Hartley's *Observations on Man* and Priestley's *Disquisitions*, which attempt to give the authority of science to the religious impulse. We can see, in fact, in Coleridge's early necessitarianism a continuation of this eighteenth-century effort. But the problem of poetry in the eighteenth century had been different; the poets then had felt, by and large, that poetry was at home in the world and in society and had its proper and well-defined function. The Romantic poets, on the other hand, felt that they had to justify their existence. However great the claims they

made for poetry and however sweeping their gestures and rolling their periods, they made those
claims because the need for justification was becoming acute. The claim they made was that poetry gives truth; or if they were as subtle as Coleridge they sought to establish an intimate and essential connection between truth and poetry on
psychological as well as metaphysical grounds. For
the Romantics, as A. E. Powell says, poetry was a
"form of knowledge, a form of action, the highest
form of either; so high that it reached their object
without their laboured process." As Keats said:
"What the Imagination seizes as Beauty must be
Truth." Over and over again, Blake affirmed that
"Imagination is Eternity."

The problem of establishing a holy alliance between poetry and truth was, however, terribly complicated by the fact that truth itself was not one
and simple. There were two truths, and they themselves might very well be in deadly competition:
the truth of religion and the truth of science. The
poets faced this situation in their various ways in
a time when one body of opinion held that with
the development of science, serious minds will turn
from poetry, whose harmony "is language on the
rack of Procrustes," whose sentiment "is canting
egotism in the mask of refined feeling," whose passion "is the commotion of a weak and selfish mind,"
whose pathos "is the whining of an unmanly spirit,"
and whose sublimity "is the inflation of an empty
head."

We know how Shelley responded to these
words of Peacock with his *Defence of Poetry,*
wherein he asserts that poetry "is at once the centre
and circumference of knowledge; it is that which
comprehends all science, and that to which all science must be referred." We know how Wordsworth had almost anticipated these very words. And
we know that, though Coleridge may have had a
deep-rooted instinctive distrust of science, he did
aim at a glorious synthesis in which all breaches
would be healed and all malice reconciled. And

though the distrust of science may have existed, Coleridge could at the same time find in poetry itself a field for the study of the "facts of mind" and could, as in some of his criticism of Shakespeare, shift the emphasis from aesthetic to scientific (i.e., psychological) interest. But the main problem of reconciliation for Coleridge was that between poetry and religion, or morality, for since those were his twin passions it was necessary for him to develop some vital connection between them if he was to be happy. His solution was, of course, one of detail and not part of the great synthesis of which he dreamed. For the age presented complications which could not, apparently, be resolved into such a system. "The fact is that the problem was," as Olwen Ward Campbell says, "gigantic, and the men were not more than great. And they seem to have suffered all of them from a kind of divided purpose and lack of conviction, which undermined their strength; part and parcel of the duality of the age. . . ."

The precarious solution which Coleridge attained was, of course, one aspect of his doctrine of the creative unity of the mind, which appears and reappears in his work and which is his great central insight and great contribution to modern thought. The opposition between thought and feeling he wished to abolish. As early as 1801, he could write to Thomas Poole: "My opinion is thus: that deep thinking is attainable only by a man of deep feeling, and that all truth is a species of revelation." And Coleridge was writing in that strain long before the composition of *The Ancient Mariner*, for instance in a letter to John Thelwall in 1796: "I feel strongly and I think strongly, but I seldom feel without thinking or think without feeling." And he proceeds to connect this proposition with his own poetic style: "My philosophical opinions are blended with or deduced from my feelings, and this, I think, peculiarises my style of writing." He is simply developing this early view when he says, in connection with Shakespeare, that the poet is "a genial understanding directing self-consciously a power and an implicit wisdom deeper even than our consciousness." And this view of the process of composition was also Wordsworth's view as we have it in the Preface: ". . . the poems in these volumes will be found distinguished at least by one mark of difference, that each of them has a worthy *purpose*. Not that I always began to write with a distinct purpose formally conceived; but habits of meditation have, I trust, so prompted and regulated my feelings, that my descriptions of such objects as strongly excite those feelings, will be found to carry along with them a *purpose*."

In all the quotations given above we find the idea that the truth is implicit *in the poetic act as such, that the moral concern and the aesthetic concern are aspects of the same activity, the creative activity, and that this activity is expressive of the whole mind.* Now, my argument is that *The Ancient Mariner* is, first, written *out of* this general belief, and second, written *about* this general belief.

As a poem written out of this belief it aims to interfuse as completely as possible its elements, that is, to present its materials symbolically, or implicitly as an absorbed import held in suspension, rather than allegorically or overtly. As a poem written about this belief, it aims to present a fable in which the moral values and the aesthetic values are shown to merge. In other words, the poem is, in general, about the unity of mind and the final unity of values, and in particular about poetry itself. It is not remarkable that Coleridge should have written on this subject, for it was the subject of his "darling studies." He had long since written, to Thelwall: "Metaphysics and poetry and 'facts of mind,' that is, accounts of all the strange phantasms that ever possessed 'your philosophy' . . . are my darling studies." And here we have the metaphysics, the poetry, and the psychology blended, as they are in the poem itself.

The fusion of the theme of the "One Life" and

the theme of imagination is the expression in the poem of Coleridge's general belief concerning the relation of truth and poetry, of morality and beauty. We find at the very turning point of the poem, the moment of the blessing of the water snakes, an explicit presentation of the idea. The sequence of events gives us, first, a recognition of the happiness of the water snakes in their fulfillment of being— they participate in the serene order of the universe. Like the stars and the moon which move unperturbed on their appointed business while the Mariner is fixed in his despair, the snakes, which appear, too, as light-giving, participate in the universal fullness of being. Seeing them thus, the Mariner can exclaim:

> *O happy living things!*

After this utterance, we have the recognition of the beauty of the water snakes under the aegis of the moon—that recognition being determined, we have seen, by the recognition of their place in the universal pattern:

> *. . . no tongue*
> *Their beauty might declare:*

Then love gushes from the Mariner's heart, the response at the level of instinctive feeling. Then he blesses them; that is, the instinctive feeling stirred by the recognition of beauty, finds its formal and objective expression. But he blesses them "unaware," and the word may be important, corresponding in this little account of the natural history of a "poem" of blessing, composed by the Mariner, to Wordsworth's word *spontaneous* in his phrase "the spontaneous overflow of powerful feelings" and Coleridge's word *unconscious* in the statement, in "On Poesy," that "There is in genius an unconscious activity; nay, that is the genius in the man of genius." So we may have here, and I do not mean this too whimsically, the case of a man who saves his own soul by composing a poem. But what Coleridge actually means is, of course, that the writing of a poem is simply a specialized example of a general process which leads to salvation. After the Mariner has composed his poem of blessing, he can begin the long voyage home.

He gets home, in the moonlight, which, we recall, is the light of imagination, and in the end he celebrates the chain of love which binds human society together, and the universe. But even here the Hermit, who officially reintroduces him into human society, is a priest of Nature as well as a priest of God; and the relation between man and Nature is established by the imagination, and so the Hermit is also a priest of imagination. In other words, imagination not only puts man in tune with the universe but puts him in tune with other men, with society: it provides the great discipline of sympathy. The socializing function of the imagination was never lost sight of by the Romantics. The poet is the man speaking of men, Wordsworth declares, and Shelley says in the *Defence:* "The great instrument of moral good is the imagination," for it leads man to "put himself in the place of another and of many others," so that "the pains and pleasures of his species must become his own." Over and over again in that generation we encounter the idea, and the Mariner returns to proclaim how sweet it is to walk "with a goodly company."

If the Mariner returns to celebrate the chain of love which binds human society and the universe, the fact should remind us that the occasion is a wedding and his audience a wedding guest. But it is sometimes argued that the Mariner repudiates marriage, contrasting it with the religious devotion indulged in "with a goodly company." [25] Now the contrast is certainly in the poem, and is involved in one of the personal themes. But in the total poem we cannot take the fact of the contrast as being unqualified. At the level of doctrine, we do not have contrast between marriage and sacramental love, but one as image of the other. It is no accident that the Mariner stops a light-hearted reveler on the way to a marriage feast. What he tells the wedding guest is that the human love, which the guest presumably takes to be an occasion for merriment, must be understood in the context of universal love and that only in such a context may it achieve its meaning. The end of the poem gives a dramatic scaling of the love, in lines 591–609.

> *What loud uproar bursts from that door!*
> *The wedding-guests are there:*
> *But in the garden-bower the bride*
> *And bride-maids singing are:*
> *And hark the little vesper bell,*
> *Which biddeth me to prayer!*
>
> *O Wedding-guest! this soul hath been*
> *Alone on a wide wide sea: . . .*
>
> *O sweeter than the marriage-feast,*
> *'Tis sweeter far to me,*
> *To walk together to the kirk*
> *With a goodly company!—*

The scale starts with the rude merriment, uninstructed and instinctive. Then the next phase, introduced by the significant word *but,* gives us the bride in the garden singing with the bridesmaids, retired from the general din and giving us, presumably, a kind of secular hymn of love. Then comes the vesper bell calling to prayer. The significance of the prayer is immediately indicated by the sudden statement that the Mariner's soul—and the use of the word *soul* here is important—has been alone on a wide sea: the Mariner now sees the chain of love which gives meaning to the marriage feast. In one of its aspects the poem is a prothalamion.

But we must ask ourselves more narrowly about the Mariner's situation, even as he proclaims his message of love. He is, we recall, a wanderer, with some shadow hanging over him of those two great wanderers, the Jew and Cain. His situation is paradoxical. Now from one point of view it is proper that the prophet of universal charity, even though he celebrates the village life of the goodly company walking to church together, should himself have no fixed address, for that would in a way deprive his message, symbolically at least, of its universality. But his wandering is not only a mark of his blessed vision: it is also a curse. So we have here a peculiar and paradoxical situation: the poem is a poem in which the poetic imagination appears in a regenerative and healing capacity, but in the end the hero, who has, presumably, been healed, appears in one of his guises as the *poète maudit*. So we learn that the imagination does not only bless, for even as it blesses it lays on a curse. Though the Mariner brings the word which is salvation, he cannot quite save himself and taste the full joy of the fellowship he advertises. Society looks askance at him. When he first returns home and is flung into the Pilot's boat (significantly by the creative storm), the ordinary mortals there are appalled: the Pilot falls down in a fit; the Pilot's boy "doth crazy go" and declares flatly that the Mariner is the devil himself; and even the Hermit has to conquer his mortal trepidations in prayer (though the priest ought to understand the artist as another person dedicated to ideal values). And even now, long after, the Wedding Guest has moments of terror under the glittering eye. The very gifts, the hypnotic eye, the "strange power of speech," set the Mariner apart.

Now, as we look back over the poem, we may see that this doubtful doubleness of the imagination has more than once been apparent. Creativity is a wind, a storm, which is sometimes inimical (as in the first storm in Part I) and is sometimes saving (as after the blessing of the snakes). But even in its most gentle manifestation, as the light breeze blows sweetly on the Mariner's brow on the voyage home, it "mingled strangely" with his "fears." There is always a strain of terror with the beauty, and in the end it is a shattering, supernatural blast which sinks the ship and delivers the Mariner to the waters of the home port even as the beneficent moon looks down.

The Mariner will be rescued and will pass like night from land to land. Let us linger on this phrase: like night. For even this tells us something. It gives us first the effortless, universal sweep, a sense of the universality of the Mariner's message which is carried from land to land. It tells us, too, by the easy, conventional equation of *dark* and *accursed* that the Mariner is the *poète maudit*. But night in this poem has a special body of associations, and with night we may have here, as a result of the long accumulation of night scenes, always with the association of the moon, a hint of the healing role of the imagination—a beneficent counterweight to the burden of the curse which is carried in the phrase. The phrase, in its special context, repeats, in little, the paradoxical situation of the Mariner.

Earlier I have said that we find in the blessing of the snakes a little fable of the creative process—the natural history of a poem of blessing. But in the end of the poem we have another fable of the creative process, and perhaps a fuller statement of Coleridge's conception of the poet, the man with the power which comes unbidden and which is an "agony" until it finds words, the power which wells up from the unconscious but which is the result of a moral experience and in its product, the poem, the "tale" told by the Mariner, will "teach"—for that is the word the Mariner uses. It is a paradoxical process.

And that paradox, the paradox of the situation of the poet, was a central fact for Coleridge and his age. The cult of Chatterton was significant, from Coleridge's boyish "Monody on the Death of Chatterton," in 1790, to the production of Vigny's *Chatterton* on the night when, as Gautier said, one could almost hear the crack of solitary pistols. In *Adonais* we do not know whether the mark on the pale brow of the last of the mourners is that of Cain or Christ,

in the "Ode" the poet falls upon the thorns of life,
and in a letter to Mrs. Shelley appears the sentence:
"Imagine my despair of good, imagine how it is
possible that one of weak and sensitive nature as
mine can run further the gauntlet through this hell-
ish society of men." And Blake, who, as his letters
and notebooks show us, frequently found himself
at odds with the world, could complain:

O why was I born with a different face?
Why was I not born like the rest of my race?

Keats was, in one respect, like the waif, as Yeats
said, looking into the window of the sweetshop.
But where Keats is a gentle outcast, Byron is a
dark and theatrical one, practicing his wild glances
before a mirror and hinting at horrid crimes. And
when he describes himself, the outcast both noble-
minded and accursed, he describes himself in *Lara*
as a figure strangely like the Mariner, with, somehow, a mysterious message and a power to compel
the listener like the power in the Mariner's glittering eye:

None knew nor how, nor why, but he entwined
Himself perforce around the hearer's mind;
There he was stamped; in liking or in hate,
If greeted once; however brief the date
That friendship, pity, or aversion knew,
Still there within the inmost thought he grew.
You could not penetrate his soul, but found,
Despite your wonder, to your own he wound;
His presence haunted still; and from the breast
He forced an all unwilling interest:
Vain was the struggle in that mental net,
His spirit seemed to dare you to forget.

But what of Wordsworth, who seems so respect-
ably rooted in social centrality and who eschewed
the opium phial of Coleridge and De Quincey, the
bottle of Lamb, the rancors of Blake, the Satanic
loves and heroic posturings of Byron, the languors
of Keats, and the shrillnesses and self-pity of
Shelley? I am not about to refer to Annette Vallon

or to the youthful ardors of revolution. I refer to
his critical theory. He says that a poet is a man
speaking to men, and affirms the universal bond,
as do his brother poets, for all that. But if we look
close we see that he also shares with his brother
poets the fascination with the outcast, the outsider.
He seeks poetry in the peasant, the idiot, the child.
We know the reasons he gives, and sound ones
they may be, for going to these figures, but we
must not forget that these figures, too, are beyond
the circle of respectable society. There is, it must
be remembered, another point, which comes out of
Wordsworth's description of the poet. He says, first,
that the poet has a "more comprehensive soul" than
other men, and second, that he is set off from them
by a certain special endowment. The first notion
refers to a difference in degree, but the second refers to a *difference in kind.* In developing this second notion Wordsworth, like other Romantic critics, comments on the special nature of the aesthetic
experience: the poet has, he says in the Preface, an
"ability of conjuring up in himself passions, which
are indeed *far from being the same as those produced by real events*, yet . . . do more nearly resemble the passions produced by real events than
anything which, from the motions of their own
minds merely, other men are accustomed to feel in
themselves. . . ."

I am not prepared, on the basis of Wordsworth's
insistence on the special quality of the creative experience, to call him, except fancifully, an example
of the *poète maudit.* The imagination was for him
a healing power, and his life was a strenuous effort
to give others something of the benefit of this
power and to make poetry genuinely social. Nevertheless, he did know something of the "distress,"
as he called it, which occasionally accompanied
the exercise of the healing power, even if his distress was a little short of the Mariner's "agony."
He says in the *Prelude* that the poet, "gentle creature as he is," has his "unruly times":

> *. . . his mind, best pleased*
> *While she as duteous as the mother dove*
> *Sits brooding, lives not always to that end,*
> *But like the innocent bird, hath goadings on*
> *That drive her as in trouble through the groves;*
> *With me is no such passion, to be blamed*
> *No otherwise than as it lasts too long.*

The dove that is goaded through the groves by its inward distress is a somewhat less compelling image than the Mariner who passes like night from land to land, but the idea is in both cases the same. But this description of the poet as cursed is not the only one in Wordsworth's work. In "Stanzas Written in my Pocket-Copy of Thomson's 'Castle of Indolence' " (1802) there is the description of a man who wanders the country in storm or heat or who sits for hours brooding apart from men.

> *What ill was on him, what he had to do*
> *A mighty wonder bred among our quiet crew.*

This man, who is compared to a "sinful creature, pale and wan," is in the end defined as a poet:

But verse was what he had been wedded to;
And his own mind did like a tempest strong
Come to him thus, and drove the weary Wight
  along.[26]

So we have, even with Wordsworth, something of the paradox which haunted Coleridge with special vindictiveness all his life: the paradox implicit in the figure of the Mariner or in that other ambiguous figure in that other poem about the imagination:

> *And all should cry, Beware! Beware!*
> *His flashing eyes, his floating hair!*
> *Weave a circle round him thrice,*
> *And close your eyes with holy dread,*
> *For he on honey-dew hath fed,*
> *And drunk the milk of Paradise.*

VI

I have tried to show, by dwelling on details as well as on the broad, central images, that there is in *The Ancient Mariner* a relatively high degree of expressive integration. There may be lags and lapses in fulfilling the basic creative idea, but, according to my reading, these lags and lapses are minor. But one school of thought has always held that the lags and lapses are far from minor, that there is no pervasive logic in the poem. Wordsworth, of course, said as much, as did Mrs. Barbauld with her complaint of improbability, and Southey in his review of the piece in *The Critical Review*. Even Lamb, in defending the poem against Southey and declaring it to have the true power of playing "tricks with the mind," was constrained to admit that parts of the poem were "fertile in unmeaning miracles." And later, in defending the poem against Wordsworth's charge that it was not integrated, he again admitted that he disliked "all the miraculous parts of it."

We must remember that the poem to which all of the critics referred was not the poem as it stands before us today. I do not argue that it would have made any difference to Mrs. Barbauld, or even to Wordsworth, but Coleridge did arrive at, by the time of the publication in *Sibylline Leaves* (1817), two major changes: he added the Gloss, which should have made the structure of the poem clearer, and he revised the text. Whether or not Coleridge was led to these changes by the criticism of the obscurity and lack of logic, the revision of the text itself was in accordance with his own theory of composition, that the parts of a work should participate in the expressiveness of the whole. So we have, in the important omissions made in the last version, a purging of at least most of the "unmeaning miracles" of which Lamb presumably complained, the descriptions of Death on the specter-bark and of the burning arms of the spirits at the time of the homecoming.[27]

The charge of the lack of integration, however, still continues to be made. One recent critic, Newton P. Stallknecht, says, for instance, that "Coleridge gives us no inkling of a possible allegorical interpretation until we reach the middle of Part III and encounter the character *Life-in-Death*." But by this critic and by others the problem is centered on the role of the supernatural in the poem. Stallknecht [28] says that "moralizing or the use of allegory in a ballad in which an imaginative use is made of the supernatural *for its own sake* is apt to seem out of place or even mechanical," and he then proceeds to define the split in the poem as one between the supernatural material and the moral which, he takes it, was grafted on the poem late in the process of composition.

This general view of the supernatural should, perhaps, be inspected in the light of Coleridge's statements regarding the place of his interest in the supernatural in his own development. We do not have, alas, the essay on "the uses of the Supernatural in poetry," which he confidently affirmed the reader would find prefixed to *The Ancient Mariner*. But we know of the childhood passion for marvels and mysteries, fairy tales and *The Arabian Nights*, and we know what value he put upon what Lamb called "that beautiful interest in wild tales" as an influence in forming the imaginative bent. For him they served the same purpose as those later and more respectable fairy tales of Plotinus and the other mystics to keep "the heart alive in the head" and save his mind from "being imprisoned within the outline of any single dogmatic system." Furthermore, we must recall the context in which the division of labor for the *Lyrical Ballads* was arrived at and in which Coleridge undertook to write the poems of a supernatural cast: the context was the passionate dialogue, protracted day after day, on the subject nearest the hearts of both the young men, the subject of the nature and function of poetry. It was a high theme for them, and in the discussion the supernatural partakes of the general seriousness: no subject for an idle shudder.

In the face of this situation, it is a little surprising to find it argued, as it is argued by Marius Bewley, that Coleridge's "motive, in the last analysis, was not substantially different from Mrs. Radcliffe's or Monk Lewis's," that the *frisson* is all except for some disjointed references to a moral preoccupation which appear in the poem only because the poet "could not help drawing in some measure from his full sensibility." But the moral element, even if it does appear thus disjointedly in the poem, "is forgotten, if indeed it was ever recognized as present; it is changed, choked out by theatrical fripperies." And he summarizes this interpretation by saying: "The moral value of the poem is sacrificed by the attainment of a somewhat frivolous distinction"—that of having successfully created an atmosphere of mystery.

Aside from the evidence in the poem itself against this view, a view not confined to Bewley's essay, one can go to Coleridge's own words concerning the use of the supernatural in those romances which Bewley takes the poet to emulate. Coleridge reviewed several of the Gothic romances, and was interested in them, but he demands in the midst of the atmosphere of terror and mystery a truth to nature, and though he recognizes in some of them moments of genius and a great deal of ingenuity, in general he estimates them "cheaply." He says: "The writer may make us wonder, but he cannot surprise us," if the order of nature is changed. "For the same reason a romance is incapable of exemplifying a moral truth." He continues: "The romance-writer possesses an unlimited power over situations; but he must scrupulously make his characters act in congruity with them. Let him work *physical* wonders only, and we will be content to *dream* with him for a while; but the first *moral* miracle which he attempts, he disgusts and awakens us." This was Coleridge's view in 1797, a few months before he began work on *The Ancient Mariner*, and it is highly improbable that in using materials similar to those of the romances he would not have attempted to avoid the defects which he had observed in the romances themselves.

The chief defect which Coleridge had observed in the romances is that, being contrary to human nature, they have no "moral" content. Presumably what Coleridge tried to do in his poem was to use the materials of "physical wonders" as expressive of spiritual truth, the physically improbable as expressive of the spiritually probable. The notion stated by Coleridge in the review of Lewis's *The Monk* can be taken as implying an awareness of the various attacks on the probability of the poem, the most famous example of which appears in Wordsworth's famous note—the "events, having no necessary connection, do not produce each other." These attacks are all based on a concern with the "physical wonders" as such, a concern which neglects the "moral truth" in the experience of the human being who endures in the midst of the wonders.

Coleridge was aware of the attacks on the poem on the grounds of the improbability caused by the use of the supernatural, and when he came to the final revision he gave us, it would seem, his answer. It is in the long motto by Burnet, which calls special attention to the supernatural element in the poem. "I readily believe," Burnet says, "that in the universe are more invisible beings than visible." He continues:

But who will expound to us the nature of them all, and their ranks and relationships and distinguishing characteristics and the functions of each? What is it they perform? What regions do they inhabit? Ever about the knowledge of these things circles the thought of man, never reaching it. Meanwhile, it is pleasant, I must confess, sometimes to contemplate in the mind, as in a picture, the image of this greater and better world: that the mind, accustomed to the little things of daily life, may not be narrowed overmuch and lose itself in trivial reflections. But meanwhile must we diligently seek after truth, maintaining just measure, that we may distinguish things certain from uncertain, day from night.[29]

It is worthy of note that this motto was added in the edition of 1817, long after the heyday of the first enthusiastic speculations on the Quantock Hills and now in the cold calculation of a critical middle age bent upon making the masterpiece more comprehensible. I have already indicated how the last sentence of the motto points to the night-day, moon-sun opposition in the poem, and ties with that basic symbol; and I take the use of the motto to be not a piece of whimsical mumbo-jumbo or a vain parade of learning, but a device for pointing at a central fact of the poem. It says that the world is full of powers and presences not visible to the physical eye (or by the "understanding"): this is a way of saying that there is a spiritual order of universal love, the sacramental vision, and of imagination; that nature, if understood aright—that is, by the imagination—offers us vital meanings. It is simply a way of underscoring the function of the supernatural machinery and atmosphere in the poem, a way of saying that it participates in the symbolic tissue of the poem.

For I take the poem to be one in which the vital integration is of a high order, not one of the "great, formless poems" which the Romantics are accused of writing,[30] and not a poem which would fit into T. S. Eliot's formula of the dissociated sensibility of the period. I take it to be a poem central and seminal for the poet himself. Though a philosopher has said that "it would be pedantry to look for philosophical doctrines" in these magical lines,[31] and though a literary scholar finds here "merely the aroma, the fine flavor," of the poet's meditations,[32] if we do look closely at the magical lines and look at them in the light of the poet's lifelong preoccupations, we may come to conclude, with Leslie Stephen, that "the germ of all Coleridge's utterances may be found . . . in the 'Ancient Mariner.'" It is central for Coleridge, but it is also central for its age, providing, not a comment on an age, but a focus of the being and issues of that age. It is, in short, a work of "pure imagination."

VII

The type of critical analysis which I have just attempted always raises certain questions. I shall state them bluntly and in the terms in which they usually appear:

1. Assuming that certain interpretations can be "drawn out of" or "put into" the poem by an "exercise of ingenuity," how do we know that the poet "intended" them?

2. If the present interpretations are "right," (a) is the poem not obscure, since good and experienced readers of the past have "missed" them, or (b) how is it that such good and experienced readers, having missed the interpretations, have still been deeply affected by the poem?

These questions, it will be readily seen, have to do, in order, with the theory of poetic creation and the theory of poetic appreciation. To answer these questions properly would require a space not here at my disposal and a competence not at my command. But it is not to be expected that a reader will accept my interpretation if I am not willing to abide his questions. And so I shall indicate, at least, the lines along which I should try to frame answers.

I should begin by saying that the questions, *as stated*, are false questions. There are real problems concealed behind these questions, but these are false because they are loaded—they will not permit an answer which does not falsify the nature of the process under discussion.

Let us take the first one.

The falsity of the first question inheres in the word *intended* as the word is intended in the context. The implication here is that the process of poetic creation is, shall we say, analogous to the process of building a house from a blueprint: the poet has an idea, the blueprint, and according to it, plank by plank and nail by nail, he makes a poem, the house. Actually, the creation of a poem is as much a process of discovery as a process of making. A poem may, in fact, start from an idea—and may involve any number of ideas—but the process for the poet is the process of discovering what the idea "means" to him in the light of his total being and his total experience (in so far as that total experience is available to him for the purpose of poetry—the degree here varies enormously from poet to poet). Or a poem may start from a phrase, a scene, an image, or an incident which has, for the poet, a suggestive quality—what, for him in the light of his total being and total available experience, we may call the symbolic potential. Then the process for the poet is the process of discovering why the item has caught his attention in the first place—which is simply another way of saying that he is trying to develop the symbolic potential. Or the original item may lead by some more or less obscure train of association to another item which will become the true germ of the poem, and whose symbolic potential may supplant that of the first item.

However the process starts, it is, of course, enormously complicated. The degree of effort may vary from instance to instance (the poet may dream up his poem in a flash or it may be laboriously accreted like coral), and the degree of self-consciousness may vary from instance to instance (the poet may or may not in the process of creation interlard his symbolical thinking with discursive and critical thinking). As Coleridge said, and as many other poets and even scientists have said, the unconscious may be the genius in the man of genius. But this is not to define the process as an irrational process. What comes unbidden from the depths at the moment of creation may be the result of the most conscious and narrowly rational effort in the past. In any case, the poet always retains the right of rejecting whatever seems to violate his nature and his developing conception of the poem. And the

process of rejection and self-criticism may be working continually during the composition of a poem.
In the case of *The Ancient Mariner* we have good
evidence that the poet was working in terms of a
preconceived theme, and we know that the original
composition required some months and that the
process of revision required years.

Whatever the amount of possible variation from
case to case in various respects, we can say that
the process is a process of discovery which objecti-
fies itself as a making. What the poet is trying to
discover, then, is what kind of poem he can make.
And the only thing he, in the ordinary sense, may
"intend" is to make a poem. In so far as his process
of discovery has been more than a rhetorical exercise, he cannot do otherwise than "intend" what
his poem says, any more than he can change his
own past as past, but he does not fully know what
he "intends" until the poem is fully composed. A
purpose "formally conceived" is not, as Wordsworth said, necessary, first to initiate the process of
creation, or second, to give the finished poem a
meaning ultimately expressive not only of the man
but of his "ideas" in a restricted sense. But, Wordsworth went on to say, "habits of meditation have, I
trust, so prompted and regulated my feelings, that
my descriptions of such objects as strongly excite
those feelings, will be found to carry along with
them a *purpose*."

If the poet does not have a blueprint of intention
(and if he does happen to have it, we ordinarily
have no access to it), on what basis may a poem be
interpreted? What kind of evidence is to be admitted? The first piece of evidence is the poem itself. And here, as I have suggested earlier, the
criterion is that of internal consistency. If the
elements of a poem operate together toward one
end, we are entitled to interpret the poem according to that end. Even if the poet himself should
rise to contradict us, we could reply that the words
of the poem speak louder than his actions.

But the application of the criterion of internal

consistency cannot be made in a vacuum. All sorts of considerations impinge upon the process. And these considerations force on the critic the criterion of external consistency. But consistency in regard to what? First, in regard to the intellectual, the spiritual climate of the age in which the poem was composed. Second, in regard to the over-all pattern of other artistic work by the author in question. Third, in regard to the thought of the author as available from non-artistic sources. Fourth, in regard to the facts of the author's life. These considerations cannot be applied in a mechanical fashion, that is, so as to confuse the material of the poem with the poem itself. If treated mechanically, the first, for example, will give us crude historicism, or the fourth will give us crude psychologism— both of which confound the material with the thing created, both of which deny the creative function of mind, both of which fail to provide any basis for distinguishing the excellent product from the conventional or inept. But treated as conditioning factors, as factors of control in interpretation, the considerations named above provide invaluable criteria.

I have said that both of the questions usually raised by the kind of interpretation I have attempted are false questions. They are false in themselves, without regard to the goodness or badness, the truth or falsity, of a particular interpretation. Just as the first question is false, as stated, because it is based on a misconception of the creative process, so the second is false because based on a misconception of the appreciative process. I shall repeat the second question: If the present interpretations are "right," (a) is the poem not obscure since good and experienced readers of the past have "missed" them, or (b) how is it that they, having missed the interpretations, have still been deeply affected by the poem?

The trouble is that the word *missed* here falsifies the relationship between the reader and the poem. It implies a matter of yes-and-no. Actually, the relationship is not one of yes-and-no, but of degree, of gradual exploration of deeper and deeper levels of meaning within the poem itself. And this process of exploration of deeper and deeper levels of the poem may be immediate and intuitive. The reader may be profoundly affected—his sense of the world may be greatly altered—even though he has not tried to frame in words the nature of the change wrought upon him, or having tried to do so, has failed (as all critics must fail in some degree, for the simple reason that the analysis cannot render the poem, the discursive activity cannot render the symbolical). As for *The Ancient Mariner* itself, the great central fact of the poem, the fact which no reader could miss—the broken tabu, the torments of guilt and punishment, the joy of reconciliation— is enough to account for the first impact of the poem upon a reader. But beyond that, the vividness of the presentation and the symbolic coherence may do their work—as blessing sprang to the Mariner's lips—unawares. For the good poem may work something of its spell even upon readers who are critically inarticulate.

If this is true—if ideally appreciation is immediate and intuitive—why should critical analysis ever be interposed between the reader and the poem? The answer is simple: in order that the intuition may be fuller, that detail may be more richly and the central images more deeply realized. But in this case what becomes of immediacy of appreciation? Nothing becomes of it, if "immediacy" is read properly—if it is read as signifying "without mediation" of critical analysis and not as signifying "upon the first instant of contact." Let me put it in this way: A poem works immediately upon us when we are ready for it. And it may require the mediation of a great deal of critical activity by ourselves and by others before we are ready. And for the greater works we are never fully ready. That is why criticism is a never-ending process.

One last word: In this essay I have not attempted to "explain" how poetry appeals, or why. I have been primarily concerned to give a discursive reading of the symbol which is the poem, in so far as I can project the import of the symbol in such a fashion. I humbly trust that I am not more insensitive than most to the "magical lines," but at the same time I cannot admit that our experience, even our aesthetic experience, is ineluctably and vindictively divided into the "magical" and the rational, with an abyss between. If poetry does anything for us, it reconciles, by its symbolical reading of experience (for by its very nature it is in itself a myth of the unity of being), the self-devisive internecine malices which arise at the superficial level on which we conduct most of our living.

And *The Ancient Mariner* is a poem on this subject.

Notes

1. *The Best of Coleridge*, ed. Earl Leslie Griggs (New York, 1934), p. 687.
2. The subtitle of *The Road to Xanadu* (Boston, 1927) is "A Study in the Ways of the Imagination." Actually, to employ the Coleridgean distinction (which Lowes explicitly repudiates) it should have been "A Study in the Ways of the Fancy," for in so far as Lowes treats the subject we have only the "fixities and definities," the units of material employed by the poet in merely new combinations of material. Lowes does nothing to show what hap-

pens in terms of imaginative meaning to these items when immersed in the "deep well." He shows how, in a factual sense, these items are transmuted, how, for instance, the "disconsolate black albatross" of *Shelvocke's Voyage*, shot by the superstitious Captain Hatley in the hope of a fair wind, becomes the albatross in the poem, but he never shows how they enter into a meaningful structure, how they become organically related to each other.

3. Humphry House, in a sympathetic criticism of this essay (The Clark Lectures, Cambridge University, published under the title *Coleridge*, London, 1953), raises a pertinent question about my method. Coleridge's important critical work, he reminds us, "was all a good deal later than most of his important creative work. We cannot thus be sure how much of his critical opinion may be carried back into 1797–8 and brought to bear on his greatest poetry" (p. 92).

By way of explaining myself, I should appeal to the principle of presumptive coherence in development, the fact that, despite waverings and false starts, a writer's history usually shows us a basic line. (In appealing to such a principle, we have to be very honest with ourselves: we have to test our congruences very scrupulously, and reason from them only when their number is massive and the negative instances very few.) I am not, however, arguing that because Coleridge held a certain doctrine of the symbol in 1817, the year of the *Biographia Literaria* and *The Statesman's Manual*, a poem written in 1797–1798 would necessarily embody that doctrine in practice. The later statements would be relevant only in so far as we can hold that those later statements represented a development of a position essentially held at the time of the composition of the poem itself. Now, there is strong evidence that this is the case.

First, Coleridge says flatly that he had become aware of the special power of the imagination at an early date, his "twenty-fourth year." In the *Biographia Literaria* (I, 58–60), he describes the effect wrought upon him by the reading of a poem by Wordsworth, a poem which exhibited "the union of deep feeling with profound thought; the fine balance of truth in observing with the imaginative faculty in modifying the objects observed; and above all the original gift of spreading the tone, the *atmosphere*, and with it the depth and height of the ideal world around forms, incidents, and situations, of which, for the common view, custom had bedimmed all the lustre, had dried up the sparkle and the dew drops" (p. 59). Then a little later in discussing the concept of the imagination, he refers to the subject as one to which a poem of Wordsworth's had "first directed my attention" (p. 64). The whole discussion of the origin of the *Lyrical Ballads* makes it clear beyond doubt that the basic conception of the imagination had been arrived at early. We also have the evidence of *The Prelude*, which grew out of these discussions— evidence that may be useful in the face of Coleridge's uneasy memory for dates.

Second, we have the evidence in certain poems. The shaping power of the mind is referred to in early poems, such as the sonnet "To Richard Brinsley Sheridan, Esq." (1795) and "Lines on a Friend Who Died of a Frenzy Fever" (1794). Shawcross points out that even in "Religious Musings" (1794) there is a volitional effort on the part of the finite mind.

Third, though Coleridge wrote *The Ancient Mariner* in 1797–1798, he worked closely on it in the period just before the publication of *Sibylline Leaves* (1817), which belongs to the same period as the *Biographià Literaria* and *The Statesman's Manual*. In other words, his careful revision of the poem apparently indicates that it satisfactorily embodies, or adumbrates, his theories of composition as held in 1817. The fact that he continued to nurse the hope of completing *Christabel* indicates the same thing about that poem. At the peak of his critical powers, and presumably under their aegis, Coleridge was revising *The Ancient Mariner*.

All in all, the evidence against this general view is based on the idea that the concept of the imagination was arrived at after the visit to Germany and the subsequent philosophical crisis. I do not deny that the crisis was real, but it seems to have resulted in a clarification of issues which had been brewing for a long time. Germany gave Coleridge form and authority, perhaps, but not the basic motivation for his final views. Yet even R. D. Havens (*The Mind of a Poet*, Baltimore, 1941), immediately after remarking on the fact that a poem by Wordsworth had provoked Coleridge to speculation about the imagination, proceeds to say that "this revolutionary conception of the imagination" was "probably derived from Kant" (p. 206). For a discussion of the date of Coleridge's study of Kant, and of the needs which led him to accept Kant, see René Wellek, *Kant in England* (Princeton, 1931), pp. 69-73.

Elsewhere in his book, Mr. House considers the idea that the poem itself "is part of the experience which led Coleridge into his later theoretic statements (as of the theory of the Imagination) rather than a symbolic adumbration of the theoretic statements themselves." It is certainly true that the poem is an element in the development of the critical theory; but it also seems true that the poem is a manifestation of that development. In practice I simply do not see how we can distinguish between these two things; they are aspects of a single process. What I am finally concerned to do, irrespective of any technical argument about the nature of symbolism, is to establish that the "import" of the poem is consistent with the declarations of the criticism, and to explore the significance of this consistency.

4. In a letter dated February 5, 1797, Lamb refers to the poem as "Your *Dream*" (*Complete Poetical Works of Samuel Taylor Coleridge*, ed. E. H. Coleridge [Oxford, 1912], I, 169). The poem is, in fact, a kind of parallel to *The Ancient Mariner* in so far as it concerns a violation of Nature: a

woodsman cuts down a tree and kills a nest of young ravens, timber from the tree is built into a ship, and when a storm sinks the ship the father raven exults in his revenge. In the *Sibylline Leaves* version, Coleridge changed the end by the addition of two lines to take the curse off the statement that revenge was sweet:

> *We must not think so;*
> *but forget and forgive,*
> *And what Heaven gives life to,*
> *we'll still let it live.*

But in a manuscript note, Coleridge commented: "Added thro' cowardly fear of the Goody! What a Hollow, where the Heart of Faith ought to be, does it not betray? this alarm concerning Christian morality, that will not permit even a Raven to be a Raven, nor a Fox a Fox, but demands conventicular justice to be inflicted on their unchristian conduct, or at least an antidote to be annexed" (*ibid.*, I, 171). It is fruitless to invoke this note as evidence that Coleridge believed in the position adopted by Griggs and Lowes. When he here says that a raven might be left a raven, he means that the raven as outside the realm of human religion and morality is entitled to gloat over revenge. When Coleridge added the last two lines he did not add a "moral" to a poem which had previously had none; he simply made explicit the distinction between raven and man, and defined man's responsibilities more closely. Without the new lines, the poem had had a "moral"— and a very unsubtle one.

5. MX. B II, Alice Snyder, Coleridge on Logic and Learning (New Haven, 1929), p. 132.

6. "Preliminary Treatise on Method," *Encyclopedia Metropolitana* (London, 1845), I, 25.

7. See John Muirhead, *Coleridge as Philosopher* (London, 1930), pp. 142–148; and later discussion in this essay.

8. *Enneads*, V, I, 7: *The Divine Mind*, trans. Stephen Mackenna (London, 1926), IV, 81–82. Another important text on the matter of self-con-

sciousness in creation appears in the account in Chapter xiv of the *Biographia Literaria* of the poet "described in ideal perfection." Here it is said that the secondary imagination is "first put into action by the will and understanding," and remains under "their irremissive, though gentle and *unnoticed control*" (italics mine).

9. The "huge ill-assorted fabric of philosophic and theological beliefs" can be read, according to Richards, as "an elaborate, transformed *symbol* of some parts of the psychology. . . . Coleridge constantly presents it [the philosophic and theological speculation] as though it were the matrix out of which he obtained his critical theories. But the critical theories can be obtained from the psychology without initial complication with the philosophical matter. They can be given all the powers that Coleridge found for them, without the use either literally, or symbolically, of the other doctrines" (*Coleridge on Imagination*, [London, 1934], pp. 58–59).

10. *The Statesman's Manual*, p. 437. See also "Lectures of 1818," Sections on Allegory and on Spenser (*Coleridge's Miscellaneous Criticism*, ed. T. M. Raysor [Cambridge, 1936], pp. 28–33). One may remember, too, the terms in which Coleridge repudiated his own early poetry: his chief charge against it is that of being—though he does not use the word—allegorical. Muirhead (*op. cit.* p. 43) comments on the abstractions which populate the poems prior to 1797, and observes that in the great poems they are "wholly subordinated to the interest of the characters and incident." But, in realizing that the great poems are not simply allegorical, he goes to the other extreme and assumes, or momentarily seems to do so, that the poems therefore have no intellectual content. He concludes with a position like that of Griggs: "It would be pedantry to look for philosophical doctrines in their magical lines." One might retort that it is exactly the same kind of pedantry to look for meaning in the "magical" events of life itself.

But to turn to Coleridge's particular doctrine of symbolism, it seems to be developed under the shadow of Plotinus. The Universe, Plotinus says, "stands a stately whole, complete within itself, serving at once its own purpose and that of all its parts which, leading and lesser alike, are of such a nature as to further the interests of the total. It is, therefore, impossible to condemn the whole on the merits of the parts which, besides, must be judged only as they enter harmoniously or not into the whole, the main consideration, quite overpassing the members which thus cease to have importance." (Mackenna, *op. cit.* II, 2, 3; *ibid.*, II, 14–15.) But the whole serves the "interests" of the parts. The following analysis can be transposed into aesthetic terms: "In what sense can we then say that the individual soul is part of the universal soul? There comes to mind here an analogy, the only one which, to speak of Plotinus, may be able to make us understand the relation between the universal soul and the individual souls. The theorem, he says, is part of the science, if one may speak thus; but the theorem, and every theorem, is the science itself, in all its extension and its life: fixed there, reduced, concentrated in that point: but in it all life is present, even if not explicitly expressed. Every scientific proposition receives life from all the science. . . . In the mind of the scientist, or of any other person whatsoever, the theorem meanwhile has value in so far as it is the entire science, regarded from one side only, in one of its particular configurations. . . . So that, as the theorem may be called part of the science and is nothing less, however, on reflection, than the science itself, so the individual soul may be called part of the universal soul, which, to consider well, is nothing more than the individual soul. And as the theorem acquires consistency and life in the articulated complex of which it forms a part, which is the scientific system, so the individual soul meanwhile affirms itself and empowers itself in so far as it is once more understood and once more understands the universal soul itself, from which Plotinus thinks it proceeds. The theorem is all the science, but the science in power, and the individual soul is all the universal soul, but in power" (Cordelia Guzzo Capone, *La Psicologia di Plotino* [Napoli, 1926], p. 52; translation mine).

11. I take it that this is what Susanne Langer means by the "unspeakable" in the import of the symbol. As applied to poetry, she puts it: "The material of poetry is discursive, but the product— the artistic phenomenon—is not; its significance is purely implicit in the poem as a totality, as a form compounded of sound and suggestion, statement and reticence, and no translation can reincarnate that. . . . An artistic symbol . . . has more than discursive or presentational meaning" (*Philosophy in a New Key* [Cambridge, 1942], pp. 261–262). Elsewhere, she distinguishes between the symbolic and the allegorical modes. In allegory, she says, "we have a literal meaning—the key to this being the accepted meanings of the words and sentence-forms—and a secondary meaning, which employs some features *of the primary* meaning," to express another structure. She continues: "But allegory is a direct and obvious form of interpretation. For the secondary meaning could really be literally expressed, being simply another story. It is verbally communicable, and does not really need the literal story for its expression. . . . But to treat a myth [or symbol in the sense used here] as an allegory in the strict sense is useless—for *all myths expressing the same fundamental idea are allegories of each other,* but they are formulations, exemplifications, not allegories of the concept they embody. Therefore, to treat a religious symbol, for instance, as an allegory of natural events, is merely substituting one language for another. The kernel of a myth is a remote idea, which is shown, not stated in the myth. It is only the myth which is stated in words" (*The Practice of Philosophy* [New York, 1930], pp. 156–158).

Following this line of thought, we can see that

when one critic makes the Pilot's boy "equal" the clergy, to take an allegorical reading in the most absurd form, the critic is merely "substituting one language for another"—is merely trying, here very unconvincingly, to make another application of the principle behind the symbol which he should try to interpret. That is to say, the boy and the clergy are on the same level of "story." And this transposition of one for the other does little to carry us toward the "kernel" or "concept" or root-attitude of the poem, which, it is true, we can never wholly frame in words but which it is the business of criticism to carry us toward.

In this connection William Blake has a most instructive passage: "The Last Judgment is not Fable or Allegory, but Vision. Fable or Allegory are a totally distinct and inferior kind of Poetry. Vision or Imagination is a Representation of what Externally Exists, Really and Unchangeably. Fable or Allegory is Form'd by the daughters of Memory. Imagination is surrounded by the daughters of Inspiration, who in the aggregate are call'd Jerusalem. Fable is allegory, but what Critics call the Fable, is Vision itself. The Hebrew Bible and the Gospel of Jesus are not Allegory, but Eternal Vision or Imagination of All that Exists. Note here that Fable or Allegory is seldom without some Vision. Pilgrim's Progress is full of it, the Greek Poets the same; but . . . Allegory and Vision . . . ought to be known as Two Distinct Things, and so call'd for the Sake of Eternal Life. Plato has made Socrates say that Poets and Prophets do not know or Understand what they write or Utter; this is a most Pernicious Falsehood. If they do not, pray is an inferior kind to be call'd Knowing? Plato confutes himself" (from "Blake's Catalogue of Pictures," *The Writings of William Blake,* ed. Geoffrey Keynes [London, 1925], III, 145–46).

12. Humphry House (*op. cit.,* p. 108) says of my use of symbolism in interpreting the poem: "I suggest that if we accept the term 'symbol' we must allow a freer, wider, less exact reference; and that

it is probably wiser to drop the term altogether. Mr. Warren himself fully allows for the possibility (even likelihood) that Coleridge did not *consciously* use symbols at all. This is consistent with Coleridge's recognition of the unconscious element in the workings of genius; but it does not therefore follow that there was a latent precision waiting for critics to elucidate."

There are several notions here. One is a technical consideration having to do with the use of the term *symbol*. I do not, as a matter of fact, feel wedded to the term: I mean it only as an image of deep import, using the word *image* in a broad sense to include event, etc. But if we discard the term *symbol*, we still have the problem of image and import. Aren't we back, for practical, immediate purposes, where we started?

Another notion above has to do with the discomfort at what is taken to be my exactness of reference and precision in interpreting the poem. I, like Mr. House, feel discomfort at the dry, schematic reading of this poem—or any poem. I, like Mr. House, take the import of this poem, and of individual items in the poem, to be massive and deep—"condensed," as I have said above; and like him I feel that when we come to the business of stating discursively that import we inevitably violate the richness of the poetic object as experienced. The violation is inevitable because we are transferring elements of the synthetic imagination into an incommensurable dimension of analysis. We are, however, committed, willy-nilly, to the attempt analytically to understand poetry: we are rational beings, and we take poetry to be, in its deepest sense, rational—that is, to have a structure, and a structure that reflects, embodies, and clarifies the secret structure of the human soul and human experience. The degree of consciousness in the creation of a poem is not necessarily relevant to its import; the real question is how fully, deeply—and veraciously because deeply— the poem renders the soul and the soul's experi-

ence, and thus enables us to understand it by living
into its structure as projected in the structure of
the poem. The only test of what, to use my critic's
word, is "latent" in a poem is the test of coherence.
(See Section VII of this essay.) In trying to determine what is latent, we may learn that the discipline of our ordinary analytic understanding,
with its apparently, and often really, barren attempts at "precision," can sometimes be a step toward that deeper, fulfilling experience which we
finally expect from the poem.

The same unease at my attempts at "precision"
is implied elsewhere: "What happens in the poem
is that the images gather their meaning by progressively rich associations, by gradual increment, and
that exact equation is never fully demanded, even
though the association is ordered and controlled"
(p. 97). Now, I think this an admirable description
of the poetic process—and a good Coleridgean one,
to boot—and also an admirable description of the
way a reader may very well experience a poem.
But—and here is a big *but*—if the associations
are "ordered and controlled," then aren't we committed to try to understand the nature of the order and control? This need not commit us to
"exact equations," but it does commit us to the attempt to disentangle, or rather to precipitate from
the solution which is the poem, the elements participating in the import of the poem. Furthermore,
we must do this as "exactly" as possible, even
while realizing the limitations of the dimension in
which we necessarily work.

A more radical criticism of my treatment than
that by Mr. House is implied in Elisabeth Schneider's very valuable and provocative *Coleridge,
Opium and Kubla Khan* (University of Chicago
Press, 1953). Her attacks on my views may be
sorted out as follows:

(1) *Coleridge had no systematic theory of symbolism, and "naturally thought in other terms than
those of dark symbol"* (p. 256).

To begin, not too seriously, the word *dark* here is

a little forensic trick. But be that as it may, I don't think that the depth and coherence of a poem depend on a poet's theory—if they did, there would be very few deep and coherent poems. It is more likely, as a matter of fact, that the theory will develop from the poetry than the poetry from the theory, or that, at least, the writing of the poetry and the development of the theory will be aspects of the same process.

The import of a poem does not depend on critical theory, and its availability for the reader does not depend—and should not depend—on our acquaintance with the poet's critical theory as such. For whatever it may signify, I may say that my basic interpretation of *The Ancient Mariner* was arrived at before I had made a systematic study of Coleridge's theory of symbolism. Some elaboration of the interpretation occurred along the way, but I cannot say how much as a logical exfoliation of the idea as I lived longer with the poem or how much as a consequence of the study of Coleridge's theory. In any case, with humility in front of Miss Schneider's learning, I still do not find Coleridge's theory quite so irresponsible as she takes it to be. There are confusions, waverings, and lags in it, perhaps more than I am aware of, but even so, we cannot, it seems to me, deny the ideas and insights embodied in it.

(2) The Ancient Mariner *is not the sort of poem* (*presumably because it is developed from the ballad tradition*) *in which Coleridge would have expressed his serious ideas.* Miss Schneider says: "In *The Ancient Mariner* the verse itself seems more consonant with Coleridge's remark that the poem has too much moral than with any elaborate cosmic interpretation: its movement does not strike my ear as sufficiently grave to bear the weight of all the meanings that have been bestowed upon it" (pp. 259–60). I honestly don't know what Miss Schneider really means to say here. I believe that what follows is a fair summary of what she actually does say.

Coleridge says the poem has "too much moral."

It does have too much moral—presumably for a poem in the ballad tradition.

Presumably because it is a poem in the ballad tradition, its movement is not "sufficiently grave" to bear the weight of the moral (i.e., the "weight of all the meanings").

But it doesn't have any meanings anyway; they have merely been "bestowed" upon it, presumably by critics.

So we get the final contradictory idea that the meanings have been merely "bestowed"—even though we start by accepting Coleridge's remark that the poem really has "too much" moral. Or perhaps Miss Schneider isn't making any connection between "moral" and "meanings." In that case, we may not have self-contradiction, but what do we have?

Let us lay aside, however, the question of what the author wants to say in the whole sentence, and fix on one of the individual ideas. Miss Schneider says that her ear tells her that this verse is not "sufficiently grave" to bear the weight of serious meaning. One might remark that if Miss Schneider is going to resort merely to her ear, then we may all resort merely to our ears and the devil take the hindmost. But more seriously, does her ear really tell her that the following lines are not sufficiently grave to bear serious meaning?

> *O happy living things! no tongue*
> *Their beauty might declare:*
> *A spring of love gushed from my heart*
> *And blessed them unaware:*

Or:

> *O Wedding-Guest! this soul hath been*
> *Alone on a wide sea:*
> *So lonely 'twas, that God himself*
> *Scarce seemed there to be.*

Miss Schneider does have a good ear, as her analysis of some of the verse of *Kubla Khan* in-

dicates, but here, anxious to grab another piece of
evidence for her argument, she cruelly slanders
that innocent member.

Continuing in her line of argument, she says in
her next sentence that when Coleridge "planned to
write on great or cosmic themes" he never thought
of using "minor poetic forms," and mentions some
of his abortive projects on a grandiose scale
(p. 260). But the mere fact that Coleridge couldn't
write those epics seems to indicate, among other
things, that his mind didn't work that way. However much his ambition urged him to draw up such
projects, his genius simply wasn't of that order.
Though his genius wasn't up to the epics, there is
no reason to assume that his native seriousness—
and ambition—was less when that genius did come
to fulfill itself on a more modest scale. And I see
no reason to assume that a minor poetic form, in
this case the ballad, would not be found worthy of
serious development and serious freighting. In fact,
there is some evidence for this in Coleridge's admiration for Wordsworth, who often worked in
terms of a very simple tradition.

(3) The Ancient Mariner *does not demand the
kind of reading which I have tried to give it.*

Presumably Miss Schneider wants us to take the
poem innocently. So do I: that is the only way to
start to take any poem. But we have to see where
our innocence will lead us—and we have to remember to keep on trusting our innocence all the way,
down no matter how unexpected, and perhaps dark,
a track. Miss Schneider says, however, that the
track doesn't run very far in *The Ancient Mariner;*
the poem doesn't demand much of our innocence.
"Symbolic meaning" is not to be expected here.

"Symbolic meaning," she says, "becomes 'trans-
lucent' [only] when the poet alters the course of
nature or heightens or distorts certain features of
his subject in ways not accounted for by the surface
meaning alone, when a particular emphasis not
otherwise explicable is laid upon a word or image,
or when his verse form takes on a special character

that is intelligible only through a symbolic meaning" (p. 261). Are we to understand that Miss
Schneider maintains that in *The Ancient Mariner*
the poet does *not* alter the course of nature or dis-
tort any matters in a way not accounted for by the
"surface meaning alone," and does *not* lay particular emphasis upon certain images in a way not
explicable at the surface level? If she does maintain this, it would be nice to know what her
"surface," or other, meaning of the poem would be,
and I cannot but feel that some burden of proof
is on her to give us a reading that proves no
significant distortions or heightenings, or special
emphases, to exist in the poem.

(4) Miss Schneider lumps the kind of reading
which I have tried to do—"symbolic," if you will—
with studies such as those of G. Wilson Knight and
Maud Bodkin, and says that the "conscious symbol-
seeking of critics or psychoanalysts," rarely succeeds in "salting the tail" of the "invisible bird,"
her image for the subconscious forces lurking beneath the "surfaces of our thought and feeling"
(p. 260). Without reference to how well or how
badly Mr. Knight, Miss Bodkin, and I have done
our work, the point here is that Miss Schneider
confuses two very different kinds of study, and
this confusion, it seems to me, haunts all her
theorizing, or implied theorizing, about the creative
process. Mr. Knight and Miss Bodkin are, if I remember them correctly, trying to give a psychoanalytic reading of poetry; the symbols they are
talking about are psychoanalytic symbols. What
I am trying to do is to talk about poetic images
and import—which may or may not overlap with
the psychoanalytic symbols.

This matter is best discussed by thinking of the
distinction between the reverie of wish-fulfillment
and the reverie of any kind of creative activity. Miss
Schneider makes the distinction: "The intense concentration of the act of composing does indeed bear
some likeness to reverie. . . . But it is creative

will that is at work and not the *wish*-fulfilment reverie of certain psychologico-aesthetic theories" (pp. 276–77).

I think that Miss Schneider is perfectly right here —and, incidentally, her notion of the will seems consistent with Coleridge's own. But we have to ask how the will works in relation to creative reverie. In a rough and ready, and tentative, way, I should hazard this: The poet wants to make a poem and is acting on his desire—is *willing* a poem. In his state of concentration certain things float into his mind; but these things are *unwilled*, for he cannot deliberately summon up any particular item; if he knew what to summon up, his work would already be done. He can envisage only the *kind* of thing, as it were, which he needs: he may see the shape of the blank spot, but he can't see—he can only feel— what ought to fill it. He can, however, reject by *will* whatever items are unsatisfactory, and he continues this process in the gradual envisagement of what he is creating. In general, he *wills* the poem. In particular, he *wills* the rejection of individual items.

In the wish-fulfillment reverie there is merely indulgence, no developing envisagement of a thing being created. The wish-fulfillment reverie is responsive only to the wish, and is merely an expression of the unconscious. The creative reverie, on the other hand, by envisagement and veto—by *will*, if you like—is responsive to various demands. It is, first, responsive to the "whole man"—to his total value-system, with its long-range as well as its short-range satisfactions. It may not adequately express this "whole man," and may even falsify him, but it cannot ignore him. Second, the creative reverie is responsive to the objective world, in respect to considerations of congruence, probability, association, etc. Third, the creative reverie is responsive to the laws of the medium, whatever that medium may be—paint, verse, mathematics, etc. The creative reverie is a massive, fluid process seeking objectification in a form that over-passes appetite.

To go further, the wish-fulfillment reverie is a surrender to the needs of the unconscious, while the creative reverie is, in the end, a liberation from the compulsiveness of the unconscious. This is not to say, however, that the creative reverie denies the needs of the unconscious, but that it gives new contexts to the images arising from the unconscious and criticizes projections of it, and in that process "liberates."

This is a way of saying that the unconscious does give materials on which the creative reverie works. The critical mischief starts when we confound those "materials" with the poem made from the materials. In any poem there may be lags, over-lays, and undigested chunks of material, but the poem, in so far as it is a good poem, survives all this by the fact of having been "created." The study of the "materials," the sort of study which Miss Bodkin and Mr. Knight, for instance, have undertaken, may lead to enlightenment in so far as it enables us to distinguish between the material of the poem and the poem itself, to understand better how such material may be absorbed, and to understand better the process of its transformation into new meanings.

I heartily agree with Miss Schneider that a poem is not a form of automatic writing. It so happens that for years I had had a nagging suspicion that Coleridge's account of the origin of *Kubla Khan* oversimplified matters. I was prepared to admit that he may have had a dream start—possibly verbal—but my guess was that then, or later, he moved over into the more ordinary process of composition to finish up. I was the more prepared to admit this because I had once dreamed up part of a poem—alas, not *Kubla Khan*—and then finished it later in colder blood. So Miss Schneider's argument about the origins of *Kubla Khan* falls on ready ground; and I think her interpretation of the poem is masterly. But for the life of me I don't see how proving that Coleridge was not asleep when he dreamed up *Kubla Khan* proves anything except that Coleridge was not asleep. I don't see how it tells us anything about the nature of the creative process, or the nature of poetry.

13. Letter to George Coleridge, April, 1798, *Letters,* I, 241–242. We also find a text on the matter of sin and grace in "Sonnet on Receiving a Letter Informing Me of the Birth of a Son." And if we look to the nightmare in Stanza VI of "Ode to the Departing Year," we find the same type of imagery which appears in the guilt dreams of "The Pains of Sleep," and which Meyer H. Abrams (in *The Milk of Paradise,* Cambridge, 1934) attributes to opium; the opium source of the imagery presumably means a guilt association. But see Schneider (*op. cit.*).

Thus far I have tried to show, in attacking the notion that the Mariner is passive and that the killing of the Albatross can therefore have no moral content, that Coleridge was not committed to no cessitarianism in any sense which would make it inevitable in the poem. But there is another line of approach to the question. If it be assumed that Coleridge did accept the doctrines of David Hartley and Joseph Priestley, it still does not follow that the Mariner's act is without moral content, for we must do Coleridge the honor of supposing that he read the works of his masters a little more closely than some of the critics seem to have done. In Priestley's *Doctrine of Philosophical Necessity Illustrated* (Birmingham, 1782, pp. 142–164), there occurs a section entitled "Of the Nature of Remorse of Conscience, and of Praying for the Pardon of Sin, on the Doctrine of Necessity," which really develops Proposition XV of Chapter I of Part II of Hartley's *Observations on Man.* Priestley writes: "It is acknowledged that a necessarian, who, as such, believes that, strictly speaking, *nothing goes wrong,* but that everything is under the best direction possible . . . cannot accuse himself of having done wrong in the ultimate sense of the words. He has, therefore, in this strict sense, nothing to do with repentance, confession, or pardon, which are all adapted to a different, imperfect, and fallacious view of things. . . . In the sublime, but accurate language of the apostle John, he will *dwell in love,* he will *dwell in God,* and *God in him;* so that, *not committing any sin,* he will have nothing to repent of. He will be *perfect, as his heavenly father is perfect.*" But man does not live at that level of enlightenment and "because of influences to which we are all exposed" cannot constantly refer "everything to its primary cause." Therefore, he will "feel the sentiments of shame, remorse, and repentance, which arise mechanically from his referring actions to himself. And, oppressed with a sense of *guilt* he will have recourse to that *mercy* of which he will stand in need." Since no man, except for rare moments in the seasons of retirement and meditations, is ever more than an "imperfect necessarian," all men have the experience of sin and remorse, and the sin, for mortal man who cannot see the complete pattern, has a content, and the content is the "almost irrevocable debasement of our minds by *looking off from God, living without him* . . . and *idolizing ourselves and the world;* considering other things as *proper agents* and *causes;* whereas, strictly speaking, there is but *one cause,* but *one sole agent* in universal nature. Thus . . . all vice is reducible to idolatry. . . ." Thus at the level of mortal experience, the level at which the Mariner must live, his shooting of the Albatross would be an act of pride, of self-idolatry—the very word Coleridge uses later in describing Original Sin.

The point I am trying to make is, finally, this: Even on the view that Coleridge is influenced by the doctrines of the necessitarians, the killing of the Albatross still has, at the level of experience, a moral content and is not to be dismissed as merely a wanton or thoughtless act. It is an act for which, at the level of experience, man takes responsibility, for, as Priestley somewhat whimsically puts it, at the end of his chapter on guilt, "If . . . we cannot habitually ascribe *all* to God, but a part only, let it be (and so indeed it naturally will be) that which is *good;* and if we must ascribe anything to ourselves, let it be that which is *evil.*"

There is, indeed, a shadowy relation between the vision of love to which the Mariner attains and the moments of vision which the necessitarians describe—the "self-annihilation" of Hartley—but the mystics had given Coleridge more rapturous descriptions of that state of bliss. Furthermore, the one thing that the poem does *not* establish is the notion that the crime and the subsequent horror are really part of a good; the Mariner never praises God for having given him the evil as a concealed good; instead, the horror of the crime and its consequences is never completely overpassed, and the agony of the Mariner continues to return at its uncertain hour. This is definitely not the way a poet of necessitarianism should end his tale.

14. *Letters of Charles Lamb,* ed. E. V. Lucas (London, 1935), I, 95. R. C. Bald ("Coleridge and *The Ancient Mariner:* Addenda to *The Road to Xanadu,*" in *Nineteenth-Century Studies* [Ithaca, 1940], p. 16) quotes from Lamb's letter and reports that Coleridge had already entered in his notebook (Gutch memorandum book, f. 21a) the topic for a projected poem: "The Origin of Evil, an Epic Poem." But Bald does not connect this with *The Ancient Mariner.* He says: "Some time in 1797, however, the subject changed; one of his other projects drew his attention to a more appropriate theme." But the case seems to be that Coleridge changed his subject, his fable, but not his theme.

There is also evidence of a more personal nature that Coleridge was obsessed by fear and guilt even before the full addiction to opium. For instance, there is his autobiographical note of January 11, 1805: "It is a most instructive part of my Life the fact, that I have been always preyed on by some Dread, and perhaps all my faulty actions have been the consequences of some Dread or other in my mind from fear of Pain, or Shame, not from prospect of Pleasure." And Coleridge lists the numerous dreads, from the boyhood horror of being detected with a sore head, through "a short-lived Fit of Fears from sex," to the "almost epileptic night-horrors in my sleep" (Bald, *op. cit.,* pp. 26–27).

Our knowledge of the poet's personal background helps us to define his dominant theme, but the critical argument can be rested on perfectly objective evidence in the poems themselves. Coleridge longed for the vision of universal love of "Religious Musings" or of the end of *The Ancient Mariner,* but we also have in "The Eolian Harp" the picture of the "sinful and most miserable man," who is "wilder'd and dark," and the nightmare in Section VI of the "Ode to the Departing Year," not to mention the later *Christabel,* "The Pains of Sleep," and *The Ancient Mariner* itself.

15. *Aids to Reflection,* pp. 268–290; quotation on p. 287. Coleridge's emphasis later on the mystery of Original Sin may find a strange echo in the famous remark about *The Ancient Mariner* in the *Table Talk,* to the effect that the poem, as a work of pure imagination, should have had no more moral than the tale in *The Arabian Nights* of the "merchant's sitting down to eat dates by the side of a well, and throwing the shells aside, and lo! a genie starts up and says he must kill the aforesaid merchant *because* one of the date shells had, it seems, put out the eye of the genie's son." But this account of the story of "The Genie and the Merchant" from the First Night, is not accurate. In fact, the careless date shell had killed the son of the genie. When the merchant begs for pity, the genie exclaims: "No mercy! Is it not just to kill him that has killed another?" And when the merchant then pleads his own lack of evil intention, the genie replies, "I must kill thee since thou hast killed my son." What is important here may be that the story referred to from *The Arabian Nights* is not merely a tale of the miraculous, but is one dealing with a random act and its apparently incommensurable punishment, much on the order of that in *The Ancient Mariner.* The mystery of sin and punishment is again before us. There is even a faint

hint of a theological parallel with Christianity, the avenging Father and the Son who suffers at the hand of man. One can see why, perhaps, this particular story sprang to Coleridge's mind. But what did he mean by the statement about the moral and the use of this story as an example? He never said, we must remember, that his own poem should be meaningless or be without a "moral." He simply said that the moral should be less obtrusive. Then he offers an example of a story wherein a mysterious factor in life is caught up without any rationalization. It may be objected that Coleridge, after all, didn't have the story straight. The error, of course, may well have been that of Henry Nelson Coleridge, who had the habit of putting down after reaching home the remarks of his distinguished kinsman (see Preface to *Table Talk*), and whose memory of *The Arabian Nights* may well have been less perfect than that of Coleridge, to whom the book had been at one time almost a devotional work. But assuming that the error is Coleridge's, we do not necessarily assume that he mistook the fundamental, mysterious drift of the tale. For a discussion of the moral significance of the story, see House, *op. cit.*, pp. 90–92.

16. P. 458. If we transfer the terminology here to the pattern of *The Ancient Mariner*, we can describe the poem as the progression of the will from abstraction and self-idolatry to the state of immanence which expresses itself as wisdom or love—those being, as Coleridge says in the passage, two aspects of the same power, the "intelligential" and the "spiritual." We may observe that, in the poem, the punishment for the sin of self-idolatry, for the resolve of the will to find in itself alone "one absolute motive," is fitted with Dantesque precision to the nature of the crime. It is, in fact, a mere extension of the crime. It is loneliness. And when the Mariner bites his own arm for the blood to drink, we have the last logical extension of "self-idolatry" converted to its own punishment.

17. The crime presented in *The Ancient Mariner*, the crime of self-assertion in the face of Law, was of peculiar appeal to the Romantics. *"Le sentiment presque ineffable, tant il est terrible, de la joie dans la damnation,"* says Baudelaire in his essay on *Richard Wagner et Tannhauser à Paris*. Another example is Shelley's interest in the crime of incest and his comments on the "poeticality" of the topic. The crime against an animal is, of course, a special case of this self-assertion, the perversity of pride. Baudelaire, in his essay on Poe, quotes his own translation of the passage given in the text from "The Black Cat" (*Revue de Paris*, March and April, 1852). Flaubert's *Légende de saint Julien l'hospitalier* is another example of this twisted rendering of the Hymn of Saint Francis or the "jubilate Agno" of Christopher Smart.

18. What of the crew? The poem says the souls "fled to bliss or woe," and that is all we have in explicit terms. But the bodies remain to be inspirited by the angelic troop. Marius Bewley ("The Poetry of Coleridge," *Scrutiny*, VIII, 406–420) comments that this episode bears a reminiscence of the Incarnation and the Resurrection, and is a further emphasis on the controlling principle of love which springs from God. But he might have gone further and pointed out that, in the general structure of the poem, these associations define the inspiriting of the corpses as an act parallel to the spiritual rebirth experienced by the Mariner. It is another example of the repetition and counterpoint in the organization of the poem. But Bewley's whole view is that the poem is basically incoherent.

19. "I never find myself alone with the embracement of rocks and hills . . . but my spirit courses, drives, and eddies like a leaf in Autumn; a wild activity of thoughts, imaginations, feelings, and impulses of motion, rises up within me; a sort of *bottom-wind*, that blows to no point of the compass, comes from I know not whence, but agitates the whole of me; my whole being is filled with waves that roll and stumble . . ." (quoted by A. E.

Powell, *The Romantic Theory of Poetry* [London, 1926], p. 99). Here Coleridge uses the storm at sea as an image to describe the state of imaginative excitement provoked by the contemplation of nature—the storm he welcomed and was to long for in the later years when the wind blew no more. I am indebted to Maud Bodkin (*Archetypal Patterns in Poetry* [Oxford, 1934], pp. 35–36) for the original suggestion for the interpretation of the wind and storm in the poem. She writes: "So, also, the image of a ship driving before the wind is used by him to express happy surrender to the creative impulse. 'Now he sails right onward' he says of Wordsworth engaged upon *The Prelude*, 'it is all open ocean and a steady breeze, and he drives before it.' In *The Ancient Mariner* the magic breeze, and the miraculous motion of the ship, or its becalming, are not, of course, like the metaphor, symbolic in conscious intention. They are symbolic only in the sense that, by the poet as by some at least of his readers, the images are valued because they give—even though this function remain unrecognized—expression to feelings that were seeking a language to relieve their own inner urgency. . . . We find graven in the substance of language testimony to the kinship, or even identity, of the felt experience of the rising of the wind and the quickening of the human spirit. 'Come from the four winds, O breath, and breathe upon these slain, that they may live.' Behind the translated words, in the vision of Ezekiel, we can feel the older meaning, strange to our present-day thought, in which the physical wind, and the breath in man's nostrils, and the power of the Divine Spirit, were aspects hardly to be differentiated." But I do not see, in the light of the poem's organization or in that of Coleridge's "Dejection" (which employs quite explicitly the wind image for creativity), that we have to assume, with the author of *Archetypal Patterns*, the image not to be symbolic in conscious intention.

The image, of course, is not uncommon in other

Romantic poetry. In Shelley, for instance, it appears as the paradoxical wind, destroying to create, in the "Ode." And in *A Defence of Poetry* we find the calm-wind opposition used precisely as in *The Ancient Mariner:* "We are aware of the evanescent visitations of thought and feeling sometimes associated with place or person, sometimes regarding our own mind alone, and always rising unforeseen and departing unbidden, but elevating and delightful beyond all expression . . . it is as it were the interpenetration of a diviner nature through our own; but its footsteps are like those of a wind over the sea, which the coming calm erases."

20. Though not in connection with the present topic, the italicized *her* in these lines is puzzling. A reasonable explanation is suggested by Frederick Pottle in a letter to the present writer: "In the version of 1798 there was an understandable contrast between *his* Death's bones and *her* the Woman's lips, *her* looks, *her* locks, and I have wondered whether the italicized *her* in the preceding stanzas (referring to the ship) did not get in by mistake. If so, the mistake was made at the very beginning, and not corrected in the many opportunities that S. T. C. had for revision."

21. It may be objected that the light of sunset is also, according to the passage from the *Biographia Literaria*, the light of the imagination. I am inclined to think that such an objection here would be legalistic, for Coleridge in the passage from the *Biographia* is thinking of a dimming light, a trick of light and shade, and the setting sun here has a "broad and burning face," and, according to the Gloss at this point, there is "No twilight within the courts of the sun." I take it that the Gloss is Coleridge's own way of anticipating the above objection, at the same time as he explains, somewhat superfluously, the statement that the dark comes at one stride.

22. Kenneth Burke is quite properly struck by the suggestive force of the phrase "silly buckets."

His interpretation involves what he takes to be the role of the Pilot's boy as a scapegoat for the Mariner's curse. He writes: "But his (the boy's) appearance in the poem cannot be understood at all, except in superficial terms of the interesting or the picturesque, if we do not grasp his function as a scapegoat of some sort—a victimized vessel for drawing off the most malign aspects of the curse that affects the 'greybeard loon' whose cure has been effected under the dubious aegis of moonlight. . . . I remember how, for instance, I had pondered for years the reference to the 'silly buckets' filled with curative rain (dew). I noted the epithet as surprising, picturesque, and interesting. I knew that it was doing something, but I wasn't quite sure what. But as soon as I looked upon the Pilot's boy as a scapegoat, I saw that the word *silly* was a technical foreshadowing of the fate that befell this figure in the poem. The structure itself became more apparent: the 'loon'-atic Mariner begins his cure from drought under the aegis of a moon that causes a silly rain, thence by synecdoche to silly buckets, and the most malignant features of this problematic cure are transferred to the Pilot's boy who now doth crazy go" (*The Philosophy of Literary Form* [Baton Rouge, 1941], pp. 287-288).

Burke emphasizes the relation of the moon and opium, and does not regard the moon as the presiding symbol of the concept of imagination at the level of an objectified, infusive theme. As for the role of the Pilot's boy, I do not feel it necessary to regard him as a scapegoat, though I do not think that this falsifies the tenor of the poem. I would make only this reservation: such an identification would be a significant connection, as I shall later point out, with the idea of the Mariner as the *poète maudit*.

But the phrase "silly buckets": We can go at this by looking at the cluster of meanings involved in the history of the word, meanings which would have been vitally present for Coleridge and the shadows of which can be detected in contemporary usage. The old meanings of *saelig-seely*, the sense of fortunate, blessed, happy, innocent, weak, still haunt the word, and fuse with the other meaning. In the poem the phrase comes in the first dream of blessedness, innocence, and happiness, just after the Albatross has dropped into the sea, and in the dream even the inanimate objects, but those associated with the longed-for water, receive the touch of this blessedness—and incidentally this blessing of the buckets by the Mariner, for it amounts to that, repeats his blessing of the snakes, so that even the inanimate objects share in the new sacramental vision. As for the senses of weakness and stupidity in the word, we have the condition of the buckets as empty and worthless. Throughout, of course, there is the man-bucket transference, empty bucket and thirsty man (lonely, accursed, foolish, weak man) that become full and blessed.

23. "Lines Left upon a Seat in a Yew Tree," which appears in *Lyrical Ballads* and which, though begun as early as 1788 or 1789, had received its final form in 1797, bears on the general question discussed here, in relation both to the sin of the Mariner and to the imagination. The poem ends with the following lines:

If thou be one whose heart the holy forms
Of young imagination have kept pure,
Stranger! henceforth be warned; and know, that pride
Howe'er disguised in its own majesty,
Is littleness; that he, who feels contempt
For any living thing, hath faculties
Which he has never used; that thought with him
Is in its infancy. The man, whose eye
Is ever on himself, doth look on one,
The least of nature's works, one who might move
The wise man to that scorn which wisdom holds
Unlawful, ever. O, be wiser, thou!
Instructed that true knowledge leads to love,
True dignity abides with him alone

Who, in the silent hour of inward thought,
Can still suspect and still revere himself,
In lowliness of heart.

Here quite clearly the sin of pride is a sin against imagination, the equation made in *The Ancient Mariner*. As Ernest de Selincourt points out (*The Poetical Works of William Wordsworth* [Oxford, 1940], I, 329), Coleridge, who heard the poem in June, 1797, was much affected by it. In July he wrote to Southey (*Letters* I, 224), though without specific reference to this poem: "I am as much a Pangloss as ever, only less contemptuous than I used to be when I argue how unwise it is to feel contempt for anything." George Wilbur Meyer (*Wordsworth's Formative Years* [Ann Arbor, 1943], p. 207) connects Wordsworth's *The Borderers* (conscious pride in Oswald, unconscious pride in Marmaduke) with the doctrine of "The Yew Tree," and says of the influence on Coleridge: "The strength of the impression which Wordsworth's philosophy of love made upon Coleridge may be approximately estimated when we observe that Coleridge expressed the same philosophy in *Osorio*, and in 'The Rime of the Ancyent Marinere,' where, it will be remembered, the wedding guest receives this good advice:
He prayeth well who loveth well, etc."
Mr. Meyer does not make any further connection of the poem with *The Ancient Mariner*, and apparently does not make this connection except with the stanzas of the moral tag.

24. The interpretation of the poem given thus far is in some points similar to those given by earlier readers. George Herbert Clarke ("Symbols in 'The Ancient Mariner,'" *Queen's Quarterly*, XL, 27-45) emphasizes the importance of the sun-moon opposition and makes this the key symbol of the poem, but he interprets the sun as the "God of Law" and the moon as the "God of Love," and with the first associates the Polar Spirit and the First Voice, and with the second the Hermit and the Sec-

ond Voice. I feel that this view is a justifiable one, but that the exploration of the symbols has been stopped at a stage which leaves much of the poem unaccounted for, and which actually falsifies certain incidents in the poem—for example, those involving the Polar Spirit, which should be connected with the moon-cluster and not with the sun-cluster. Another study which emphasizes the importance of the sun-moon opposition is by Kenneth Burke (*op. cit.*, pp. 24–33, 33–66, 93–102). He notes that punishment is under the sun, and recovery and forgiveness under the moon. But his concern is with the personal themes, and not with the other types of theme. In this particular study he is primarily concerned with the creative process and not with the thing created, though, of course, it is difficult to treat one without treating the other. In any case, he makes some extremely valuable comments on *The Ancient Mariner* and "The Eolian Harp."

In neither of the above studies is the theory of the imagination connected with the poem. But that idea does appear in two other studies, one by Dorothy Waples and one by Newton P. Stallknecht. Miss Waples ("David Hartley in 'The Ancient Mariner,'" *Journal of English and Germanic Philology*, XXXV, 337–351) takes the view that Coleridge denied the moral of the poem in his conversation with Mrs. Barbauld because the moral is Hartleyan, in her view, and Coleridge had repudiated Hartley. She interprets the poem as a strict, two-dimensional allegory of the Hartleyan progression, by association, from imagination, through ambition, self-interest, sympathy, and theopathy, to the moral sense. After the killing of the bird, imagination introduces the Mariner to fear; ambition and shame are involved in the repudiation of the Mariner by his fellows, who hang the bird at his neck; his acquaintance with death and horror appeals to self-interest and refines it to repentance; the incident of the snakes shows the development of sympathy; the return to the power of prayer indicates the transition

to theopathy; the return to human society affirms
the moral sense. There are several lines of comment due here. First, the author plainly misreads,
as do a number of other critics, what Coleridge actually said in the *Table Talk*. He did not repudiate
the moral of the poem, he simply said that its "obtrusion" was too open. So she starts her argument
from a false premise. Second, she makes Coleridge
a doctrinaire follower of Hartley in a way which
denies the rich complexity of his development.
Third, her narrow allegory leaves large tracts of
the poem unaccounted for. Why, for example, does
the Polar Spirit pursue the ship? What do the
various storms have to do in the poem? Is there
any symbolic content for the sun-moon opposition?
Why does the Mariner, if he has achieved the moral
sense, have to wander the world with his recurring
agony? She does use the imagination as a starting
point for her interpretation, but it is the imagination according to Hartley, and not according to
Coleridge, which is a very different kettle of fish.
According to Hartley, the pleasures of the imagination, "the first of our intellectual pleasures, which
are generated from the sensible ones by association" (*Observations on Man,* [London, 1834], p.
475), belong primarily to youth, and are of value
only as they lead, as a kind of bait, to higher pleasures. It follows that Hartley has a contempt for
and fear of the arts as connected with "evil com-
munications," the "pagan show and pomp of the
world," and vanity and waste of time. They are only
disinfected when "devoted to the immediate service
of God and religion in an eminent manner," and
when "profane subjects" arc abjured (p. 481). It is
unnecessary to develop the point that this view,
which makes the imagination a mode of memory,
is absolutely opposed to the theory of the relation
of art and morality held by both Wordsworth and
Coleridge at the time of the composition of the
Lyrical Ballads. In any case, if *The Ancient Mariner* involves the concept of the imagination, the
Coleridgean imagination presides, as the moon,

over the end of the poem, and is not something which merely serves as a starter and is abandoned after its usefulness is over.

Stallknecht ("The Moral of the *Ancient Mariner*," *Strange Seas of Thought* [Durham, N. C., 1945], pp. 141–171: slightly revised version of an article "The Moral of the 'Ancient Mariner,'" PMLA, XLVII, 559–569) presents a much more valuable consideration of the poem. His thesis is that it, like *The Prelude* (1805, Bk. xi, lines 75 ff. and 133 ff.), gives the account of the world apprehended through the lower faculty of mere reason as a universe of death and then the redemption from the horror of this mechanistic interpretation by the discovery of the imaginative love of nature, which "strengthens the human spirit, raising it also to a life of moral freedom and happiness" (p. 148). I think that this is a good statement of the general background of the poem if the critic does not mean to imply that in *The Ancient Mariner* the imagination does not participate in the final freedom and happiness and is overpassed. My criticism of the essay is primarily directed at the application of his view to the poem itself. The critic treats the idea of the poem as a late excrescence, really separate from the "fine dramatic use of incident" and the "simple and lively imagery" and the materials drawn from the books of travel; for him the poem is not "dominated by a subtle moral." In other words, he limits his interpretation to: "(1) the incident of Part IV where the spell begins to break . . . and (2) the last stanzas, wherein the Mariner is rewarded with a deep sense of human love and sympathy" (p. 151). The intention of my essay, however, is to demonstrate that the poem taken as a whole is meaningful.

Stallknecht argues that since Coleridge, in the account of the origins of the poem (*Biographia Literaria,* chapter xiv), makes no reference to any meaning in the original plan, and since Wordsworth suggested the shooting of the Albatross, Coleridge had no intention of a meaning for his poem

when he began it and did not discover one until
he had reached the third and fourth parts. On the
first part of his argument, we can merely appeal to
the poetic theory of both Coleridge and Wordsworth
—a point discussed elsewhere in this essay. The
fact that Coleridge did not give an abstract statement of his idea, or did not say that the poem was
intended to have one, may prove nothing more sinister than that Coleridge did not envisage a reader
who would entertain the theory that poetry may
have no meaning and still be poetry; and anyway,
it is not to be taken as a proof that the poem as
finished twenty years later would still have all the
lags and meaninglessness attributed to it by Stallknecht. (A poem may have such defects, but we
have to discover them by going to the poem and not
by going to some remark about the origin of the
poem or to a discussion of its mere materials—so
much philosophy, so much supernatural machinery, so much dramatic incident, all weighed out
like so much bread, cheese, and pickle for a sand-
wich.)

As to the second part of his argument—that
Coleridge did not discover a meaning until he
reached the middle of the poem—there is some evidence that the general idea which was finally embodied in the poem had been occupying Coleridge's mind for some time. Aside from the general
discussions of the subject recounted in the *Biographia Literaria*, we can point to three items:
First, De Quincey's remark that Coleridge told him
that he had at first intended to embody his "idea"
in a dream poem involving imagery drawn from
high latitudes; second, Lamb's letter to Coleridge
about the epic on the origin of evil (see Note 14);
and third, Coleridge's statement in the preface to
"The Wanderings of Cain" that the crime of Cain involved a crime against "sense" (a crime concerned
with man's proper relation to nature) and that *The
Ancient Mariner* was written "instead" of the poem
about Cain, the other accursed wanderer. These
two items of evidence indicate that Coleridge had

had in mind the general idea embodied in *The Ancient Mariner* and that it involved a crime against
nature. It does not matter, then, that Wordsworth
happened to suggest the particular piece of narrative machinery, the shooting of the Albatross,
which was to embody the idea. Further, at what
point in the process of composition Coleridge happened to grasp his total vision of the poem is irrelevant; the important thing is that we can go to
the poem and discover the embodiment.

25. Burke, op. cit., p. 71; Hugh l'Anson Fausset,
Samuel Taylor Coleridge (London, 1926), p. 166.

26. I am indebted to Frederick Pottle for this
piece of evidence.

27. The following stanzas are omitted. The description of death:

> His *bones were black with many a crack,*
>   *All black and bare I ween;*
> *Jet-black and bare, save where with rust*
> *Of mouldy damps and charnel crust*
>   *They're patch'd with purple and green.*
>
> . . . . .
>
> *A gust of wind sterte up behind*
>   *And whistled thro' his bones;*
> *Thro' the holes of his eyes and the hole of*
>   *his mouth*
>   *Half-whistles and half-groans.*

The return:

> *The moonlight bay was white all o'er,*
>   *Till rising from the same,*
> *Full many shapes, that shadows were,*
>   *Like as of torches came.*
>
> *A little distance from the prow*
>   *Those dark-red shadows were;*
> *But soon I saw that my own flesh*
>   *Was red as in a glare.*
>
> *I turn'd my head in fear and dread,*
>   *And by the holy rood,*

The bodies had advanc'd and now
   Before the mast they stood.

They lifted up their stiff right arms,
   They held them strait and tight;
And each right-arm burnt like a torch,
   A torch that's borne upright.
Their stony eye-balls glitter'd on
   In the red and smoky light.

28. *Op. cit.*, p. 150.

29. The translation used here is from the edition of the poem by Carleton Noyes (New York, 1900).

30. A. E. Powell (*op. cit.*, pp. 1–14), in following Croce's distinction between classic and romantic art as given in *I Problemi*, describes the romantic artist as one who values content more than form, who "has a practical as well as an artistic interest in his matter," who "prizes emotional experience for its own sake, and aims at enlarging men's power to experience" (p. 1). But this is a dangerous distinction in practice, for it tends to lead to an arbitrary definition of form, to a conception corresponding to Coleridge's notion of "superimposed form" as opposed to "organic form," or Blake's notion of mathematic form as opposed to living form. Dr. Boyer taught Coleridge that poetry has "a logic of its own, as severe as that of science" (*Biographia Literaria*, I, 4), and Coleridge's total effort in criticism may be taken as tending toward a description of that logic, or that formal principle. And it is a very dangerous and narrow conception of form that would equate it with mere syllogistic deployment of argument in a poem, with neatness of point and antithesis, or consecutiveness or realism of action. Who can maintain Pope's *Essay on Man* has form and that Keats's odes do not?

31. Muirhead, *op. cit.*, p. 43.

32. S. F. Gingerich, "Coleridge," *Essays in the Romantic Poets* (New York, 1924), p. 29.

Robert Penn Warren was born in Guthrie, Kentucky, in 1905. He entered Vanderbilt University at the age of sixteen and graduated *summa cum laude;* he went to the University of California for his master's degree, then to Yale University, and in 1928 to Oxford as a Rhodes Scholar.

Mr. Warren began his teaching career at Southwestern College (1930–31) and Vanderbilt University (1931–34). He moved to Louisiana State University in 1934, and was one of the founders and editors of *The Southern Review.* From 1942 to 1950 he was Professor of English at the University of Minnesota (and Consultant in Poetry at the Library of Congress, 1944–45). From 1951 to 1956 he was a member of the faculty of Yale University.

In 1939 Mr. Warren published his first novel, *Night Rider* (reissued by Random House in 1948) and won his first Guggenheim Fellowship. In 1943 came *At Heaven's Gate* and in 1946, *All the King's Men* (Pulitzer Prize). His fourth novel was *World Enough and Time* (Random House, 1950). *Brother to Dragons: A Tale in Verse and Voices* appeared in 1953, and his most recent novel, *Band of Angels,* in 1955. Mr. Warren has also published four volumes of poetry, of which the most recent is *Promises* (National Book Award, 1958); a short-story collection, *The Circus in the Attic;* and such influential textbooks (with Cleanth Brooks) as *Understanding Poetry* and *Understanding Fiction.*

Mr. Warren lives in Connecticut with his wife, Eleanor Clark, whose most recent book is *Rome and a Villa,* and their two children, Rosanna and Gabriel.